PEACE
IN THE MAKING

PEACE
IN THE MAKING

THE MENACHEM BEGIN–ANWAR EL-SADAT
PERSONAL CORRESPONDENCE

EDITED BY
HARRY HURWITZ
AND YISRAEL MEDAD

Additional Research and Annotations:
Yisrael Medad and Kezia Raffel Pride

Published by
Gefen Publishing House

in cooperation with
the Menachem Begin Heritage Center
Jerusalem, Israel

Typesetting and Cover Design: S. Kim Glassman

ISBN 978-965-229-456-2

Edition   1   3   5   7   9   8   6   4   2

Gefen Publishing House Ltd.   Gefen Books
6 Hatzvi Street, Jerusalem 94386, Israel   600 Broadway, Lynbrook, NY 11563, USA
972-2-538-0247 • orders@gefenpublishing.com   1-800-477-5257 • orders@gefenpublishing.com

www.gefenpublishing.com

Printed in Israel   *Send for our free catalogue*

"Peace is not the absence of war;
it is a virtue, a state of mind,
a disposition for benevolence, confidence, and justice."

–Baruch Spinoza (1632–1677)

CONTENTS

THE CORRESPONDENCE, SPEECHES AND INTERVIEWS

Part 1
First Overtures:
The Prelude to and the Visit in Jerusalem
May–November 1977

Part 2
Post-Visit Doldrums
December 1977–August 1978

Part 3
From Camp David to the White House Lawn
September 1978–March 1979

Part 4
Constructing Peace
April 1979–April 1982

FOREWORD

This important project of publishing the collection of historical documents relating to the Israel-Egypt Peace Process was born in the small apartment on the edge of the Jerusalem Forest in which Menachem Begin lived after his retirement from office in 1983.

After the first year of almost total seclusion, he was pleased to welcome a small group of longtime personal friends who had accompanied him much of the way in his years of struggle at this small apartment every *motzei Shabbat* (at the conclusion of the Sabbath). They had special permission to enter and were speedily cleared by the security guards in the hut on street level. From there they had to descend several flights of stairs or take the elevator down.

On entering the apartment they were warmly received by Menachem Begin himself, most times with a smile and sometimes with a worried look. On occasion, he was up and about, usually wearing his dressing gown, but on those days when he did not feel well, he was in bed and his friends gathered near and around him.

They saw that his small bedroom table had several piles of thick books which he was constantly reading.

The discussion was always on events of the past, on personalities of the past and on events in other parts of the world. He refused to be drawn into discussions on current affairs in Israel.

Thus we spoke, week after week, about the imminent breakdown of the Soviet Union, which he had foreseen and predicted in his book *White Nights*, written prior to Stalin's death and published in early 1953. Later, he spoke with great admiration of Nelson Mandela in South Africa, who had already spent more than twenty years in detention and his spirit remained unbroken. "He is a formidable man," said Begin, who had himself been a political prisoner in a Soviet "correctional labor camp" in Russia's far north at the Pechora Gulag.

Sometimes he spoke simply about the books he was reading – an occasional novel, but his favorites were biographies of political leaders, books on history and major political issues. Most of the books in his room were in mint condition. He had either received them from publishers abroad or from friends who had brought them on their visits to Israel from the US, Britain or elsewhere. Local publishers or distributors had made it a practice to send him books on political subjects, which they released hoping that he would comment, but this never happened.

At one point, he was very busy reading – or devouring – a tome on the exchange of letters between Winston Churchill and Franklin Delano Roosevelt. He followed and digested every word, every turn of phrase – which he admired greatly. At our *motzei Shabbat* "sessions" he spoke of Churchill's great pride in the British fleet, of the courage of his people in World War II and Roosevelt's readiness first to help Britain and then to become involved in the war after Pearl Harbor.

These discussions gave me the idea of compiling a book covering the exchange of letters and documents between Prime Minister Menachem Begin of Israel and President Anwar Sadat of Egypt. I turned to my friend who was in charge of Prime Minister Begin's personal archives in the Prime Minister's Office and shared my idea with him. I asked him to let me have copies of all such letters and documents that were not classified and, after several weeks, he handed me a file for which I was most grateful.

After perusing it several times, I took this file with me on a subsequent *motzei Shabbat* visit to Menachem Begin.

"And what have you got there?" he asked.

I replied that it was a file containing declassified letters between him and Anwar Sadat.

"Really? That is interesting. May I see it?"

"Of course. They are your letters or letters addressed to you." He glanced through the file and asked if he could keep it for a week or two.

"Certainly," I said. My hope was that he would become more and more involved in the material in the file.

The following week that file became the main point of discussions with our *motzei Shabbat* group. "What do you want to do with it?" he asked.

"Well, just as there is the Churchill-Roosevelt book, I am thinking of publishing this Begin-Sadat book."

He raised his eyebrows and said, "A book? But there is not enough material here for a serious book."

"If there is not enough for a book," I said, "we may include the exchange of speeches between you on some of the occasions when you met, or interviews you both gave to foreign television journalists like Walter Cronkite or Barbara Walters."

"That makes it all very interesting," he said. And we left it at that for another two weeks, during which he obviously reread the material.

When we discussed the matter again a few weeks later, he said, "You still want to publish it as a book?"

When I replied in the affirmative, he raised his hands as if to say "stop" and said, "*Yesh od zman* (There is still time)."

We need not have heeded his announcement, as we need not have asked his permission to publish such a book at all, but our respect for him was so great that I simply abided by his wish and judgment.

But now, with a delay of almost a quarter of a century and to mark the various ceremonies and events connected with the thirtieth anniversary of Sadat's visit to Jerusalem and the subsequent peace process, the time has come to publish this important book as an expression of our admiration for Menachem Begin and his peace partner, Anwar Sadat, who together achieved the breakthrough to peace and brought about the turning point in the relations between Israel and Egypt.

There are those who say that the peace agreement that they signed has resulted in a "cold peace," to which I have always replied: "Rather a cold peace than a hot war."

And the fact is that since those dramatic days, there has been no war between Israel and Egypt. Moreover, Egypt has stayed out of subsequent wars between Israel and other Arab countries.

Harry Hurwitz

PREFACE

The above foreword was penned early in 2008. Harry Hurwitz died on October 1, 2008, and we are leaving his words essentially unchanged. This book was among his top priorities for the last three years of his life, and its publishing is a memorial to his devotion to Menachem Begin and the skills he brought with him as advisor to the prime minister, to his diplomatic service on behalf of the State of Israel as well as his efforts in the founding of the Menachem Begin Heritage Center in Jerusalem.

The peace treaty that was the result of the efforts of these two leaders, whose intimate correspondence we can now read fully and thereby understand their thinking, was viewed by both of them as the crowning achievement of their lives. Both paid a political and personal price: in Begin's case, significant elements within his party and coalition left him with rancor, while Sadat fell to the bullets of assassins from amongst the fundamentalist Islamic forces. The peace has held, however, between the two countries despite strains and some unrealized expectations. In reading this book's contents, the hope is that an additional peacemaking project will benefit from the lessons and experiences described in this volume.

Herzl Makov
Chairman
Menachem Begin Heritage Center

This book, which includes the personal correspondence between Israel's Prime Minister Menachem Begin and Egypt's President Anwar Sadat during the period of their peacemaking endeavors culminating in the signing of the first peace treaty between an Arab country and Israel in 1979, has been expanded to include additional material. The editors and publishers have made extensive efforts to present to the public a true record of the three years from 1977 to 1979, although a full diplomatic history is not the intention. This is not an academic research work but is characterized by a more personal and intimate view, from the inside, of how peace was made.

In addition to the footnotes, the introductory notes, the additional material including speeches, press conference transcripts and other items, the reader can find in the bibliography a more detailed and diverse perspective on all the aspects of the peace process. Both English and Hebrew works can be found there for the researcher.

In our editorial text and in transcripts of speeches, we have standardized spellings of names and places, using American spelling and punctuation conventions. Despite our wish for a standardized text, nevertheless, so as to reflect as authentically as possible the actual correspondence, in the letters themselves we have reproduced the original spellings and punctuation, including those of datelines and signatures. Since the letters were translated and transcribed by different individuals over a period of time, some names, including that of President Sadat, appear in the book with more than one spelling, and British spelling and punctuation conventions are used for some of the letters.

Taking up the task to complete the book, I have been aided by Kezia Raffel Pride, senior editor at Gefen Publishing House. Her queries and prodding have produced a better book. The enthusiasm of the publishers, Michael Fischberger and Ilan Greenfield of Gefen Publishing House, has been a great impetus. The book was greatly enhanced by the talented design work of S. Kim Glassman.

I wish to thank Shulamit Margolit, who retyped the letters and additional texts.

I acknowledge, too, the assistance of Iris Berlatzky, Ilana Brown, Moshe Fuksman-Sha'al, Bruriah Romanov, Ziv Rubinovitz and Rami Shtivi, as well as the encouragement of Herzl Makov, all of the Menachem Begin Heritage Center in Jerusalem. Yechiel Kadishai, Mr. Begin's personal assistant, was helpful, as always. Dan Pattir responded to inquiries in a helpful fashion, as did Yehuda Avner.

Yisrael Medad
Director, Information Resources
Menachem Begin Heritage Center

INTRODUCTION BY
AMBASSADOR YEHUDA AVNER

Menachem Begin was the most ideological prime minister Israel had ever
elected, an iron-core patriarch, neutral in nothing that intruded upon
the protection of the territorial integrity of the Land of Israel to which he
devoted his life; that, and the pursuit of peace. Ample testimony to these
truths is contained in the letters and speeches in this important volume.

Always a grand raconteur and an aficionado of history, Begin was a
man of words – an intellectual of the Polish mold but in the Jewish idiom.
When he was an underground commander, words were often his sole
arsenal as he battled the British for freedom. It was a time of sharp wits
and subterfuge, when survival hung on knowing what the other side was
thinking, saying, planning, writing, reading and broadcasting. Words were
weapons. He had to learn them. So, day by day, night by night, he sat glued
to the British radio frenetically mastering the news and the King's English,
an exercise which endowed him with a lush English vocabulary.

A man of passionate polemic and gripping oratory, he loved the
Knesset, he loved to debate, he loved to write, he loved to read, he loved to
preach, he loved journalism, he loved letters. Letter writing, he lamented,
was a dying skill. Language was being robbed of precision and clarity. Politicians were prime pirates of this despoilment. Parliamentary debate was
everywhere on the wane. Congress and Westminster were still relatively
decent chambers, and the Knesset, too, had its rare moments. But, generally
speaking, good talk for good talk's sake was gone. He once remarked that
politicians had become bottom-line pragmatists, bereft of humor. "Where
is the parliamentarian today," he chortled in a sudden flash of wit, "who can
dispose of an opponent with the elegance of a Benjamin Disraeli calling
across the aisle to Gladstone, 'The Honorable Gentleman is a sophistical
rhetorician inebriated with the exuberance of his own verbosity'?"

A liberal democrat and parliamentarian to the core, he publicly declared
on the very first day of Israel's independence in 1948, upon emerging from
his perilous years in the underground: "Henceforth, God forbid that a decision of a democratically elected government of Israel shall ever be defied

by force. Whatever our differences, however strongly held are our differing convictions, however raucous the debate – these shall be expressed only through the legal avenues of legitimate dissent, as befits our parliamentary democracy. It is thanks to this democracy, set in a sea of despotism, that we shall weather every storm, overcome every hurdle, and withstand every test, as we shall grow, with God's help, from strength to strength."

This was the ethos that inspired his every speech and his every letter. Unlike his predecessors, he wrote his own speeches and drafted his own letters, never putting his signature to anything he had not composed himself in his tight, taut and cramped handwriting, which was sometimes excruciatingly difficult to decipher. I know, because I was the decipherer. On his first day in office in June 1977, he handed me the draft of a response to a letter he had received from the president of the United States, and impishly instructed me, "You shall please polish my Polish English. You shall be my Shakespeare. Please shakespearize it."

I was quick to learn that Begin delighted in inventing such neologisms – creating new words or new meanings for established words. Henceforth, shakespearize meant stylize.

When giving dictation, he would habitually make a Norman arch of his long fingers, pause in thought to mentally organize what he wanted to say and then say it with an amazing rhetorical flow, all preassembled in the alcoves of his mind.

His exchange of correspondence with President Anwar Sadat of Egypt began with the president's surprise acceptance of Prime Minister Begin's invitation to visit him in Jerusalem, in November 1977, to talk peace. An air of expectancy gripped the nation when Sadat arrived, as if some miracle was in the offing, some redeeming formula for a speedy treaty of peace with the largest, most influential and the strongest of all of Israel's Arab enemies: Egypt. But it was not that simple. Always the autocrat, Anwar Sadat assumed that his grand reconciliatory gesture of coming to Jerusalem would automatically be rewarded by a grand reconciliatory gesture on the part of Begin in the form of an unconditional Israeli withdrawal on all fronts back to the indefensible 1967 pre-Six-Day War lines, and Israeli acquiescence to the establishment of a Palestinian state. Small wonder, then, that whenever the Egyptian and Israeli negotiating teams met, they faced an unbridgeable abyss of misunderstanding and deadlock. By the spring of 1978 the talks were totally in the doldrums, and like the legendary Sisyphus, whenever Begin pushed his boulder up the steep hill of negotiation it always came rolling down again over his toes. Letters, some of them indignant, were exchanged between the two leaders, most notably during the tense and frustrating months of the summer of 1980, as featured in this volume.

The reader will note that the letters were often loquacious, most particularly those of Sadat, one of which was thirty-five pages long in the original. All of them are instructive for the insights they reveal about the personalities and temperaments of the two men. In the case of Sadat, but for a personal passage here and there, his letters were drafted by a committee of presidential advisers – this on the admission to me by a member of his staff; Begin's were written in his own hand.

Whereas the prime minister's opening paragraphs could be chatty, followed by meticulous, hard-hitting, and often legalistic argumentations, Sadat's were invariably grandiloquent, replete with a penchant for long-winded obfuscations and even bouts of mysticism. Religion shaped the minds of both men, yet Sadat was not averse to catapulting his policies into the realm of the supernatural. Thus, in one of his letters he writes: "The thoughts which I am sharing with you now occurred to me as I was on the peak of Mount Moses, reciting the Koran and worshiping God in this sacred part of the land of Egypt.... I became more certain of a fact I have stated before[:] that my peace initiative was a sacred mission. The story of the Israelites began in the land of Egypt. It is apparent that it is the will of God Almighty that the story will find its completion in Egypt also." He then went on to insist that Israel surrender east Jerusalem, where Jewry's most sacred shrines are situated, and which the Arabs had despoiled until they were liberated in the Six-Day War.

Begin was so beguiled by Sadat's mystical hyperbole that he took counsel with a couple of ministers to assist him in composing a judicious point of reply, but they could find none. So, as was his wont, he mounted an even higher plateau of moral certitude, and being a leader possessing a unique, all-encompassing sense of Jewish history, with a Jewish memory that went back thousands of years and a Jewish vision that went forward thousands of years, he answered Sadat in his own coinage, telling him: "We hate war and yearn for peace. But let me say this: should anybody at any time raise against us a modern sword in the attempt to rob us of Jerusalem, our capital, the object of our love and prayers, we Jews will fight for Jerusalem as we have never done since the days of the Maccabees.

And how Judah the Maccabee fought and won the day, every student of history and strategy knows." This was the original, hand-written version given to me to "shakespearize." Although this wording did not appear in the final letter delivered to Sadat, it is typical of the sort of verbal sparring that characterized the Begin-Sadat correspondence.

Such caustic barrages, one would think, would have caused the two men to take umbrage and mount the barricades. But no. With the passage of time, they met ever more frequently, and in the process learned to respect and trust each other ever more, so that what had begun with written duels between belligerents ended in an embrace of personal friendship that ran deep.

Begin was to mourn Sadat's assassination not only because he had lost a peace partner but, equally, because he had lost a true friend. With pained nostalgia he confided to us, his personal staff, "Anwar and I used to open up our hearts to one another. Often we would speak about our beliefs and our ancient traditions, and our experiences, and how they impacted on our lives and made us what we are. We once said to each other that our lives are short, but the peace must surely outlive us. We were sitting on his terrace in Alexandria, just the two of us, he puffing on his pipe and looking out to sea, and he said, 'You know, Menachem, there will come a time and I will no longer be president of Egypt.' And I said to him, 'You know, Anwar, there will come a time and I will no longer be prime minister of Israel.' And then we laughed, and embraced, and we said to one another with true affection that while we will inevitably go the way of all flesh, our nations will never pass away, and neither, with the grace of God, will the peace."

In time, the peace between the two countries did cool under the tutorship of Hosni Mubarak, President Sadat's successor, and Menachem Begin was heard to sigh, "Were Anwar still alive today, things might have turned out a little different."

Yehuda Avner served as advisor to Prime Minister Menachem Begin, and as Israeli Ambassador to Australia and the UK. He is the author of *The Prime Ministers: An Intimate Narrative of Israeli Leadership* (Jerusalem: Toby Press, 2010).

BIOGRAPHICAL SKETCH OF MENACHEM BEGIN

Menachem Begin was born in Brest-Litovsk on August 16, 1913, son of Zeev-Dov and Hassia Begin. He was educated at the Mizrachi Hebrew School and the Polish Gymnasium. Until the age of thirteen he belonged to the Hashomer Hatza'ir movement, and at the age of sixteen he joined Betar (Brit Trumpeldor) nationalist youth movement associated with the Zionist Revisionist movement of Ze'ev Jabotinsky.

In 1931, he entered Warsaw University and took his law degree in 1935. In 1932 he became head of the Organization Department of Betar in Poland. In 1936, he was sent to Czechoslovakia to head the movement there. In 1937 he returned to Poland, and for a time was imprisoned for leading a demonstration in front of the British Legation in Warsaw protesting against British policy in Palestine. He organized groups of Betar members who went to Palestine as illegal immigrants, and in 1939 became the head of the movement in Poland. He married Aliza (née Arnold) in May.

Upon the outbreak of World War II, he fled to Vilna and eventually was arrested by the Russian authorities in September 1940. In May 1941, he was transferred to a Gulag camp in Pechora but was released under the terms of the Stalin-Sikorski agreement in September 1941.

He then joined the Polish Free Army and reached Mandate Palestine. Achieving a leave of absence in 1943, he was appointed to command the Irgun Zvai Leumi (National Military Organization), known by the initials of its Hebrew name as "Etzel." He led the underground's operations against the British regime. The government offered a reward of £10,000 for information leading to his arrest, but he evaded capture by living under assumed identities.

After the establishment of the State of Israel, he founded the Herut movement and headed the party's list of candidates for the Knesset. He was a member of the Knesset from the first elections in 1949 until 1984. On June 1, 1967, Mr. Begin joined the National Unity government in which he served as minister without portfolio until August 4, 1970.

Begin, at the head of the Likud party, won the ninth Knesset elections of May 17, 1977, and presented his government to the Knesset on June 20, becoming prime minister of Israel. The Likud also gained the largest numbers of seats in the tenth Knesset elections of 1981.

Begin's premiership was marked by a liberalization of the economy, increased construction of Jewish communities throughout the Jewish national homeland, Project Renewal to correct negligence of disadvantaged neighborhoods, the bombing of the Iraqi atomic reactor and the First Lebanon War.

Begin resigned as prime minister in September 1983, retired from public office and died on March 4, 1992.

His publications include *The Revolt*, his memoirs as Irgun commander, and *White Nights*, his diary as a Soviet prisoner. His son, Benny, is a member of Knesset and minister. He has two daughters, Hasia and Leah.

BIOGRAPHICAL SKETCH OF MUHAMMAD ANWAR EL-SADAT

Muhammad Anwar el-Sadat was born on December 25, 1918, in Mit Abu al-Kum, al-Minufiyah, Egypt to a poor family, one of thirteen brothers and sisters. He graduated from the Royal Military Academy in Cairo in 1938 and entered the army as a second lieutenant, posted in Sudan. There he met Gamal Abdel Nasser, and along with several other junior officers they formed the secret Free Officers movement committed to freeing Egypt from British domination and royal corruption.

During the Second World War he was imprisoned by the British for his efforts to obtain help from Germany. In 1952, he took part in the military coup that overthrew King Farouk. In 1954, Sadat was appointed minister of state and in 1959 became secretary general of the National Union political party. Sadat was president of the People's Assembly (1960–1968) and also eventually vice president of Egypt.

After Nasser's death in 1970, Sadat succeeded him as president. He implemented policies that sought to curb government corruption and limit the power of the Nasserists. In 1971 the Americans tried to initiate a peace treaty between Israel and Egypt, with mediation by the Swedish UN negotiator Gunnar Jarring, but it was not successful.

On October 6, 1973, Sadat launched the October War, also known as the Yom Kippur War, together with Syria. It was a two-pronged surprise attack against the Israeli forces occupying the Egyptian Sinai Peninsula and the Syrian Golan Heights in an attempt to retake the territory captured by Israel six years earlier in the 1967 Six-Day War.

During the last years of Sadat's rule, extreme Islamists initiated riots based on economic issues as well as cultural developments. In September 1981, Sadat ordered mass arrests of more than fifteen hundred people. However, on October 6, 1981, a month after the crackdown, Sadat was assassinated during the annual victory parade in Cairo by Lieutenant Khalid Islambouli. Sadat was succeeded by his vice president, Hosni Mubarak.

Sadat was married twice. He was first married to Ehsan Madi; after divorcing her he married Jehan (née Raouf). His children from his first marriage are three daughters, Rokaya, Rawia and Camelia; from his second marriage he had a son, Gamal, and three more daughters: Lobna, Noha and Jehan.

He authored *Revolt on the Nile* and an autobiography, *Search for Identity*.

OVERVIEW OF THE ISRAEL-EGYPT PEACE PROCESS

A BIT OF HISTORY

Egypt, as the largest and most powerful of Israel's neighbors, also was Israel's biggest enemy. Within a period of just twenty-five years, five wars were conducted between the two countries – the War of Independence (1948–1949), the Sinai Campaign (1956), the Six-Day War (1967), the War of Attrition (1968–1970) and the Yom Kippur War (1973).

After conquering northeastern Sinai in the War of Independence, Israel was forced by international pressure to withdraw. During the Sinai Campaign, Israel took over the entire Sinai Peninsula and again, due to international pressure, withdrew. In 1967, the Sinai Peninsula again fell into Israel's hands but remained under Israeli administration this time. In the aftermath of the 1973 conflict, Egyptian president Anwar Sadat came to the recognition that the Arabs could not defeat Israel on the field of battle and that the return of Sinai would be facilitated only through American diplomatic pressure. This fact, and his desire to rehabilitate Egypt's economy, altered his political thrust – from a dependence on the Soviet Union to one on the United States. American involvement with interim agreements between Egypt and Israel following the war strengthened this trend.

Menachem Begin, then the leader of the opposition, did not support these interim agreements because they included transferring territorial acquisitions without a final peace treaty.

In May 1977, following the elections and immediately after his confirmation as Israel's prime minister in June, Menachem Begin decided to further the cause of peace. His foreign minister, Moshe Dayan, was a partner to this initiative. Begin declared that he was prepared for peace talks within the Geneva Conference framework. Through the offices of the Romanian president and the king of Morocco, Israel made it clear to the Egyptian president that Israel was ready for talks and open to engage in negotiations.

In July 1977, Begin visited American president Jimmy Carter in Washington. In August, he went to Romania and met with Nicolae Ceausescu. The advancement of the peace process was a central agenda item in each of these visits. In September, Dayan secretly met with Hassan al-Tahomi, Egyptian deputy prime minister, in Morocco. At this stage, Sadat estimated that there was a firm base for an agreement. Additional messages that Begin was interested in meeting him and that there were grounds for talks had also been passed on to Sadat via the Shah of Iran and the prime minister of India. Nevertheless, the breakthrough was not achieved. The dramatic turning point was made by the Egyptian president himself, in a courageous move that surprised all – Israel, the Arab countries and the rest of the world.

SADAT'S ANNOUNCEMENT

On November 9, 1977, Sadat addressed the People's Assembly in Cairo and proclaimed: "I am ready to go to the Israeli parliament itself in order to further the efforts to make peace in our region so that not even one Egyptian soldier should be harmed…." His words caused a storm of reactions in the Arab world, foremost among his detractors being the "Rejectionist Front" countries: Syria, Libya, Iraq and Algeria. He was opposed at home as well and the foreign minister, Ismail Fahmi, resigned.

Sadat's closest advisors were prepared for such an announcement but since nothing had been finalized, they, too, were surprised. Sadat's move was meant to circumvent the inconvenient Geneva Conference still being promoted by the United States in which the Soviets and other were involved. Begin, too, was unenthused by the idea of an international conference at Geneva and was pleased to avoid it despite the two leaders insisting that their move was a preliminary conference matter.

The Israeli response to Sadat's words was immediate. On November 11, Begin announced over Israel's Arabic-language radio that Sadat would be accorded full hospitality and, turning to the Egyptian people, said:

> We wish you well…. We, the Israelis, stretch out our hand to you…. [I]t will be a pleasure to welcome and receive your president with the traditional hospitality you and we have inherited from our

common father, Abraham. And I, for my part, will of course be ready to come to your capital, Cairo, for the same purpose: no more wars – peace – a real peace and forever.

Sadat responded, saying that his visit would be conducted without prior conditions.

The secret contacts between Israel and Egypt had been kept from the knowledge of the head of military intelligence, the army's chief-of-staff and the defense minister. This intense secrecy surrounding the diplomatic maneuvering led to a warning from military intelligence that Sadat's visit was actually an Egyptian plot and Chief of Staff Motta Gur gave a newspaper interview warning of such a possible attack. In the ten days leading up to Sadat's arrival, the American media served as a platform for communication between the two leaders. It was in a TV interview with Walter Cronkite that Sadat confirmed his willingness to travel to Israel within the week, and later the same day Begin made clear he was inviting Sadat to Jerusalem. Begin conveyed an official written invitation to the American ambassador to Israel, Sam Lewis. Sadat accepted it immediately but, concerned for his personal safety, did not publicly agree until he finished his visit to Damascus.

SADAT'S VISIT TO JERUSALEM

After the Sabbath, on Saturday night, November 19, 1977, President Sadat's plane landed at 8:00 PM thus making him the first Arab leader ever to visit Israel in an open manner. He was received in an official protocol ceremony at a state-sponsored event. He was greeted by the president of Israel, Professor Efraim Katzir, Prime Minister Menachem Begin and the entire senior echelon of the state's institutions. As the doors of the plane opened, horns were trumpeted, a red carpet was laid out and the IDF orchestra played the national anthems of both states. The flags of Israel and Egypt lined the highway from the airport to Israel's capital, Jerusalem. The ceremony took place despite the fact that there was technically still a state of war existing between the two countries.

All of Israel was prepared for the visit and the operation was given the security code name "Hour of Good Will." Tens of thousands of police personnel and army soldiers provided security. During his two-day visit, Sadat visited the Knesset and Yad Vashem (The Holocaust Martyrs' and

Heroes' Remembrance Authority), prayed at the al-Aqsa Mosque and met Begin many times. In his speech before the Knesset plenum, the climax of the visit, he demanded total withdrawal from the disputed territories and a solution to the "Palestinian problem."

On November 20, 1977, President Sadat addressed the Knesset. He stressed the heavy toll that both Egyptians and Israelis had suffered in the wars fought between the two countries, and he extended a hand in peace to the citizens of Israel. He also presented a very hard line on territorial questions, stressing that Israeli "expansionism" would not be permitted, and demanding that Israel withdraw from all "Arab territory," including Arab Jerusalem.

Mr. Begin followed President Sadat at the podium, emphasizing the historic Jewish connection to the Land of Israel while expressing Israel's goodwill towards creating peace.

THE CAMP DAVID PEACE TALKS

Following Sadat's dramatic visit to Israel, direct peace talks between Egypt and Israel commenced. Over the next few months, a difficult and drawn-out process took place with no real results and a few crises. Meetings were conducted in Ismailia, Jerusalem, Cairo, Morocco and the United States. When they reached an impasse, United States president Jimmy Carter invited the two sides to him. On September 5, 1978, the talks renewed at the presidential retreat of Camp David, near Washington.

At the core of the dispute between Israel and Egypt was the issue of autonomy for the Arabs of the disputed territories and the Egyptian insistence that Israel withdraw to the international boundary. The idea of autonomy, as proposed by Begin in December 1977, established that the Arabs of Palestine would be permitted control over the civilian aspects of their lives but not matters such as security and foreign affairs. The plan was intended to ensure that the areas of Judea, Samaria and Gaza remained under Israeli authority due to its legitimate demand for ownership of the territory. According to Begin's autonomy plan, Israel would not assert its sovereignty over the area and this concern would be left open.

For thirteen tense and difficult days, the two delegations headed by Begin and Sadat held talks. Members of the Israeli delegation included

Foreign Minister Moshe Dayan, Defense Minister Ezer Weizmann and the Israeli government's legal advisor, Aharon Barak, among others. President Carter had instructed that the conference be closed to the media and all visitors. No member of the delegations was permitted to leave during the entire period of the talks.

Sensitive issues were not lacking. Begin understood that the matter of the Israeli communities in Sinai were non-negotiable for Sadat, and Carter and Sadat understood that Begin would not yield on the matter of a Palestinian state. The peace framework that eventually was signed included an Israeli commitment to grant autonomy to the "Arabs of Eretz-Yisrael," in Begin's terminology, as he refused to recognize a separate national identity of "Palestinians"; he would recognize them as individuals but not as a collective people. The agreement could have been signed earlier but Carter stubbornly sought to pressure Begin on the Palestinian issue even beyond what Sadat dared to hope for. The talks almost broke down the night before the signing.

In the end, on September 17, 1978 (15 Elul 5738), Begin and Sadat signed, together with Carter, the historic first peace framework agreement with an Arab state. On September 27, the peace accord was brought before the Knesset for confirmation. The vote was eighty-four for, nineteen against and seventeen abstentions. Six months later, the full peace treaty was signed.

At Camp David, two accords were signed. (Both documents are reproduced in the appendix.) The first, "A Framework for Peace in the Middle East," declared that the legal bases for peace were Security Council Resolutions 242 and 338 and dealt with the areas of Judea, Samaria and Gaza. Autonomy would last for five years and would be replaced by a permanent status agreement. The second agreement, "A Framework for the Conclusion of a Peace Treaty between Egypt and Israel," dealt with a normalization process between Israel and Egypt on the assumption that future treaties would be made with Jordan, Lebanon and Syria.

The Egypt-Israel accord was predicated on Israel's complete withdrawal from the Sinai Peninsula, to "the internationally recognized border between Mandate Palestine and Egypt." The withdrawal included dismantlement of the Jewish communities in Sinai, in exchange for which normal relations would be established. These were to include diplomatic relations as well as cultural and economic relations, an end to economic boycotts, free travel of goods and persons and defense of citizens through recourse to courts, military arrangements in the peninsula such as demilitarization and limitations on numbers of troops, kinds of personnel and equipment, and so on, as well as the supervision mechanism (that is, a determination of who would supervise the implementation of the agreements reached).

It was important for Egypt to forge a link between the accords dealing with Judea, Samaria and Gaza and the peace process between it and Israel. This was intended to avoid accusations within the Arab world of a separate peace and the abandonment of the Palestinian issue. Israel's main concern was to protect a future claim for sovereignty over these same territories. Israel, for the first time, recognized "the legitimate right of the Palestinian peoples and their just requirements" in connection with final arrangements in those areas (although Israel delineated those rights as pertaining to individuals, not to a unified people). Israel even agreed that Jordan would be involved in the interim period of autonomy.

The agreements had letters attached on the issue of Jerusalem. Begin declared that the city would not be divided and would remain as Israel's capital. Sadat, for his part, announced that the city was Arab and a part of the "West Bank" and it must be returned to Arab sovereignty.

Despite the fact that not all issues were resolved, a great deal of progress was made. In recognition of their labors, Begin and Sadat were awarded the Nobel Peace Prize, which was awarded on December 10, 1978. Sadat, however, did not attend and delegated his aide Sayed Marei in his stead.

THE PEACE TREATY

Prime Minister Menachem Begin waves his hand at a member of his faction
in the Knesset. On the right: Yigael Yadin and Moshe Dayan.

For the next three months, marathon negotiations were conducted, accompanied by demonstrations and protests in Israel both pro and con. Egypt was attacked verbally by the Arab League. Cyrus Vance, US secretary of state, traveled many times to the area and between the two countries, as well as other Middle East nations. A main issue of contention was Egypt's demand to place Egyptian liaison officers in Gaza, which Begin refused, viewing it as a symbolic presence of Egyptian sovereignty within the borders of the original mandated area of the Jewish national home. President Carter then took the unusual step of visiting the two leaders in their respective countries at the beginning of March to conclude the negotiations.

The peace treaty was signed on the White House lawn on March 26, 1979, before fifteen hundred invited guests and the world's media in a forty-five-minute ceremony, after being ratified by the Israeli Knesset on March 22 by a ninety-five to eighteen vote.

POST-TREATY EVENTS

Prime Minister Menachem Begin and President Sadat share a private talk, Beersheba

In May 1979, autonomy discussions commenced at Beersheba, based on the framework accords. Kamal Hassan Ali, Egyptian foreign minister, and Israeli minister for the interior Dr. Avraham Burg chaired the two delegations. The opening positions expressed indicated a large gap between expectations, almost impossible to bridge. The talks soon came to a halt and were not renewed. In October 1979, Moshe Dayan resigned as foreign minister over disagreements with Prime Minister Begin over the nature of the autonomy talks. In May 1980, Defense Minister Ezer Weizmann also resigned in protest and Begin assumed the position of defense minister until the June 1981 elections.

On April 25, 1982, following an intense and at times violent struggle, the Rafiah Salient was evacuated of its seven thousand Jewish inhabitants and the communities, including the towns of Yammit and Ophira and a number of agricultural villages, as well as all Israeli armed forces and their military bases and also oil fields in the Sinai Peninsula.

President Anwar Sadat with Prime Minister Menachem Begin (left)
before departing for Egypt

The fixing of the new international border between the two countries
was no easy task. It was based on the 1906 boundary line set between the
Ottoman Empire and Great Britain. A special problem was Taba, some
five miles west of Eilat. Due to a certain lack of clarity in the delineations
on the maps of the time, it appeared to Israel that Taba should be included

in Israeli territory, and so it did not withdraw from the area and a hotel and other tourist infrastructures were built. Egypt asserted that the border passed east of Taba. An international arbitration panel eventually declared, after more than seven years, that Taba should revert to Egypt. Israel's inner cabinet voted nine to one (Ariel Sharon was the dissenting minister) on February 26, 1989, to accept the agreement. On March 15, the evacuation took place. The border crossing was to be open twenty-four hours a day and Egypt agreed to allow Israelis carrying a passport, but not a visa, to visit Taba. Israeli currency continued to be accepted at the hotel, and Israel continued to supply water and electricity to the strip. There was a dramatic change in Egypt's international status. In rejecting links to Russia and establishing firm ties with the United States, Egypt became isolated in the Arab world and was expelled temporarily from the Arab League, affecting Egypt's Pan-Arab moves. The Islamic Jihad movement strengthened and during 1981, some sixteen hundred extremists were arrested in Egypt. In 1989, Arab League membership was renewed and its headquarters returned to Cairo.

On October 6, 1981, Sadat was assassinated by Islamic extremists. Of twenty-four Arab League countries, only three sent representatives to the funeral. Menachem Begin resigned as prime minister in September 1983 and died on March 4, 1992.

THE CORRESPONDENCE, SPEECHES AND INTERVIEWS

Part 1

First Overtures:
The Prelude to and the Visit in
Jerusalem
May–November 1977

JUNE 20, 1977

PRIME MINISTER BEGIN'S FIRST SPEECH TO THE KNESSET

Menachem Begin's peace initiative was not a sudden impulse. He had developed the idea over a number of years and referred to it in private talks and later in various public addresses. Many had heard his outline of the subject several times and then heard him proclaim it openly at a Likud party convention.

On May 17, 1977, Menachem Begin led the Likud to a decisive victory in Israel's general elections. In his first appearance in the Knesset as prime minister of Israel, on June 20, 1977, he presented his new government and submitted his policy, saying, among other things:

> Our prime concern is the prevention of a new war in the Middle East. I call upon King Hussein, President Sadat and President Assad to meet with me – whether in our capitals or on neutral ground, in public or away from the spotlights of publicity – in order to discuss the establishment of true peace between their countries and Israel. Much blood, too much, has been shed in the region – Jewish and Arab. Let us put an end to the bloodshedding that is abhorrent to us, and sit down at the negotiating table in sincerity and seriousness. Should this plea encounter refusal, we shall take note of the Arab intransigence. It will not be new. Five prime ministers who preceded me – David Ben-Gurion, Moshe Sharett and Levi Eshkol, of blessed memory, and Mrs. Golda Meir and Yitzhak Rabin, to whom I wish long life – repeatedly called for holding such meetings. And there was no response – or rather, there was a negative response – from the other side. But we shall not weary of sounding the call – not for propaganda purposes, but for the vital needs of our people and our countries.

NOVEMBER 9, 1977

PRESIDENT SADAT'S ADDRESS TO THE EGYPTIAN PARLIAMENT

Following are excerpts of President Sadat's address to the People's Assembly, Egypt's parliament, in the course of which he first publicly stated his willingness to travel to Israel.

Let me now pause for a moment and talk to you and our people and the Arab nation about the latest developments as regards the [Geneva] Conference, which is being proposed at both the Arab and international levels not as an end in itself but as a means that could lead to that end. If we succeed in exploiting our strength so as to face Israel with the choice between a peace based on justice and legality and a confrontation with incalculable consequences, it will be a confrontation in which the Arab nation will employ all its resources, material and moral. You are well aware of what efforts have been made in recent months towards convening the Geneva Conference as soon as possible – before the end of this year, in fact – on condition that, before it is convened, proper preparations are made to ensure that the aims for which it is convened are realized. Such preparation will enable us to reach a just and comprehensive peaceful settlement within a reasonable time and prevent the Conference being turned into a platform for rhetoric or an arena for verbal fencing, the exchange of accusations and the striking of attitudes for propaganda purposes.

It is only fair to say that a greater part of these efforts has been made by the US and that President Carter has devoted a great part of his time and attention to the problem and given it a high priority over many of the problems that confront him at home and abroad. We greatly appreciate this attitude of his, for it reflects a penetrating view of the nature of the conflict and its regional and international dimensions and of the consequences it could lead to all over the world should it continue. There is also the question of the special responsibility borne by the United States in this conflict because of the military, political, economic and diplomatic support it has supplied and is still supplying to Israel.

Perhaps the most important of President Carter's achievements in this field is the way he has come to understand the problem of the Palestinian people, the problem which Israel, with her lying propaganda and her notorious influence in American society, has succeeded in concealing and misrepresenting for more than a quarter of a century. In the space of a few months, President Carter has succeeded in removing the veil from the eyes of the American people and placing the Palestine problem within its true frameworks.

As we approach this delicate stage, I want to submit to you and to the Arab nation the main guidelines we have set for ourselves in our quest for liberation. Firstly, we are not at all afraid of any kind of confrontation with Israel, for we appreciate her real significance, without either exaggerating her strength so as to raise her to the status of a mighty power capable of anything, or so underestimating her as to believe that she is a puny entity with no strength at all.

Secondly, in every move we make a point of safeguarding the Arab nation's strongest and most effective weapon – the genuine Arab solidarity which is an expression of faith in the Arabs' unity of goal and destiny, of their unity of interest and strategic line, even though we differ in our views of what efforts and circumstances will lead to the common goal.

Thirdly, in every move we make and every step we take we must concentrate on the substance and not be distracted from it by the form or allow ourselves to be immobilized by rigid forms that have nothing to do with the essence of the problem and have no effect on the outcome of the conflict. History teaches us that true revolutionaries are those who clearly set themselves an objective and strive to realize it whatever the cost to them in sacrifices, without bothering about the form or allowing their attention to be diverted from the essence of the cause they are fighting for to forms and formulas that have nothing to do with the matter....

We are therefore determined not to spend more time than is necessary on procedural matters and forms and thus prevent Israel attaining her goal. We refuse to play her game – indeed we insist on her facing up to things in such a way that the heart of the matter is reached immediately, and that not a moment passes before discussion of the source and basis of the conflict – the Israeli occupation of Arab territory in violation of the rights of the people of Palestine. We must relentlessly insist on this. Then no one will be able to ask us or oblige us to do what we do not want, and we shall achieve our goal. For in defining that goal we have not been excessive; as all agree, we have adhered to international legality and the rule of law and the standards accepted by all civilized countries for distinguishing between right and wrong.

You heard me saying just now that we do not set great store by procedural matters. I say this frankly, in your presence, to our people, to the Arab nation and to the whole world. We are ready to go to Geneva and to sit down on behalf of peace regardless of the procedural problems raised by Israel in the hope of spoiling our chances or of so exasperating us that we say, as we have done in the past, No, we do not want to go and we shall not go, so that she may appear to the world as the advocate of peace....

I am ready to agree to any procedural points. When we go to Geneva we shall refuse to give up the territory, the Arab territory occupied in 1967, and neither Israel nor any other power will be able to prevent me demanding the legitimate rights of the Palestinians, their right to self-determination and to establish their state.

I am ready to go to Geneva – and I do not conceal this from you who are the representatives of the people and I say it in the hearing of our people and of the Arab nation. You heard me saying that I am prepared to go the ends of the earth if my doing so will prevent any of my officers or men being killed or wounded. I really am ready to go to the ends and Israel will be amazed to hear me say that we do not refuse them – I am prepared to go to their very home, to the Knesset itself and discuss things with them.

Brothers and sisters, members of the People's Assembly, no time must be lost; it is for us to decide, and there can be no decision without the permission of the people, and the people want us to look ahead so as to make up for lost time, and much time has been lost. The people want us to act rather than talk. The people want us to do all in our power to build a new future, and it is no good quarrelling about the past that has gone, or weeping or shedding crocodile tears over debris that has piled up and blocked the road; if there is a will to work, the road can always be paved, if men are ready to make every effort they can always clear the debris to make space for building and construction.

NOVEMBER 11, 1977

BEGIN BROADCASTS DIRECTLY TO THE EGYPTIAN PEOPLE

Begin had been making general appeals to the leaders of all the surrounding countries since his installation as prime minister. When he spoke to a delegation of members of the US Armed Services Committee, who were touring the Middle East and proceeding to Cairo the next day, Begin again extended his invitation to Sadat. More dramatically, he broadcast a special appeal in English directly to the Egyptian people:

Citizens of Egypt, this is the first time that I address you directly, but it is not the first time that I think and speak of you. You are our neighbors and always will be.

For the last twenty-nine years a tragic, completely unnecessary conflict has continued between your country and ours. Since the time when the government of King Farouk ordered to invade our land, Eretz Israel, in order to strangle our newly restored freedom and independence, four major wars took place between you and us.

Much blood was shed on both sides. Many families were orphaned and bereaved, in Egypt and Israel. In retrospect, we know that all those attempts to destroy the Jewish state were in vain, as all the sacrifices you were called upon to make – in life, in development, in economy, in social advancement – all these superfluous sacrifices were also in vain. And may I tell you, our neighbors, that so it will be in the future.

You should know that we have come back to the land of our forefathers, that it is we who…established independence in our own land, for all generations to come.

We wish you well. In fact, there is no reason whatsoever for hostility between our peoples. In ancient times, Egypt and Eretz Israel were allies; real friends and allies, against a common enemy from the north. Yes, indeed, many changes have taken place since those days, but perhaps the intrinsic basis for friendship and mutual help remains unaltered.

Nov

1977

1978

1979

1980

1981

We, the Israelis, stretch out our hand to you. It is not, as you know, a weak hand. If attacked, we shall always defend ourselves, as our forefathers, the Maccabees, did – and won the day.

But we do not want any clashes with you. Let us say one to another, and let it be a silent oath by both peoples, of Egypt and Israel: no more wars, no more bloodshed and no more threats.

Let us not only make peace, let us also start on the road of friendship, sincere and productive cooperation. We can help each other. We can make the lives of our nations better, easier, happier.

Your president said, two days ago, that he will be ready to come to Jerusalem, to our parliament – the Knesset – in order to prevent one Egyptian soldier from being wounded. It is a good statement. I have already welcomed it, and it will be a pleasure to welcome and receive your president with the traditional hospitality you and we have inherited from our common father, Abraham.

And I for my part will, of course, be ready to come to your capital, Cairo, for the same purpose: no more wars – peace, a real peace, and forever.

It is in the Holy Koran, in Surah 5, that our right to this land was stated and sanctified. May I read to you this eternal surah:

> Recall when Moses said to his people, O my people, remember the goodness of Allah towards you when He appointed prophets among you. O my people, enter the Holy Land which Allah hath written down as yours.

It is in this spirit of our common belief in God, in Divine Providence, in right and in justice, in all the great human values which were handed down to you by the Prophet Muhammad and by our prophets – Moses, Joshua, Jeremiah, Ezekiel – it is in this human spirit that I say to you with all my heart: shalom (peace), [which in Arabic is] *Sulkh*.

NOVEMBER 14, 1977

A VIRTUAL "JOINT" INTERVIEW WITH WALTER CRONKITE

The subject of Begin's invitation and Anwar Sadat's willingness to go to Israel was in the air. Wanting to pin down the story, American journalist Walter Cronkite pressed Sadat in a satellite interview from New York on November 14, 1977. When Sadat responded with an unambiguous declaration of willingness, CBS scrambled to set up a separate satellite interview in Tel Aviv with Begin for that very evening, and broadcast it together with the Sadat interview, with Begin and Sadat shown answering questions as if they were in an actual dialogue. American pundits at the time called it "Cronkite diplomacy," although the other major American news networks groused that they also had been working on the story. Following is an abbreviated transcript of the "joint" interview.

Sadat: I'm just waiting for the proper invitation.

Cronkite: You must get something directly from Mr. Begin, not through the press?

Sadat: Right. Right.

Cronkite: And how would that be transmitted, sir, since you do not have diplomatic relations with Israel?

Sadat: Why not through our mutual friend, the Americans…

Begin: …I will, during the week, ask my friend the American ambassador to Israel to find out in Cairo from his colleague, the American ambassador to Egypt, whether he will be prepared to give us his good offices, and transmit a letter from me to President Sadat inviting him, formally and cordially, through the good offices of the United States, to come to Jerusalem.

Cronkite: *(To Sadat.)* If you get that formal invitation, how soon are you prepared to go?

Sadat: Really, I'm looking forward to fulfill this visit in the…in the earliest time possible.

Cronkite: Would that…that would be, say, within a week?

Sadat: You can say that, yes.

Cronkite: You said that you wished to address the Knesset, the parliament in Israel…

Sadat: That's right.

Cronkite: Would you also engage in substantive discussions?

Sadat: I may exchange our views or so with Begin…yes.

Cronkite: What about the opposition from some of your fellow leaders in the Arab world to this visit…they have expressed this to you, I gather?

Sadat: I didn't tell any one of my colleagues and I didn't ask them to agree or not agree upon this. I felt that my responsibility as president of Egypt is to try all means to reach peace. And I took this decision – for sure, there are those who are against it, but as much as I am convinced that this is the right way and my people back me, I shall be fulfilling the whole thing.

Cronkite: Has the PLO leader, Yasser Arafat, expressed any opinion on this visit to Premier Begin?

Sadat: Not at all. Not at all because as I told you, Walter, this is my initiative.

Cronkite: What is the ultimate that could result from such a meeting… what's the best way you could hope for?

Sadat: We are in a crucial moment. There has never been a suitable moment in the Arab world to reach genuine peace like we are now. So I want to put the fact before them and in the same time we want to discuss what will be the other alternative if we can't achieve peace. It will be horrible. Believe me, horrible.

Cronkite later asked Begin how he was prepared to parlay Sadat's declaration into a face-to-face meeting. Begin responded:

Begin: Tomorrow I will make a statement in our parliament in the afternoon and I think that immediately after this statement I will get in touch with Mr. Lewis, my good friend the American ambassador [to Israel], and so find out. But I can assure you,

Mr. Cronkite, as we really want the visit of President Sadat – we really want to negotiate the peace, to establish permanent peace in the Middle East – I will not hesitate to send such a letter.

Cronkite: Are there any preconditions under which you will be inviting him?

Begin: No preconditions and I understand that also President Sadat doesn't put forward any preconditions. He has got his position, we have our position; let us sit together around the table and talk peace, and everybody will bring his position.

Cronkite: He hinted to me this morning that he thought it might be possible that he would be going to Israel if the invitation was forthcoming within a week or so. Do you think that's realistic?

Begin: Very good news. Well, if President Sadat is ready to come next week, if he tells me that he will come next week, I will have to postpone my trip to Britain because I am supposed to go next Sunday to London at the invitation of Prime Minister Callaghan. But I suppose that Prime Minister Callaghan will also be agreeable to postpone that meeting for a week and rather have President Sadat in Jerusalem, because it is hoped to have peace in the Middle East. But if President Sadat would come after my return from Europe I will come back home next Friday after my visit to London and to Geneva and then he may come the next Monday. But anyhow, any time, any day he's prepared to come, I will receive him cordially at the airport, and go together with him to Jerusalem, also represent him to the Knesset and let him make his speech to our parliament. I will follow him onto the platform and greet him, receive him. I think it's now up to President Sadat to carry out his, let me say, promise, or bring into fruition his readiness to come to Jerusalem.

NOVEMBER 15, 1977

BEGIN'S OFFICIAL INVITATION

Begin made good on his promise the following day. This is the official letter of invitation from Prime Minister Menachem Begin, which he handed to US Ambassador to Israel Samuel Lewis; it was then conveyed to President Sadat via US Ambassador to Egypt Hermann Frederick Eilts.

Jerusalem, November 15, 1977

His Excellency
Mr. Anwar Sadat
President of the Arab Republic of Egypt
Cairo

Dear Mr. President,

On behalf of the government of Israel I have the honour to extend to you our cordial invitation to come to Jerusalem and to visit our country.

Your Excellency's readiness to undertake such a visit as expressed to the People's Council of Egypt, has been noted here with deep and positive interest, as has been the statement that you would wish to address the members of our parliament, the Knesset, and to meet with me.

If, as I hope, you will accept our invitation, arrangements will be made for you to address the Knesset from its rostrum. You will also, should you so desire, be enabled to meet with our various parliamentary groups, those supporting the government as well as those in opposition.

As to the date of the proposed visit we shall be glad to meet [at] your convenience. It so happens that I am scheduled at the invitation of Prime Minister Callaghan to leave for London on Sunday, 20 November, on an official visit to Great Britain. Should you advise me, Mr. President, that you would be ready to come to Jerusalem on Monday, 21 November, I would ask Prime Minister Callaghan's indulgence and arrange to postpone

my visit to Britain, so as to be able to receive you
personally and to initiate together with you talks on the
establishment of peace, for which, as we both know, the
peoples of the Middle East yearn and pray.

   Alternatively, should you decide to come here on
Thursday, 24 November, or thereafter, I would be back
from London by Wednesday afternoon, and greet you upon
your arrival.

   May I assure you, Mr. President, that the parliament,
the government and the people of Israel will receive you
with respect and cordiality.

Yours sincerely,
Menachem Begin

...AND SADAT'S ACCEPTANCE

Samuel Lewis cabled Begin's invitation to the American ambassador in Egypt, Hermann Frederick Eilts, early in the morning on Wednesday, November 16. President Sadat was to leave that day for a trip to Damascus. Egyptian vice president Hosni Mubarak suggested to Sadat that he not respond to Begin's invitation before the Damascus trip; should his acceptance become public while he was in Damascus, Mubarak felt that Sadat would be in danger. In order to give the Israelis time to prepare for the visit, Eilts was given reluctant permission to cable to the Israeli government, via Lewis, "If a certain president wants to visit Israel, what is the earliest time on Saturday he should arrive?" Sadat's official reply to the invitation, however, came only on Thursday, November 17, after his return from Damascus. At a press conference at his home in Ismailia, Sadat had Eilts give him the invitation in front of the cameras as if delivering it for the first time. Since the actual invitation had been misplaced, Eilts handed Sadat a letter Sadat himself had addressed to Eilts, and Sadat, carefully positioned so the cameras could not see the letter, read it and publicly accepted the invitation.[1] Afterwards President Sadat wrote Prime Minister Begin an official letter:

---

1. Kenneth W. Stein, *Heroic Diplomacy: Sadat, Kissinger, Carter, Begin, and the Quest for Arab-Israeli Peace* (London: Routledge, 1999), 224–25.

بسم الله الرحمن الرحيم

*The President
of the Arab Republic of Egypt*

الرئيس

Dear Mr. Prime Minister,

I have the pleasure to accept the invitation extended to me to come to Jerusalem and address the representatives of your people on one of the most important issues to both of us, an issue of war and peace.

I am pleased to hear that my readiness to undertake such a visit has been met with deep and positive interest by the Government of Israel.

I hope that my initiative, which reflects our sincere desire to establish a just and durable peace in the Middle East, would find a positive response on your part, not only at the present time but first and foremost in the future, when historical decisions have to be made in the direction of ending an era of devastating war and tension.

As has been agreed upon,[2] I shall start my visit on November 19. I shall have the pleasure of addressing the Knesset and later to meet with your parliamentary groups as well as with other officials.

Yours sincerely,
Mohamed Anwar El Sadat

---

2. In the absence of diplomatic relations between the two countries, messages were relayed indirectly between Sam Lewis, the American ambassador to Israel, and Hermann Frederick Eilts, the American ambassador to Egypt. Begin's written invitation arrived in Cairo on November 16 but with a visit to Damascus planned for the next day, Sadat's official public acceptance was publicized late Thursday on his return from Syria.

NOVEMBER 20, 1977

SADAT ADDRESSES THE KNESSET IN JERUSALEM

The visit was set up without delay. In a surreal scene, at 8:00 PM on Saturday evening, November 19, 1977 (after the Sabbath), President Sadat arrived at Ben-Gurion Airport with an entourage of Egyptian military and political personnel. The moment of arrival was extremely tense. Egypt and Israel were officially still in a state of war with each other. Many in Israel were convinced that Sadat's visit was a military ploy, and half-expected a commando troop to burst out of the plane. The Egyptian delegation, for their part, were also not fully convinced that they wouldn't be shot down on the tarmac. Instead, the visitors were received with full honors and a military band played, though no speeches were given. President Sadat and President Katzir drove directly to Jerusalem, where President Sadat met Prime Minister Begin. On Sunday morning, November 20, President Sadat prayed at the al-Aqsa Mosque in Jerusalem, and visited the Church of the Holy Sepulcher and Yad Vashem. Then President Sadat, Prime Minister Begin and Labor Party Chairman Peres addressed a special session of the Knesset, President Sadat speaking in Arabic. The following translation of his speech was issued by the Office of the President of Egypt.

FROM LEFT TO RIGHT: Prime Minister Menachem Begin,
Egyptian president Anwar Sadat and Knesset chairman Yitzhak Shamir
at the Knesset in Jerusalem during Sadat's visit to Israel

In the name of God, the Gracious and Merciful.

Mr. Speaker, Ladies and Gentlemen:

Peace and the mercy of God Almighty be upon you and may peace be for us all, God willing. Peace for us all on the Arab land, and in Israel as well, as in every part of this big world, which is so complexed by its conflicts, disturbed by its sharp contradictions, menaced now and then by destructive wars launched by man to annihilate the fellow man. Finally, amidst the ruins of what man has built and the remains of the victims of Mankind, there emerges neither victor nor vanquished. The only vanquished remains man, God's most sublime creation, man whom God has created – as Ghandi the apostle of peace puts it: to forge ahead to mould the way of life and worship God Almighty.

I come to you today on solid ground, to shape a new life, to establish peace. We all, on this land, the land of God; we all, Muslims, Christians and Jews, worship God and no one but God. God's teachings and commandments are love, sincerity, purity and peace.

I do not blame all those who received my decision – when I announced it to the entire world before the Egyptian People's Assembly – with surprise and amazement. Some, ripped by the violent surprise, believed that my decision was no more than verbal juggling to cater for world public opinion. Others, still, interpreted it as political tactics to camouflage my intention of launching a new war. I would go as far as to tell you that one of my aides at the President['s] Office contacted me at the late hour following my return home from the People's Assembly and sounded worried as he asked me: "Mr. President, what would be our reaction if Israel should actually extend an invitation to you?" I replied calmly, I will accept it immediately. I have declared that I will go to the end of the world: I will go to Israel, for I want to put before the People of Israel all the facts.

I can see the point of all those who were astounded by my decision or those who had any doubts as to the sincerity of the intentions behind the declaration of my decision. No one would have ever conceived that the President of the biggest Arab State, which bears the heaviest burden and the top responsibility pertaining to the cause of war and peace in the Middle East, could declare his readiness to go to the land of the adversary while we were still in a state of war. Rather, we all are still bearing the consequences of four fierce wars waged within thirty years. The families of the 1973 October War are still moaning under the cruel pains of widowhood and bereavement of sons, fathers and brothers.

As I have already declared, I have not consulted, as far as this decision is concerned, with any of my colleagues and brothers, the Arab Heads of State or the confrontation States.[3] Those of them who contacted me, following the declaration of this decision, expressed their objection, because the feeling of utter suspicion and absolute lack of confidence between the Arab States and the Palestinian People on the one hand, and Israel on the other, still surges in us all. It is sufficient to say that many months in which peace could have been brought about had been wasted over differences and fruitless discussions on the procedure for the convocation of the Geneva Conference, all showing utter suspicion and absolute lack of confidence.

But, to be absolutely frank with you, I took this decision after reaching thoughts knowing that it constitutes a grave risk for, if God Almighty has made it my fate to assume the responsibility on behalf of the Egyptian People and to share in the fate-determining responsibility of the Arab Nation and the Palestinian People, the main duty dictated by this responsibility is to exhaust all and every means in a bid to save my Egyptian Arab People and the entire Arab Nation the horrors of new, shocking and destructive wars, the dimensions of which are foreseen by no other than God himself.

After […] thoughts, I was convinced that the obligation of responsibility before God, and before the people, make it incumbent on me that I should go to the farthest corner of the world, even to Jerusalem, to address Members of the Knesset, the representatives of the People of Israel, and acquaint them with all the facts surging in me. Then, I would leave you to decide for yourselves. Following this, may God Almighty determine our fate.

Ladies and Gentlemen, there are moments in the life of nations and peoples when it is incumbent on those known for their wisdom and clarity of vision to overlook the past, with all its complexities and weighing memories, in a bold drive towards new horizons. Those who, like us, are shouldering the same responsibility entrusted to us, are the first who should have the courage to take fate-determining decisions which are in

---

3. Confrontation states is a military term meaning all those who view themselves as being in a state of war (in this case, with Israel); rejectionist states is by contrast a political term meaning those who do not engage in negotiations.

consonance with the circumstances. We must all rise above all forms of fanaticism, self-deception and obsolete theories of superiority. The most important thing is never to forget that infallibility is the prerogative of God alone.

If I said that I wanted to save all the Arab People the horrors of shocking and destructive wars, I most sincerely declare before you that I have the same feelings and bear the same responsibility towards all and every man on earth, and certainly towards the Israeli People.

Any life lost in war is a human life, irrespective of its being that of an Israeli or an Arab. A wife who becomes a widow is a human being entitled to a happy family life, whether she be an Arab or an Israeli. Innocent children who are deprived of the care and compassion of their parents are ours, be they living on Arab or Israeli land. They command our top responsibility to afford them a comfortable life today and tomorrow.

For the sake of them all, for the safeguard of the lives of all our sons and brothers, for affording our communities the opportunity to work for the progress and happiness of man and his right to a dignified life, for our responsibilities before the generations to come, for a smile on the face of every child born on our land – for all that, I have taken my decision to come to you, despite all hazards, to deliver my address.

I have shouldered the prerequisites of the historical responsibility and, therefore, I declared – on 4 February 1971, to be precise – that I was willing to sign a peace agreement with Israel. This was the first declaration made by a responsible Arab official since the outbreak of the Arab-Israeli conflict.

Motivated by all these factors dictated by the responsibilities of leadership, I called, on 16 October 1973, before the Egyptian People's Assembly, for an international conference to establish peace with Israel.

Motivated by all these factors dictated by duties of history and leadership, we signed the first disengagement agreement, followed by the second disengagement agreement in Sinai. Then we proceeded trying both open and closed doors in a bid to find a certain path leading to a durable and just peace. We opened our hearts to the peoples of the entire world to make them understand our motivations and objectives, and to leave them actually convinced of the fact that we are advocates of justice and peace-makers.

Motivated by all these factors, I decided to come to you with an open mind and an open heart, and with a conscious determination, so that we might establish permanent peace based on justice.

It is so fated that my trip to you, the trip of peace, should coincide with the Islamic feast, the holy Feast of Sacrifice when Abraham – peace be upon him – great-grandfather of the Arabs and Jews, submitted to God: I say when God Almighty ordered him, and to Him Abraham went, with dedicated sentiments, not out of weakness, but through a giant spiritual force and by a free will, to sacrifice his very own son, prompted by a firm and unshakable belief in ideals that lend life a profound significance.

This coincidence may carry a new meaning to us all, which may become a genuine aspiration heralding security and peace.

Ladies and Gentlemen, let us be frank with each other, using straight-forward words and a clear conception, with no ambiguity. Let us be frank with each other today while the entire world, both East and West, follows these unparalleled moments which could prove to be a radical turning point in the history of this part of the world, if not in the history of the world as a whole. Let us be frank with each other as we answer this important question: how can we achieve permanent peace based on justice?

I have come to you carrying my clear and frank answer to this big question, so that the people in Israel as well as the whole world might hear it, and so that all those whose devoted prayers ring in my ears, pleading to God Almighty that this historic meeting may eventually lead to the results aspired to by millions, might also hear it.

Before I proclaim my answer, I wish to assure you that, in my clear and frank answer, I am basing myself on a number of facts which no one can deny.

The first fact: no one can build his happiness at the expense of the misery of others.

The second fact: never have I spoken or will ever speak in two languages. Never have I adopted or will adopt two policies. I never deal with anyone except in one language, one policy, and with one face.

The third fact: direct confrontation and a straight line are the nearest and most successful methods to reach a clear objective.

The fourth fact: the call for permanent and just peace, based on respect for the United Nations resolutions, has now become the call of the whole world. It has become a clear expression of the will of the international community, whether in official capitals, where policies are made and decisions taken, or at the level of world public opinion which influences policy-making and decision-taking.

The fifth fact: and this is probably the clearest and most prominent, is that the Arab Nation, in its drive for permanent peace based on justice, does not proceed from a position of weakness or hesitation, but it has the potential of power and stability, which tells of a sincere will for peace. The Arab-declared intention stems from an awareness prompted by a heritage of civilization that, to avoid an inevitable disaster that will befall us, you and the entire world, there is no alternative to the establishment of permanent peace based on justice – peace that is not shaken by storms, swayed by suspicion, or jeopardized by ill intentions.

In the light of these facts which I meant to place before you the way I see them, I would also wish to warn you in all sincerity: I warn you against some thoughts that could cross your minds. Frankness makes it incumbent upon me to tell you the following:

First: I have not come here for a separate agreement between Egypt and Israel. This is not part of the policy of Egypt. The problem is not that a peace between Egypt and Israel, or between any Arab confrontation State and Israel, will not bring permanent peace based on justice in the entire region. Rather, even if peace between all the confrontation States and Israel were achieved, in the absence of a just solution to the Palestinian problem, never will there be that durable and just peace upon which the entire world insists today.

Second: I have not come to you to seek a partial peace, namely to terminate the state of belligerency at this stage, and put off the entire problem to a subsequent stage. This is not the radical solution that would steer us to permanent peace.

Equally, I have not come to you for a third disengagement agreement in Sinai, or in the Golan and the West Bank. For this would mean that we are merely delaying the ignition of the fuse; it would mean that we are lacking the courage to confront peace, that we are too weak to shoulder the burdens and responsibilities of a durable peace based on justice.

I have come to you so that together we might build a durable peace based on justice, to avoid the shedding of one single drop of blood from an Arab or an Israeli. It is for this reason that I have proclaimed my readiness to go to the farthest corner of the world.

Here, I would go back to the answer to the big question: how can we achieve a durable peace based on justice?

In my opinion, and I declare it to the whole world from this forum, the answer is neither difficult nor impossible, despite long years of feud, blood vengeance, spite and hatred, and breeding generations on concepts of total rift and deep-rooted animosity. The answer is not difficult, nor is it impossible, if we sincerely and faithfully follow a straight line.

You want to live with us in this part of the world. In all sincerity, I tell you, we welcome you among us, with full security and safety. This, in itself, is a tremendous turning point: one of the landmarks of a decisive historical change.

We used to reject you. We had our reasons and our claims, yes. We used to brand you as "so-called" Israel, yes. We were together in international conferences and organizations and our representatives did not, and still do not, exchange greetings, yes. This has happened and is still happening.

It is also true that we used to set, as a precondition for any negotiations with you, a mediator who would meet separately with each party. Through this procedure, the talks of the first and second disengagement agreements took place.

Our delegates met in the first Geneva Conference without exchanging a direct word. Yes, this has happened.

Yet, today I tell you, and declare it to the whole world, that we accept to live with you in permanent peace based on justice. We do not want to encircle you or be encircled ourselves by destructive missiles ready for launching, nor by the shells of grudges and hatred. I have announced on more than one occasion that Israel has become a *fait accompli*, recognized by the world, and that the two super powers have undertaken the responsibility of its security and the defense of its existence.

As we really and truly seek peace, we really and truly welcome you to live among us in peace and security.

There was a huge wall between us which you tried to build up over a quarter of a century, but it was destroyed in 1973. It was a wall of a continuously inflammable and escalating psychological warfare. It was a wall of a fear of the force that could sweep the entire Arab Nation. It was a wall of propaganda, that we were a Nation reduced to a motionless corpse. Rather, some of you had gone as far as to say that, even after fifty years, the Arabs would not regain any strength. It was a wall that threatened always with the long arm that could reach and strike anywhere. It was a wall that warned us against extermination and annihilation if we tried to use our legitimate right to liberate the occupied territories. Together we have to admit that that wall fell and collapsed in 1973.

Yet, there remained another wall. This wall constitutes a psychological barrier between us. A barrier of suspicion. A barrier of rejection. A barrier of fear of deception. A barrier of hallucinations around any action, deed or decision. A barrier of cautious and erroneous interpretations of all and every event or statement. It is this psychological barrier which I described in official statements as representing 70 percent of the whole problem.

Today, through my visit to you, I ask you: why don't we stretch out our hands with faith and sincerity so that, together, we might destroy this barrier? Why shouldn't ours and your will meet with faith and sincerity, so that together we might remove all suspicion of fear, betrayal and ill intentions? Why don't we stand together with the bravery of men and the boldness of heroes who dedicate themselves to a sublime objective? Why don't we stand and not destroy? An edifice that is a beacon for generations to come – the human message for construction, development and the dignity of man? Why should we bequeath to the coming generations the plight of bloodshed, death, orphans, widowhood, family disintegration, and the wailing of victims?

Why don't we believe in the wisdom of God conveyed to us by the Proverbs of Solomon:

> Deceit is in the heart of them that imagine evil; but to the counselors of peace is joy. [Proverbs 12:20] Better is a dry morsel, and quietness therewith, than a house full of sacrifices with strife. [Proverbs 17:1]

Why don't we repeat together from the Psalms of David:

> Hear the voice of my supplications, when I cry unto thee, when I lift up my hands toward thy holy oracle. Draw me not away with the wicked and with the workers of iniquity, which speak peace to their neighbours, but mischief is in their hearts. Give them according to their deeds, and according to the wickedness of their endeavours. [Psalms 28:2–4]

To tell you the truth, peace cannot be worth its name unless it is based on justice, and not on the occupation of the land of others. It would not be appropriate for you to demand for yourselves what you deny others.

With all frankness, and with the spirit that has prompted me to come to you today, I tell you: you have to give up, once and for all, the dreams of conquests, and give up the belief that force is the best method for dealing with the Arabs. You should clearly understand and assimilate the lesson of confrontation between you and us.

Expansion does not pay. To speak frankly, our land does not yield itself to bargaining. It is not even open to argument. To us, the national soil is equal to the holy valley where God Almighty spoke to Moses – peace be upon him. None of us can, or accept to, cede one inch of it, or accept the principle of debating or bargaining over it.

I sincerely tell you that before us today lies the appropriate chance for peace, if we are really serious in our endeavours for peace. It is a chance that time cannot afford once again. It is a chance that, if lost or wasted, the plotter against it will bear the curse of humanity and the curse of history.

What is peace for Israel? It means that Israel lives in the region with her Arab neighbours, in security and safety. To such logic, I say yes. It means that Israel lives within her borders, secure against any aggression. To such logic, I say yes. It means that Israel obtains all kinds of guarantees you envisage and accept. We declare that we accept all the guarantees you want from the two super powers or from either of them, or from the Big Five, or some of them.

Once again, I declare clearly and unequivocally that we agree to any guarantees you accept because, in return, we shall obtain the same guarantees.

In short, then, when we ask: what is peace for Israel, the answer would be: it is that Israel live within her borders with her Arab neighbours, in safety and security within the framework of all the guarantees she accepts and which are offered to the other party. But how can this be achieved? How can we reach this conclusion which would lead us to permanent peace based on justice?

There are facts that should be faced with all courage and clarity. There are Arab territories which Israel has occupied by armed force. We insist on complete withdrawal from these territories, including Arab Jerusalem.

I have come to Jerusalem, as the City of Peace, which will always remain as a living embodiment of coexistence among believers of the three religions. It is inadmissible that anyone should conceive the special status of the City of Jerusalem within the framework of annexation or expansionism, but it should be a free and open city for all believers.

1 9 7 7

Nov

1 9 7 8

1 9 7 9

1 9 8 0

1 9 8 1

Above all, the city should not be severed from those who have made it their abode for centuries. Instead of awakening the prejudices of the Crusaders, we should revive the spirit of Omar ibn el Khattab and Saladdin, namely the spirit of tolerance and respect for rights. The holy shrines of Islam and Christianity are not only places of worship, but a living testimony of our uninterrupted presence here politically, spiritually and intellectually. Let us make no mistake about the importance and reverence we Christians and Muslims attach to Jerusalem.

Let me tell you, without the slightest hesitation, that I did not come to you under this dome to make a request that your troops evacuate the occupied territories. Complete withdrawal from the Arab territories occupied in 1967 is a logical and undisputed fact. Nobody should plead for that. Any talk about permanent peace based on justice, and any move to ensure our coexistence in peace and security in this part of the world, would become meaningless, while you occupy Arab territories by force of arms. For there is no peace that could be in consonance with, or be built on, the occupation of the land of others. Otherwise, it would not be a serious peace.

Yes, this is a foregone conclusion which is not open to discussion or debate – if intentions are sincere and if endeavours to establish a just and durable peace for ours and the generations to come are genuine.

As for the Palestinian cause, nobody could deny that it is the crux of the entire problem. Nobody in the world could accept, today, slogans propagated here in Israel, ignoring the existence of the Palestinian People, and questioning their whereabouts. The cause of the Palestinian People and their legitimate rights are no longer ignored or denied today by anybody. Rather, nobody who has the ability of judgment can deny or ignore it.

It is an acknowledged fact received by the world community, both in the East and in the West, with support and recognition in international documents and official statements. It is of no use to anybody to turn deaf ears to its resounding voice which is being heard day and night, or to overlook its historical reality. Even the United States, your first ally which is absolutely committed to safeguard Israel's security and existence, and which offered and still offers Israel every moral, material and military support – I say – even the United States has opted to face up to reality and facts, and admit that the Palestinian People are entitled to legitimate rights and that the Palestinian problem is the core and essence of the conflict and that, so long as it continues to be unresolved, the conflict will continue to aggravate, reaching new dimensions. In all sincerity, I tell you that there can be no peace without the Palestinians. It is a grave error of unpredictable consequences to overlook or brush aside this cause.

I shall not indulge in past events since the Balfour Declaration sixty years ago. You are well acquainted with the relevant facts. If you have found the legal and moral justification to set up a national home on a land that did not all belong to you, it is incumbent upon you to show understanding of the insistence of the People of Palestine on establishing, once again [*sic*] a state on their land. When some extremists ask the Palestinians to give up this sublime objective, this, in fact, means asking them to renounce their identity and every hope for the future.

I hail the Israeli voices that called for the recognition of the Palestinian People's rights to achieve and safeguard peace. Here I tell you, Ladies and Gentlemen, that it is no use to refrain from recognizing the Palestinian People and their rights to statehood and rights of return.

We, the Arabs, have faced this experience before, with you and with the reality of Israeli existence. The struggle took us from war to war, from victims to more victims, until you and we have today reached the edge of a horrifying abyss and a terrifying disaster, unless, together, we seize the opportunity, today, of a durable peace based on justice.

You have to face reality bravely as I have done. There can never be any solution to a problem by evading it or turning a deaf ear to it. Peace cannot last if attempts are made to impose fantasy concepts on which the world has turned its back and announced its unanimous call for the respect of rights and facts. There is no need to enter a vicious circle as to Palestinian rights. It is useless to create obstacles. Otherwise the march of peace will be impeded or peace will be blown up.

As I have told you, there is no happiness to the detriment of others. Direct confrontation and straight-forwardness are the short-cut and the most successful way to reach a clear objective. Direct confrontation concerning the Palestinian problem, and tackling it in one single language with a view to achieving a durable and just peace, lie in the establishment of their state. With all the guarantees you demand, there should be no fear of a newly born state that needs the assistance of all countries of the world. When the bells of peace ring, there will be no hands to beat the drums of war. Even if they existed, they would be soundless.

1
9
7
7

Nov

1
9
7
8

1
9
7
9

1
9
8
0

1
9
8
1

Conceive with me a peace agreement in Geneva that we would herald to a world thirsty for peace, a peace agreement based on the following points:

First: ending the Israeli occupation of the Arab territories occupied in 1967.

Second: achievement of the fundamental rights of the Palestinian People and their right to self-determination, including their right to establish their own state.

Third: the right of all states in the area to live in peace within their boundaries, which will be secure and guaranteed through procedures to be agreed upon, which provide appropriate security to international boundaries, in addition to appropriate international guarantees.

Fourth: commitment of all states in the region to administer the relations among them in accordance with the objectives and principles of the United Nations Charter, particularly the principles concerning the non-resort to force and the solution of differences among them by peaceful means.

Fifth: ending the state of belligerency in the region.

Ladies and Gentlemen, peace is not the mere endorsement of written lines: rather, it is a rewriting of history. Peace is not a game of calling for peace to defend certain whims or rewriting of history. Peace is a giant struggle against all and every ambition and whim. Perhaps the examples taken from ancient and modern history teach us all that missiles, warships and nuclear weapons cannot establish security. Rather, they destroy what peace and security build. For the sake of our peoples, and for the sake of the civilizations made by man, we may endow the rule of humanity with all the power of the values and principles that promote the sublime position of Mankind.

Allow me to address my call from this rostrum to the People of Israel. I address myself with true and sincere words to every man, woman and child in Israel.

From the Egyptian People who bless this sacred mission of peace, I convey to you the message of peace, the message of the Egyptian People who do not know fanaticism, and whose sons, Muslims, Christians, and

Jews, live together in a spirit of cordiality, love and tolerance. This is Egypt whose people have entrusted me with that sacred message, the message of security, safety and peace. To every man, woman and child in Israel, I say: encourage your leadership to struggle for peace. Let all endeavours be channeled towards building a huge edifice for peace, instead of strongholds and hideouts defended by destructive rockets. Introduce to the entire world the image of the new man in this area, so that he might set an example to the man of our age, the man of peace everywhere.

Be the heralds to your sons. Tell them that past wars were the last of wars and the end of sorrows. Tell them that we are in for a new beginning to a new life – the life of love, prosperity, freedom and peace.

You, bewailing mother; you, widowed wife; you, the son who lost a brother or a father; you, all victims of wars – fill the earth and space with recitals of peace. Fill bosoms and hearts with the aspirations of peace. Turn the song into a reality that blossoms and lives. Make hope a code of conduct and endeavour. The will of peoples is part of the will of God.

Ladies and Gentlemen, before I came to this place, with every beat of my heart and with every sentiment, I prayed to God Almighty, while performing the Qurban Bairam prayers, and while visiting the Holy Sepulchre, to give me strength and to confirm my belief that this visit may achieve the objectives I look forward to, for a happy present and a happier future.

I have chosen to set aside all precedents and traditions known by warring countries, in spite of the fact that occupation of the Arab territories is still there. Rather, the declaration of my readiness to proceed to Israel came as a great surprise that stirred many feelings and astounded many minds. Some opinions even doubted its intent. Despite that, the decision was inspired by all the clarity and purity of belief, and with all the true expression of my People's will and intentions.

And I have chosen this difficult road which is considered, in the opinion of many, the most difficult road. I have chosen to come to you with an open heart and an open mind. I have chosen to give this great impetus to all international efforts exerted for peace. I have chosen to present to you, and in your own home, the realities devoid of any schemes or whims, not to maneuver or to win a round, but for us to win together, the most dangerous of rounds and battles in modern history – the battle of permanent peace based on justice.

It is not my battle alone, nor is it the battle of the leadership in Israel alone. It is the battle of all and every citizen in all our territories whose right it is to live in peace. It is the commitment of conscience and responsibility in the hearts of millions.

When I put forward this initiative, many asked what is it that I conceived as possible to achieve during this visit, and what my expectations were. And, as I answered the questioners, I announce before you that I have not thought of carrying out this initiative from the concept of what could be achieved during this visit, but I have come here to deliver a message. I have delivered the message, and may God be my witness.

I repeat with Zechariah, "Love right and justice."

I quote the following verses from the holy Koran:

We believe in God and in what has been revealed to us and what was revealed to Abraham, Ismail, Isaac, [Jacob,] and the tribes and in the books given to Moses, Jesus, and the prophets from their Lord. We make no distinction between one and another among them and to God we submit. [Koran 3:84]

NOVEMBER 20, 1977

BEGIN ADDRESSES THE KNESSET AFTER SADAT

After President Sadat addressed the Knesset, Prime Minister Begin spoke as well. In advance of Sadat's visit Begin had indicated that if Sadat spoke in English, he would as well, but that if Sadat spoke in Arabic, he would address the Knesset in Hebrew, and so he did. He answered Sadat's territorial demands by speaking passionately about the historical Jewish connection to the Land of Israel, yet emphasized Israel's willingness to enter into negotiations on all issues.

Mr. Speaker. Honorable President of the State of Israel. Honorable President of the Arab Republic of Egypt. Worthy and learned Knesset Members:

We send our greetings to the president and to all adherents of the Islamic faith, in our own country and wherever they may be, on the occasion of the Feast of Sacrifice, Id el-Adha.

This feast reminds us of the binding of Isaac on the altar, the test with which the Creator tried the faith of our forefather Abraham – our common father; the challenge which Abraham met. But, from the point of view of morality and the advancement of Mankind, this event heralded the principle of a ban on human sacrifice. Our two peoples, in their ancient tradition, learned and taught that humanitarian prohibition, while the nations around us continued to offer human sacrifices to their idols. Thus we, the people of Israel, and the Arab people contributed to the advancement of Mankind, and we continue to contribute to human civilization until this very day.

I greet the president of Egypt on the occasion of his visit to our country and his participation in this session of the Knesset. The duration of the flight from Cairo to Jerusalem is short but, until last night, the distance between them was infinite. President Sadat showed courage in crossing this distance. We Jews can appreciate courage, as exhibited by our guest, because it is with courage that we arose, and with it we shall continue to exist.

Mr. Speaker, this small people, the surviving remnant of the Jewish people which returned to our historic homeland, always sought peace. And, when the dawn of our freedom rose on the fourteenth of May, 1948, the fourth of Iyar, 5708, David Ben-Gurion said, in the Declaration of Independence, the charter of our national independence:

> We extend our hand to all neighboring states and their peoples
> in an offer of peace and good neighborliness, and appeal to them
> to establish bonds of cooperation and mutual help with the
> sovereign Jewish people settled in its own Land.

A year earlier, in the midst of the fateful struggle for the liberation of the Land and the redemption of the Nation, while still in the underground, we issued the following call to our neighbors:

> Let us live together in this Land and together advance towards
> a life of freedom and happiness. Our Arab neighbors – do not
> reject the hand that is outstretched to you in peace.

Nov

1977

1978

1979

1980

1981

But it is my duty – my duty, Mr. Speaker, and not only my privilege – to assert today in truth that our hand, extended in peace, was rejected. And, one day after our independence was renewed, in accordance with our eternal and indisputable right, we were attacked on three fronts, and we stood virtually without arms – few against many, weak against strong. One day after the declaration of our independence, an attempt was made to strangle it with enmity, and to extinguish the last hope of the Jewish people in the generation of Holocaust and resurrection.

No, we do not believe in might, and we have never based our relations with the Arab Nation on force. On the contrary, force was exercised against us. Throughout all the years of this generation we have never ceased to be attacked with brute force in order to destroy our nation, to demolish our independence, to annul our right. And we defended ourselves.

True, we defend our right, our existence, our honor, our women and our children against recurrent attempts to crush us by brute force, and not on one front alone. This, too, is true: with the help of God we overcame the forces of aggression and assured the survival of our nation, not only for this generation, but for all those to come.

We do not believe in might; we believe in right, only in right. And that is why our aspiration, from the depths of our hearts, from time immemorial until this very day, is peace.

Mr. President, in this democratic chamber sit commanders of all the Hebrew underground fighting organizations. They were compelled to conduct a battle of few against many, against a mighty world power. Here sit our top military commanders, who led their forces in a battle that was imposed on them, and to a victory that was inevitable, because they defended right. They belong to various parties, and have different outlooks. But I am sure, Mr. President, that I am expressing the views of them all, without exception, when I say that we have one aspiration at heart, one desire in our souls, and we are all united in this aspiration and this desire – to bring peace: peace to our nation which has not known it for even one day since the beginning of the return to Zion; and peace to our neighbors to whom we wish all the best. And we believe that if we achieve peace, true peace, we shall be able to assist one another in all realms of life, and a new era will be opened in the Middle East: an era of flourishing and growth, of development and progress and advancement, as in ancient times.

Therefore, allow me today to define the meaning of peace as we understand it. We seek a true, full peace, with absolute reconciliation between the Jewish people and the Arab people. We must not permit memories of the past to stand in our way. There have been wars; blood has been shed; our wonderful sons have fallen in battle on both sides. We shall always cherish the memory of our heroes who gave their lives so that this day, yea even this day, might come. We respect the valor of an adversary, and we pay tribute to all members of the young generation of the Arab Nation who have fallen as well.

Let us not be daunted by memories of the past, even if they are bitter to us all. We must overcome them, and focus on what lies ahead: on our peoples, on our children, on our common future. For, in this region, we shall all live together – the Great Arab Nation in its states and its countries, and the Jewish people in its Land, Eretz Israel – forever and ever. For this reason the meaning of peace must be defined.

As free men, Mr. President, let us conduct negotiations for a peace treaty, and with the help of God, so we believe with all our hearts, the day will come when we will sign it, with mutual respect. Then will we know that the era of wars has ended, that we have extended a hand to one another, that we have shaken each other's hand, and that the future will be glorious for all the peoples of the region. Of prime significance, therefore, in the context of a peace treaty, is a termination of the state of war.

I agree, Mr. President, that you have not come here and we did not invite you to our country in order, as has been suggested in recent days, to drive a wedge between the Arab peoples, or, expressed more cleverly in accord with the ancient saying *"divide et impera."* Israel had no desire to rule and does not wish to divide. We want peace with all our neighbors – with Egypt and with Jordan, with Syria and with Lebanon.

There is no need to differentiate between a peace treaty and the termination of the state of war. We neither propose this, nor do we seek it. On the contrary, the first article of a peace treaty determines the end of the state of war, forever. We wish to establish normal relations between us, as exist among all nations after all wars. We have learned from history, Mr. President, that war is avoidable. It is peace that is inevitable.

Many nations have waged war against one another, and sometimes they have made use of the foolish term "eternal enemy." There are no eternal enemies. After all wars comes the inevitable: peace. Therefore, in the context of a peace treaty, we seek to stipulate the establishment of diplomatic relations, as is customary among civilized nations.

Today, Jerusalem is bedecked with two flags – the Egyptian and the Israeli. Together, Mr. President, we have seen our little children waving both flags. Let us sign a peace treaty and establish such a situation forever, both in Jerusalem and in Cairo. I hope the day will come when Egyptian children will wave Israeli and Egyptian flags together, just as the Israeli children are waving both of these flags together in Jerusalem; when you, Mr. President, will be represented by a loyal ambassador in Jerusalem, and we, by an ambassador in Cairo and, should differences of opinion arise between us, we will clarify them, like civilized peoples, through our authorized emissaries.

We propose economic cooperation for the development of our countries. God created marvelous lands in the Middle East – virtual oases in the desert – but there are also deserts, and these can be made fertile. Let us join hands in facing this challenge, and cooperate in developing our countries, in abolishing poverty, hunger and homelessness. Let us raise our nations to the status of developed countries, so that we may no longer be called developing states.

With all due respect, I am prepared to endorse the words of His Highness, the King of Morocco, who said, publicly, that, if peace were to be established in the Middle East, the combination of Arab and Jewish genius can together convert the region into a paradise on earth.

Let us open our countries to free movement, so that you shall come to us and we will visit you. I am prepared today to announce, Mr. Speaker, that our country is open to the citizens of Egypt, and I do not qualify this announcement with any condition on our part. I think it would be only proper and just that there be a mutual announcement on this matter. And, just as Egyptian flags are flying in our streets, there is also an honored Egyptian delegation in our capital and in our country today. Let there be many visitors. Our border will be open to you, just as will be all the other borders, for, as I noted, we would like the same situation to prevail in the south, in the north and in the east.

Therefore, I renew my invitation to the president of Syria to follow in your footsteps, Mr. President, and to come to our country to begin negotiations on the establishment of peace between Israel and Syria and on the signing of a peace treaty between us. I am sorry to say, there is no justification for the mourning that has been decreed on the other side of our northern border. On the contrary, such visits, such contacts and discussions, can and should be a cause of happiness, a cause of elation for all peoples.

I invite King Hussein to come here and we shall discuss with him all the problems that exist between us. I also invite genuine spokesmen of the Palestinian Arabs to come and to hold talks with us on our common future, on guaranteeing human freedom, social justice, peace and mutual respect.

And, if they should invite us to come to their capitals, we shall respond to their invitation. Should they invite us to begin negotiations in Damascus, Amman or Beirut, we shall go to those capitals in order to negotiate there. We do not wish to divide. We seek true peace with all our neighbors, to be expressed in peace treaties, the context of which shall be as I have already clarified.

Mr. Speaker, it is my duty today to tell our guests and all the nations who are watching us and listening to our words about the bond between our people and this Land. The president mentioned the Balfour Declaration. No, sir, we took no foreign land. We returned to our homeland. The bond between our people and this Land is eternal. It was created at the dawn of human history. It was never severed. In this Land we established our civilization; here our prophets spoke those holy words you cited this very day; here the kings of Judah and Israel prostrated themselves; here we became a nation; here we established our kingdom and, when we were exiled from our country by the force that was exercised against us, even when we were far away, we did not forget this Land, not even for a single day. We prayed for it; we longed for it; we have believed in our return to it ever since the day these words were spoken:

> When God caused the return to Zion, we were like dreamers. At that time, our mouths filled with laughter, and our tongues with song. [Psalms 126:1–2]

That song applies to all our exiles, to all our sufferings, and to the consolation that the return to Zion would surely come.

This, our right, has been recognized. The Balfour Declaration was included in the Mandate which was recognized by the nations of the world, including the United States of America. And the preamble to that authoritative international document states:

Nov

1977

1978

1979

1980

1981

> Whereas recognition has thereby been given to the historical connection of the Jewish People with Palestine (or, in Hebrew, "Eretz Israel") and to the grounds for reconstituting their National Home in that country (that is, in "Eretz Israel")…

In 1919, we also gained recognition of this right from the spokesman of the Arab people. The agreement of 3 January 1919, signed by Emir Feisal and Chaim Weizmann, states:

> Mindful of the racial kinship and ancient bonds existing between the Arabs and the Jewish People, and realizing that the surest means of working out the consummation of their national aspirations is through the closest possible collaboration in the development of the Arab State and of Palestine.

Afterwards, follow all the articles on cooperation between the Arab state and Eretz Israel. That is our right; its fulfillment – the truth.

What happened to us when our homeland was taken from us? I accompanied you this morning, Mr. President, to Yad Vashem. With your own eyes you saw what the fate of our people was when this homeland was taken from it. It is an incredible story. We both agreed, Mr. President, that whoever has not himself seen what is found in Yad Vashem cannot understand what befell this people when it was homeless, robbed of its own homeland. And we both read a document dated 30 January 1939, in which the word *Vernichtung* appears – "if war breaks out the Jewish race in Europe will be annihilated." Then, too, we were told to pay no heed to such words. The whole world heard. No one came to our rescue; not during the nine critical, fateful months following this announcement – the likes of which had never been heard since God created man and man created Satan – and not during those six years when millions of our people, among them a million and a half small Jewish children, were slaughtered in every possible way.

No one came to our rescue, not from the East and not from the West. And therefore we, this entire generation, the generation of Holocaust and resurrection, swore an oath of allegiance: never again shall we endanger our people; never again will our wives and our children – whom it is our duty to defend, if need be even at the cost of our own lives – be put in the devastating range of enemy fire.

And further: ever since then it has been, and will continue to be, our duty, for generations to come, to remember that certain things said about our people are to be related to with all seriousness. We must not, Heaven forbid, for the future of our people, accept any advice suggesting that we not take such words seriously.

President Sadat knows, as he knew from us before he came to Jerusalem, that our position concerning permanent borders between us and our neighbors differs from his. However, I call upon the president of Egypt and upon all our neighbors: do not rule out negotiations on any subject whatsoever. I propose, in the name of the overwhelming majority of this parliament, that everything will be negotiable. Anybody who says that, in the relationship between the Arab people – or the Arab nations in the area – and the State of Israel there are subjects that should be excluded from negotiations, is assuming an awesome responsibility. Everything is negotiable. No side shall say the contrary. No side shall present prior conditions. We will conduct the negotiations with respect.

If there are differences of opinion between us, that is not exceptional. Anyone who has studied the history of wars and the annals of peace treaties knows that all negotiations for peace treaties have begun with differences of opinion between the parties concerned, and that, in the course of the negotiations, they have reached solutions which have made possible the signing of agreements of peace treaties. That is the path we propose to follow.

We shall conduct the negotiations as equals. There are no vanquished and there are no victors. All the peoples of the region are equal, and all will relate to each other with respect. In this spirit of openness, of readiness of each to listen to the other – to facts, reasons, explanations – with every reasonable attempt at mutual persuasion – let us conduct the negotiations as I have asked and propose to open them, to conduct them, to continue them persistently until we succeed, in good time, in signing a peace treaty between us.

We are prepared, not only, to sit with representatives of Egypt and with representatives of Jordan, Syria and Lebanon – if it so desires – at a peace conference in Geneva. We proposed that the Geneva Conference be renewed on the basis of Resolutions 242 and 338 of the Security Council. However, should problems arise between us prior to the convening of the Geneva Conference, we will clarify them today and tomorrow and, if the President of Egypt will be interested in continuing to clarify them in Cairo – all the better; if on neutral ground – no opposition. Anywhere. Let us clarify – even before the Geneva conference convenes – the problems that should be made clear before it meets, with opened eyes and a readiness to listen to all suggestions.

Allow me to say a word about Jerusalem. Mr. President, today you prayed in a house of worship sacred to the Islamic faith, and from there you went to the Church of the Holy Sepulchre. You witnessed the fact, known to all who come from throughout the world, that, ever since this city was joined together, there is absolutely free access, without any interference or obstacle, for the members of all religions to their holy places. This positive phenomenon did not exist for nineteen years. It has existed now for about eleven years, and we can assure the Muslim world and the Christian world – all the nations – that there will always be free access to the holy places of every faith. We shall defend this right of free access, for it is something in which we believe – in the equality of rights for every man and every citizen, and in respect for every faith.

Mr. Speaker, this is a special day for our parliament, and it will undoubtedly be remembered for many years in the annals of our nation, in the history of the Egyptian people, and perhaps, also, in the history of nations. And on this day, with your permission, worthy and learned members of the Knesset, I wish to offer a prayer that the God of our common ancestors will grant us the requisite wisdom of heart in order to overcome the difficulties and obstacles, the calumnies and slanders. With the help of God, may we arrive at the longed-for day for which all our people pray – the day of peace.

For indeed, as the Psalmist of Israel said, "Righteousness and peace have kissed" [Psalms 85:10], and, as the prophet Zechariah said, "Love truth and peace" [Zechariah 8:19].

NOVEMBER 21, 1977

JOINT PRESS CONFERENCE IN JERUSALEM

Sadat's visit to Israel concluded with a joint press conference given by Prime Minister Begin and President Sadat in Jerusalem. Prime Minister Begin began by reading the text of a "communiqué" that officially summarized the understandings reached during the visit. Afterwards journalists questioned the two leaders, sometimes in surprisingly confrontational tones, indicative of the high state of tension between the two countries. Both Begin and Sadat showed a combination of strength, resolve, and even humor, as they shared the spotlight on this extraordinary occasion.

Begin: With the permission of the President, our noble guest, I will read to you, Ladies and Gentlemen, the text of the agreed communiqué issued at the conclusion of the visit to our country of President Sadat:

> In response to the sincere and courageous move by President Sadat, and believing in the need to continue the dialogue along the lines proposed by both sides during their exchanges and the presentation of their positions in the historic meeting in Jerusalem, and in order to enhance the prospect of a fruitful consummation of this significant visit, the Government of Israel, expressing the will of the people of Israel, proposes that this hopeful step be further pursued through dialogue between the two countries concerned, thereby paving the way towards successful negotiations, leading to the signing of peace treaties in Geneva with all the neighbouring Arab states.

Q: Mr. Prime Minister, have you received an invitation to go to Cairo and, if so, when will you go?

Begin: We discussed this issue, with complete candor. I think that President Sadat would like to reciprocate. I would like to see Cairo, but

I do understand the reasons why, at this stage, such an invitation was not issued. I would like to say, I do hope to visit Cairo.

Q: In addition to agreeing, in principle, that the dialogue between the two countries will continue, did the two of you, during the course of President Sadat's visit, work out specific, practical details for the continuation of this dialogue, even before the Geneva Peace Conference?

Sadat: Well, for sure, we had a big survey of all the problems that we are facing. We gave great importance to the convening of the Geneva Conference, but not more than this, the time was so short.

Q: I would also like Prime Minister Begin to respond to that question. How do you continue a dialogue without an Israeli ambassador in Cairo and an Egyptian ambassador in Jerusalem? How will you do it, practically?

Begin: The establishment of diplomatic relations usually goes together with the signing of peace treaties. In fact, sometimes the establishment of diplomatic relations does precede the signing of a peace treaty, as was the case between the Soviet Union and Japan, when, in Moscow, in October 1956, they signed a peace declaration which, though not a peace treaty, included the establishment of diplomatic relations. But in our case, I suppose it will be logical to have diplomatic relations established as an integral part of the peace treaty which, in God's good time, we hope to sign.

Q: Mr. President, why aren't you inviting the prime minister of Israel to visit Cairo at this stage?

Sadat: Well, after I was invited here by the prime minister, and after I addressed the Knesset and the Israeli people through the Knesset, the prime minister has the full right to come and address our parliament in Cairo. For certain reasons that we discussed together, we have found that we should postpone this issue for the future.

Begin: Mr. Kital, you heard from the president that I have a right, and we have only postponed the exercise of this right.

Q: Mr. Prime Minister, in view of the political and physical risks that the president of Egypt took by coming to Israel, do you feel that you have gone far enough in giving him something that he can take back home?

Begin: We appreciate very much the courage of the president, in his decision to come from Cairo to Jerusalem. We did our best to make his stay enjoyable. I think he enjoyed his stay, and we had a frank discussion, both in public, from the rostrum of the Knesset, our parliament, and in private. It is not a matter of a kind of compensation. What we wanted to achieve during this visit was to make sure that we started a serious direct dialogue about the ways to establish peace in the Middle East – not only between Egypt and Israel, but also between Israel and all the other neighboring countries. I think we can say that we made progress on this issue, and the key word is "continuation." We agreed that we are going to continue our dialogue and ultimately, out of it will come peace.

Q: Mr. President, my name is Abie Nathan. I am from *The Voice of Peace* – the peace ship that sailed into the Suez Canal, thanks to your permission, early this year. My question to you, sir, is: how did you get the idea, and who were the leaders around the world who encouraged you to take this bold initiative for peace, to help to bring our peoples together? And, when can I hope to come with an Israeli football team to Cairo to play against the Cairo eleven?

Sadat: Well, for the first part of the question – about this initiative and if I have already discussed it with any other leader – my answer is this: it started before I began my last trip to Romania, Iran and Saudi Arabia. I didn't discuss it with anyone except my foreign minister and, for sure, our Security Council in Egypt. The whole situation needed action, the peace process needed momentum again, and these are the motives behind this initiative.

Q: A common key question to President Sadat and Prime Minister Begin: After so many conversations, did you really reach an agreement on the meaning of the word "security" concerning Israel and the neighboring countries? The second question is directed to President Sadat: Arab hospitality is very well known all over the world. Did you feel a little bit embarrassed about the fact that you had to postpone the invitation of Mr. Begin to Cairo?

Begin: I am not embarrassed.

Sadat: Well, the first question about security – with the premier and with the various parties in the Knesset today, we agreed upon the principle. Upon security we agree. But, on the meaning of security, we differ. I think that, through Geneva, we can reach an agreement, and let us hope that what I have said already today in the Knesset – let us hope that the two slogans that I want everyone to say are: "Let us have no war after October" [the reference is to the October 1973 Yom Kippur War] and "Let us agree upon security." I think those are the main issues.

For the second question, on hospitality – very sly – either I am an Arab and hospitable or not. No, as I said before, we have discussed this, Premier Begin and myself, and we have agreed together to postpone it for the time being.

Begin: I would like to add one remark. I would say to the questioner and all of you, Ladies and Gentlemen, that, during the visit of President Sadat to our country and to Jerusalem, a momentous agreement has been achieved, already, namely: no more war, no more bloodshed, no more attacks, and collaboration in order to avoid any event which might lead to such tragic developments. When I addressed the Egyptian people directly, I said, let us give a silent oath, one to another: no more war, no more bloodshed, no more threats. May I say that that mutual pledge was given in Jerusalem, and we are very grateful to President Sadat that he said so from the rostrum of the Knesset, personally to me, and today also to my colleagues in parliament, both the supporters and the opponents of the government. It is a great moral achievement for our nations, for the Middle East and, indeed, for the whole world.

Q: Mr. Prime Minister, according to the joint communiqué, it is understood that the dialogue is going to be resumed. How is it going to be resumed, where, and will there be any place for the Palestinians to participate in this dialogue, now or later on in the Geneva Conference?

Begin: In the Geneva Conference the proper representation of Palestinian Arabs will take place. We agree on it. As far as the places in which the dialogue will continue, believe me, President Sadat and I know some geography.

Q: Mr. President, as you prepare to leave Israel, do you have a message for the people of Israel, with whom you are, after all, still at war?

Sadat: If I may say anything through you to the people of Israel, I must say this: that I am really deeply grateful for the very warm welcome and the marvelous sentiments that they have shown to me.

Q: Mr. President, I am Shmuel Segev from [the Israeli newspaper] *Maʾariv*. The Israeli government has allowed many Egyptian journalists to come and cover your visit. Will you now be prepared to open the doors of Egypt for Israeli journalists?

Sadat: When Mr. Begin visits us, for sure you will be coming.

Q: Not before?

Begin: Mr. Segev, *l'hitraʾot be'Kahir* [see you in Cairo]….

Q: Mr. President, what psychological and what substantive progress have you made in Israel on your visit?

Sadat: Well, maybe you have heard me say before, that one of the main motives behind this visit to Israel was to give the peace process new momentum and to get rid of the psychological barrier that, in my opinion, was more than 70 percent of the whole conflict, the other 30 percent being substance. For the substance, as I told you, we have made a very big survey, but the time is too short to have progress in this way.

Begin: The time was so short that I think that, before I go to Cairo, I will have to invite President Sadat to Jerusalem for a second time.

Q: I have two questions for President Sadat. The first: after your meeting with the delegation of the Armed Services Committee of the US House of Representatives, you were quoted as saying: "The Soviet Union will for sure make difficulties for me and I am making my calculations so that this attitude should not create any obstacles at Geneva." Mr. President, was the Soviet Union, in the circumstances, blocking the road to Geneva?

Sadat: You must have heard of the communiqué that was issued by the Soviet Union and the United States for the convening of the

Geneva Conference. What I told the committee you mentioned is this: that my relations with the Soviets are strained and it appears that whatever I do doesn't go to their liking at all. For instance, the visit here also, in their comments, doesn't go to their liking at all. I fear that the same attitude could be adopted in Geneva, and they are one of the co-sponsors. But, in the same answer, I said that, whenever the parties concerned reach an agreement, no one, neither a big power nor a small power, can prevent us from fulfilling it, as much as we have agreed upon it.

Q: Egypt agreed to a joint venture with the blacklisted US Ford Motor Company. Mr. Muhammad Mabruk, head of the Arab boycott of Israel, attacked the government of Egypt. Don't you think, Mr. President, that the time has come to put an end to the boycott?

Sadat: Well, I have an idea on this. I consider all these to be side issues. Let us try to solve the main issue, then all the side issues, automatically, will be solved.

Q: Mr. President, I thought it was significant that you went out of your way this morning to congratulate Mr. Peres on his speech. You called it constructive. Could you tell us what, precisely, in Mr. Peres's speech you found constructive?

Sadat: I said that, and said it in spite of the fact that we differ on several issues; don't forget that. I said, "…in spite of the fact that we differ on several issues," but his speech was still constructive.

Q: You repeated several times in the Knesset this morning that, whatever happens again between Egypt and Israel, the solutions must be sought not through war. Does this repeated statement cancel your previous repeated statements in Egypt that, if you cannot get back the territories by diplomatic means, you will get them back by force of war?

Sadat: For sure, I must tell you quite frankly that I am issuing this after I made my visit here and at the same time when we are preparing for Geneva. Well, after we had this new momentum and this new spirit, let us agree that, whatever happens between us, we should solve it together through talks rather than going to war. Because, as I told you, really, I was very deeply touched when I saw the children, the Israeli children, hailing me here…the Israeli women. Really, I was very touched, and the same thing happens in Egypt also. Maybe you know that my people now are 100 percent behind me. They don't want any war. They want that we settle our differences on the table. But, mark this. I also said in the Knesset, and on this I differed with Premier Begin – he considered this as a condition – I said that the issue of the withdrawal from the occupied territories should not even be put on the table, except for the details of it, not as a principle. We differ on this. But when I made my statement, this is behind it. I mean this will be automatically, in Geneva, negotiated and decided.

Q: Mr. President, have you discussed today with the West Bank personalities [the reference is to local Arab leaders] the political future of the West Bank, and do you think they should participate in Geneva? When are you going to visit King Khalid?

Sadat: Well, for the first question, I received them. They were very kind to come and apologize for those who are abusing me in the outside world, from their patriots. I was very happy and elated when I prayed yesterday in al-Aqsa, and I met with our Arab citizens. I was very happy and elated regarding their representation. I should not say anything about this because the Palestinians should decide this for themselves.

About the visit to Saudi Arabia: whenever there is any issue, there are very close contacts together, and whenever there is any need to discuss anything, I may go at any time, or King Khalid may come to Cairo at any time. We do not have protocols and so on between us.

Q: Mr. President, now that you are more acquainted with the facts of the Nazi Holocaust, do you have a better insight into Israel's determination to maintain appropriate security positions against the extremist elements that are openly committed to the destruction of the Jewish state?

Sadat: Could you repeat the question?

Q: Mr. President, now that you are more acquainted with the facts of the Nazi Holocaust, do you have a better insight into Israel's determination to maintain appropriate security positions against the extremist elements that are openly committed to the destruction of the Jewish state?

Sadat: As you have heard me say just now, security is one of the two main issues or two main slogans that should be raised now. I quite agree. I quite understand the point of view of security for the Israelis but, on the other hand, it shouldn't be through any compromise on land, because that would mean expansion. And, in my opinion, we shall discuss this thoroughly afterwards. A few kilometers here, or a few kilometers there, will not provide security. The intention is what provides security.

Q: Mr. President, you have faced very strong attacks from much of the rest of the Arab world for your visit here. You've even been faced with the threat of assassination for what you have done. What do you say to these people?

Sadat: I shall not be saying anything to those people. I think I shall be telling my people in Egypt what has happened here. I shall be giving a speech before the parliament a few days after my arrival. I need not answer all those who have attacked me. Let me remind you that, after the disengagement agreement, for one continual year I was much more vehemently attacked than I am now.

Q: I have a question for both Prime Minister Begin and for President Sadat, and the premise is the same for both questions. Since there are twenty-three other Arab countries, with millions and millions of miles and plenty of money, and since Israel's territory is so small, by comparison, and since, as President Sadat just said, some of this land was not acquired by what he termed expansion, but was actually acquired by defensive war, after it was started, does Premier Begin believe that any of this land should be given up, in view of the biblical injunction not to surrender one inch of land acquired with the help of God?

And my question to President Sadat, would a larger demilitarized Sinai with joint development of the oil resources or the other resources of the area and with economic development and cooperation required to help his battered economy – wouldn't this and tourism be better for Egypt and for Israel than giving any of the land; or is vanity to win territory more important?

Sadat: Two words only for my answer – our land is sacred.

Begin: My friend, if you asked me a question about security…

Q: No, the question was about territory, not about security.

Begin: Will you please allow me to reply?

Q: OK.

Begin: Thank you for your permission. I will explain now what security is to us: the lives of every man, woman and child. This is what national security means to us. We have long experience: in one generation we lost a third of our people and, in this country, eleven times we had to defend ourselves against repeated attempts to destroy us. With such an experience we will care for our people, for our women and children, as I said yesterday in parliament. I think that we have almost a complete national consensus – with the exception of one party, the Communist Party, which is completely subservient to Moscow. This is the consensus by the overwhelming majority of our parliament, whether in coalition or in opposition, and this is going to be our attitude during negotiations. Of course, I can respect a statement as was made just now by President Sadat: "Our land is sacred," and, because I respect it, I can say now: "Our land is sacred."

Q: Mr. Prime Minister, do you note a certain lack of symmetry in the fact that President Sadat is crossing a political canal and exposing himself to risks vis-à-vis his own people, while you stayed within the relative safety of Israeli official concept? In other words, while President Sadat came to Jerusalem and addressed himself to us, you came to Jerusalem and addressed yourself to us. Is this symmetry?

Begin: As I told you, my friend, I am ready to go to Cairo any day. And then, if to accept your statement, I will take that risk. So, if taking risks is a problem, both of us, I suppose, are prepared to take risks.

Q: Yesterday, in his speech, President Sadat spoke about the Palestinian problem being the crux of the Mid-East conflict. Israel, in his view, would have nothing to fear if a new state were established. No peace can be established without solving the problem. I should

Nov

like to ask the Prime Minister, why did you not relate by so much as a word to what Mr. Sadat had to say?

Begin: I did, but I spoke in Hebrew. And I must correct you as I do always. Palestine is the name of a country, and in this country there are two nationalities. There are Palestinian Jews and Palestinian Arabs. When you say "Palestinians," you do not explain the problem at issue. We do recognize the Arab nationality in our country, and therefore I always say: "Please, the question of the Palestinian Arabs." And in Hebrew I say "*ha-be'ayah shel Arviyei Eretz-Yisrael*," because in Hebrew, the name of this country is Eretz-Yisrael. Since the book of Samuel, and President Sadat knows the Bible perfectly well, no less than the Koran – so he knows the book of Samuel as well – where it is written for the first time: "And no locksmith shall be found throughout Eretz-Yisrael." The translation of Eretz-Yisrael is Palestine. I spoke about the Arabs of Eretz-Yisrael, or, in other words, about Palestinian Arabs. It is an issue, and we have proposals to solve this issue.

Q: Mr. President, do you have any plans to meet with President Assad and persuade him maybe to join you?

Sadat: From time to time we do meet in the Arab world. I was asked in Damascus, before I came here, whether President Assad tried to put pressure on me not to complete this visit. I told them that no one put pressure on the other. This is our way.

Q: The fact that you have come on this visit, is it really a breakthrough towards peace?

Sadat: We have always been speaking about and, indeed, the most important thing today is that we should go to Geneva. And that is what we have been talking about – going to Geneva.

Q: …May I ask you, since you have been here in the last twenty-four hours, do you feel closer to reconciling the just rights and needs of the Israeli people and the just rights and needs of the Palestinians?

Sadat: I am sure that the progress that we started through my visit here will enable us to solve all the problems.

For example, we consider that there is an urgent problem of security. I also consider that the Palestinian state is very important. In spite of our differences upon this issue, we can decide in Geneva on all these. If you ask me whether I am optimistic or pessimistic, I can tell you, I am optimistic.

Begin: Ladies and gentlemen, it will take another two hours until President Sadat will be on his way to his country, to Cairo. May I now sum up this momentous visit. It is indeed a momentous visit. We are formally in a state of war, our two countries. As far as I can remember, I do not know of precedent that the leader of a country that finds itself in a state of war with another country paid such a visit to that country, and was received with so much warmth and sincerity. The reaction was positive in the government, in parliament, but first and foremost, among our people.

We drove, President Sadat and I, several times together. We have seen our people in the streets, in the thousands – men, women and little children – all of them greeting the President, taking him to their hearts. The children waved both flags, the Egyptian flag and the Israeli flag. I wish, with your permission, Mr. President, to express the hope that the day is not too far when Egyptian children will have the Israeli flag and the Egyptian flag. This visit is a real success for both countries, and the cause of peace.

And, as we both believe, the President and I, in Divine Providence, before the departure of the President and his party, we pray to the Almighty that he give all of us the wisdom to continue in our efforts to bring peace to our nations – real peace – and so to make sure that this region, with all the nations dwelling here, achieves peace, advances, and lives in liberty, in justice and in happiness. Thank you.

Sadat: Well, Ladies and Gentlemen, may I take this opportunity to thank Prime Minister Begin, the Israeli people and President Katzir for the very warm welcome that was accorded to me here. We are at a crucial moment. Let us hope, all of us, that we can keep the momentum in Geneva and may God guide the steps of Premier Begin and the Knesset, because there is a great need for hard and drastic decision. I already did my share in my decision to come

1977

Nov

1978

1979

1980

1981

here, and I shall be really looking forward to those decisions from Premier Begin and the Knesset.

All my best wishes to my friend Premier Begin and his family, and all my deep gratitude to the Israeli people, whose welcome I can never forget. Thank you.

Part 2

Post-Visit Doldrums
December 1977–August 1978

DECEMBER 26, 1977

THE ISMAILIA SUMMIT

After the high of the Jerusalem visit, reality set in. Negotiations commenced, but the two leaders were still very far apart in their positions and expectations. The Ismailia summit, a month after the historic Jerusalem visit, was Sadat's first opportunity to welcome the Israeli leader to Egypt. But despite the excitement of the two historic first visits, the momentum was not enough to bridge the serious gaps. The main achievement of the Ismailia summit was an agreement to convene meetings of joint military and political committees. The first would meet in Cairo and the second in Jerusalem. The chairmen would rotate. But beyond this procedural matter, no real agreement could be reached, despite the fact that an extra day was added on to the conference schedule. On December 26, 1977, at the conclusion of the summit, the two leaders conducted a press conference with statements and a question-and-answer session.

SADAT'S STATEMENT

In the name of God, let me seize this opportunity to express my gratitude for the efforts you have done to cover the historical moments here in Ismailia. As you know, after my visit to Jerusalem on the twentieth of November, a new spirit prevails in the area and we have agreed in Jerusalem and in Ismailia also to continue our efforts towards achieving a comprehensive settlement.

We have agreed upon raising the level of the representation in the Cairo conference to ministerial level and as you have heard yesterday we have agreed upon two committees: a political committee and a military committee headed by ministers of foreign affairs and ministers of defense. The military committee will convene in Cairo. The political committee will convene in Jerusalem.

Those committees shall work in the context of the Cairo conference, meaning that they will report to the plenary whenever they reach any decision. The question of the withdrawal we have made progress, but on the Palestinian question, which we consider the core and crux of the problem here in this area, the Egyptian and Israeli delegations here discussed the Palestinian problem.

The position of Egypt is that on the West Bank and the Gaza Strip a Palestinian state should be established. The position of Israel is that Palestinian Arabs in Judea, Samaria, the West Bank of Jordan and the Gaza Strip should enjoy self-rule.

We have agreed that because we have differed on the issue, the issue will be discussed in the political committee of the Cairo preparatory conference.

I hope I have given you some light upon our work and thank you again.

BEGIN'S STATEMENT

Mr. President, Ladies and Gentlemen. I have come here a hopeful prime minister and I am leaving a happy man. The conference in Ismailia has been successful. We will continue with the momentum of the peacemaking process.

Now starts the phase of the most serious negotiations – how to establish peace between Egypt and Israel as part of a comprehensive settlement throughout the Middle East. These two days are very good days for Egypt, Israel and for peace.

May I express our gratitude to the President for his gracious hospitality he bestowed upon me, upon my friends and colleagues, the foreign minister Moshe Dayan and the defense minister Ezer Weizman and our collaborators and advisers. This is the second meeting between President Sadat and myself after the historic event of his breakthrough visit to Jerusalem.

Here, too, may I say, we spoke as friends. We want to establish real peace. There are problems to discuss and in these two committees, the chairmanship of which we will rotate between our respective ministers, those serious negotiations and talks will take place.

Now my friends and I will leave Ismailia and Egypt with the faith that we contributed to the peacemaking process and there is hope that, with God's help, President Sadat and I and our friends will establish peace.

Thank you, Ladies and Gentlemen.

[Following the statements Prime Minister Begin and President Sadat took questions from journalists.]

Q: Mr. Begin, what are the advantages of two or three committees working in tandem rather than a cohesive peace forum, and since you and President Sadat obviously coordinated these discussions, do you expect to meet soon and frequently?

Begin: The committees will start with their work quite soon. In the first week of January they will work every day. We hope for good and concrete results. President Sadat and I also agreed during our private talks, if necessary, from time to time we shall meet again.

Q: Mr. Begin and Mr. Sadat, would you say Egypt and Israel are about to achieve a peace treaty in a couple of months?

Sadat: We are working towards a comprehensive settlement. As I said before, we want to establish peace in the area. Without a comprehensive settlement we can't achieve peace.

Begin: I agree with the President.

Q: Looking beyond a peace settlement, can you tell us something about your long-term grand designs for peace? How to satisfy your people's expectations of a better life, of a renaissance in this Middle East cradle of civilization? Are you in favor of cooperation in science, education, agriculture, industry, trade and cultural exchanges between your two countries and eventually between Israel and the Arab world as a whole?

Sadat: Well, the two committees will start, and, as I said, will report to the plenary. Let me say this: we are working towards a comprehensive settlement in the area here and the nature of peace is on the agenda between both sides of the two committees, and all that you have mentioned will be discussed in the committees.

Begin: May I congratulate you, Mr. Carr, on the poetry you read to us and I think this is a very good vision and when we establish peace, all those good things you put into your question will be put into realization.

Q: Mr. President, is the gap on the Palestinians unbridgeable?

Sadat: Inasmuch as we shall be continuing in the Cairo conference to discuss whatever points of difference between us, we shall continue. As Prime Minister Begin has said, if need be we shall meet again. I don't think there is any gap that cannot be bridged between us.

Dec

1977

1978

1979

1980

1981

Q: President, do you agree that Egypt not only holds the key to peace in the Middle East, but also that no combination of Arab countries can wage war in the foreseeable future against Israel?

Sadat: Well, maybe you have heard my speech. We were sincere in war and we are sincere for peace since my visit to Jerusalem last November. Let us sit together like civilized people and discuss whatever problem between us. Let us agree upon the fact that the October War should be the last war. We did not differ upon this at all. The continuation of our efforts will answer all this.

Q: What about waging war without Egypt?

Sadat: Well, we have here, for sure, in the Arab world, in this area here, the key to war and peace. In Egypt here, this is a fact, a historic fact. Well, I can't speak for anyone but I can say this.

Q: Mr. President, can the West Bank Palestinian issue be solved without a role for the PLO?

Sadat: There should be a solution for this problem. We have passed it to the political committee that we have agreed upon in the Cairo conference. For sure, we shall find a solution. Because, as I have said before, the Palestinian question is the crux of the whole problem. Maybe in the future, after the political committee works and the discussions start, a new situation will develop.

Begin: The organization called the PLO is bent on the destruction of Israel. It is written in their charter. They never changed their position. As I stated time and again, from our point of view everything is negotiable except the destruction of Israel. Therefore, this organization is no partner to our negotiations. Now as I read before I reached Ismailia, the spokesman of this organization threatened the life of President Sadat – speaking about one bullet that may change the course of events. So now we have a situation, after Tripoli,[4] in

---

4.   The reference is to a meeting held by the Palestine Liberation Movement in Tripoli, Libya, on December 4, 1977, when the "rejectionist front" of groups and states was created to try to isolate Egypt from making peace with Israel. Their summation statement rejected UN Security Council Resolutions 242 and 338 as well as all international conferences based on these two resolutions (including the Geneva Conference), and announced a striving for the interim realization of Palestinian self-determination and return without reconciliation,

which such threats are issued both against Israel and Egypt. We want to discuss the problem of the Palestinian Arabs with our Egyptian friends. We want to negotiate with the representatives of the Palestinian Arabs and this we are going to do in the first week of January.

Q: Is there any possibility that other Arab countries will join the conference? Will you keep King Hussein of Jordan informed?

Sadat: For sure I will be informing King Hussein of all the developments that have taken place here in Ismailia and let us hope that others will join yet in the next stage.

Q: In view of the dramatic changes that have taken place, have you, Mr. President, changed your mind about delaying diplomatic relations for future generations?

Sadat: As I have said before, the nature of peace is one of the important points that is on the agenda for the two committees and for the plenary session after that. Let me tell you this: it is now not more than thirty-five or forty days since my visit to Jerusalem. Everything has changed. Everything has changed since that visit took place. I quite agree with those who say that the world after the Jerusalem visit is completely different to the world before the visit.

Q: Seven years ago the US and China started ping-pong diplomacy. Will you open the borders to allow sportsmen of both sides, even at this stage, and in that way to allow people to know each other and play together? The Egyptian football team – which I'm told is better than Israel's – could play the Israel team.

Sadat: It is not yet ripe. But for sure we shall be continuing our discussions in our meetings. As you have heard, there will be a committee here and a committee there and gradually we shall be in a position to reach agreement upon all what you are proposing here.

Begin: Until the day the President agrees to exchange sportsmen on both sides, do something to strengthen our football team. [*Laughter.*]

---

recognition or negotiations. In addition, they declared a political boycott of the Sadat regime.

Q: Mr. President, in view of the disagreement on the Palestinians, can an interim accord be reached between Egypt and Israel?

Sadat: The differences should be overcome in the committees. It is a fact.

Q: You are not seeking an alternative to peace?

Sadat: As I have already stated before the Knesset, this time we are not either for a disengagement agreement or a partial agreement – trying to reach some stages and then postponing other steps after that. No. This time we are for peace. Genuine peace. Comprehensive settlement.

Begin: May I add, Mrs. Zemer, the President and I agreed that there is no alternative to peace.

Q: How do you explain the abrupt change from years of enmity and distrust to friendliness and trust?

Sadat: It is not abrupt. It must have been in the subconscious of all of us and when I made my step, in my calculation, really, I knew my people would agree to it. But I never thought that they would go to this extent. It is a natural feeling and there is no fear at all. There will be no revival of anything that has happened in the past.

Q: Mr. President, Mr. Begin, have you reached the stage where mutual troop reductions in the Sinai are possible?

Sadat: Let us hope that in a few weeks we shall be in a position to report.

Begin: Yes. Yes. We hope so. When peace comes on, both countries, all countries, in the Middle East will be able to reduce their military forces and expenditure which is eating up our substance and rather devote our sources and resources to the liquidation of poverty, development of agriculture and industry. This is our common aim.

Q: I was asking about troop reduction at this stage.

Begin: We do hope for the possibility of reducing troops from all sides.

Q: On what moral grounds, Mr. Begin, are you denying the Palestinians, the West Bank and Gaza their right to self-determination? And you, Mr. President, on what moral grounds can you negotiate about the future of the Palestinians without a single Palestinian representative present?

Begin: One correction, my friend. I belong to the Palestinian people too. Because I am a Palestinian Jew and there are Palestinian Arabs. But, of course, we want to live in human dignity, in liberty, justice and equality of rights. Therefore, I brought the President a proposal of self-rule for the first time in the history of the Palestinian Arabs. Now we have established a political committee. We stated our positions clearly and the political committee will continue the discussion of this very serious problem.

Sadat: What we are discussing really is within the Arab strategy that was agreed upon in the Arab summit conference. But in the details I shall not negotiate for the Palestinians. So they should take their share. But in this Arab strategy, what I am doing really is that I am not speaking for myself but for this strategy in its principles. But I shall not put myself as a spokesman for them or speak for them. They should join in the next stage.

Q: Is Israel's demand for a military presence in the West Bank a major stumbling block?

Sadat: I do not want to reveal what we have already discussed in the proposals that have been made by Prime Minister Begin. He has shown his will to end the military government on the West Bank. But we differ upon the issue, as I have told you, of a Palestinian state on the West Bank and the Gaza Strip. That means self-determination.

Q: Did you discuss the future of the Golan Heights?

Sadat: I cannot speak for Syria or the Golan Heights; as I told you, now we are concerned with the main principles in the Arab strategy. And whenever we reach agreement upon those points between us in the committees, in the political and military committees, after that everyone should negotiate for himself.

Begin: I do want to express the hope that President [Hafez] Assad [of Syria] will join our common effort. We want a comprehensive peace treaty. We want peace with all our neighbors to the south, to the north and to the east, and when President Assad agrees to negotiate with us, we will be willing to negotiate with him. This is a problem of the northern border of Israel and the common border of Israel and Syria.

Q: I am an Egyptian journalist and I want to ask Mr. Begin in his language.

Begin: You want to speak to me in Hebrew? I understand Hebrew. [*Laughter.*]

Q: [*In Hebrew.*] Mr. Prime Minister, I want to ask you whether the initiative of President Sadat brought about profound changes in your thinking and outlook, and also how you see the future of Israel and the Middle East after peace.

Begin: [*In Hebrew.*] Firstly, I want to tell you, you speak better Hebrew than I do. [*In English, addressing Sadat.*] I want you to know he speaks better Hebrew than I do. [*Laughter.*] Congratulations. No, I want to answer. I thank you for your question. [*In Hebrew.*] I want to say that the visit of President Sadat to Jerusalem was a visit of historic significance, for the whole Israeli people, for the whole Egyptian people, for all the peoples, and we appreciate it. Since the visit we have worked well on a peace plan, and I brought this peace plan before the President, and we explained it in detail yesterday in the joint meeting, when we were alone, and when the two delegations met.

The future of Israel after peace is achieved, as in the case of Egypt – I have no doubt, it will be glorious and that peace will be achieved between the peoples, the Middle East will develop, and as His Majesty the king of Morocco has said, it can become a sort of paradise on earth. This is the cradle of human civilization and from here came the tidings of peace and progress. Therefore, I was very happy to hear your question and that is my answer. Now I shall translate into English with a Hebrew accent. [*Begin then translated his remarks into English.*]

Q: Now that you have raised the level of the talks, how do you see the role of the US? Will you be inviting Secretary of State Vance to take part in some of your talks and is there a role for the Soviet Union?

Sadat: I foresee for the US and the UN in the political committee [*inaudible*] but the military committee will be bilateral; as for the US, it will be in the political committee without the Soviet Union. We didn't exclude them. They excluded themselves. Well, we have no objection from our side.

Q: Mr. President, will you call an Arab summit, and will the other parties be invited to the Cairo conference when the level is upgraded?

Sadat: Until we reach in the committee agreement on the main issues and mainly the Palestinian issue, on which we have differed – until we reach this point, as it is part of our Arab strategy, I shall not be in a position to ask for an Arab summit meeting. But whenever we reach this, I think that after that, I shall be in a position to discuss with my Arab colleagues the possibility of a summit.

Q: Do you feel that Mr. Begin's proposals contain sufficient concessions to have justified your trip to Jerusalem?

Sadat: Well, we have agreed on certain points. We have made progress on the withdrawal. We have differed among us on certain points, namely the Palestinian question. These proposals that have been made by Premier Begin will be put before the committee, political or military, and other counterproposals will be submitted to these committees, and until we reach them we think that the momentum that we have given to the peace process is continuing.

Q: What do you think of Begin's proposals?

Sadat: Well, as I have told you, we have points of difference and points of agreement.

Q: Can you be more specific on what progress was made on Sinai? And does this mean foreign ministers exclusively in the Cairo conference?

Sadat: I have stated before that in the political committee there will be the foreign ministers, and in the military committee there will be the defense ministers. For the first part that you have asked, I have heard the proposals Premier Begin told us about and we are preparing our counterproposal in the military committee. But really what concerns us in this respect is a comprehensive settlement.

This is not the Sinai that is the problem now, because as I told you, after peace, after a genuine peace in the area, regarding Sinai, this is a side issue and, of course, in a comprehensive settlement it will be part of it. And as I told you, I prefer not to reveal anything, and leave the military committee to work on the details and discuss proposals and counterproposals until we reach agreement.

Q: Mr. President, what about the PLO? Don't you feel the Palestinians have the right to choose their representatives? What role do you think the PLO should play in the peacemaking process?

Sadat: I have stated before the Knesset that the Palestinians should be a part of the settlement because, as I said, the Palestinian question is the core of the whole problem. The PLO is now in the rejection camp. I sent them an invitation and they refused and excluded themselves. Well, I didn't exclude them. For the future, let us wait for what will develop.

Q: Mr. President, is it still your position that Israel must withdraw from all occupied land, including East Jerusalem?

Sadat: That's right.

Q: When you speak of progress on the question of withdrawal, may I ask Mr. Begin how he interprets that progress?

Begin: Well, Resolution 242 does not commit Israel to total withdrawal, and therefore this matter is a matter for negotiation, to establish those secure and recognized boundaries which are mentioned in the second paragraph of Resolution 242. And this is the crux of our problem – to negotiate the conditions of peace in order to establish peace throughout the Middle East. This is what we are going to do in the next few weeks and months.

Q: Will Syria eventually join the talks, and what would be the effect?

Sadat: I can't answer this. You should ask President Assad; I can't speak for him. As I told you, whenever they find it convenient for them to join, we shall welcome them.

Q: Will the Cairo conference reconvene simultaneously with the two ministerial committees? Or alternately?

Sadat: It has always been my position that without good preparation, Geneva will be a failure. I said this during my visit last April in the US. I made my first proposal for a working group under [US Secretary of State] Vance to start contacting all the parties concerned and a meeting to be prepared before Geneva.

Q: But what about simultaneous meetings of the two committees?

Sadat: They will be working in the context of the Cairo conference, and as I said, they will report to the plenary.

Q: Does this mean the Cairo conference will continue on the foreign minister level, that Mr. Vance and [UN secretary general] Mr. Waldheim will come here?

Sadat: Let us hope so. But for sure, we shall not go back. We are going forward.

Q: But the political committee is meeting in Jerusalem. Does this mean that Mr. Vance and Mr. Waldheim will also be in Jerusalem?

Sadat: Well, we shall leave this to them.

Q: Mr. Begin, do you accept the principle of non-acquisition of territory by force and are you going to apply it to a comprehensive settlement?

Begin: Yes, we are for a comprehensive settlement and I accept the principle established under law attesting that there mustn't be any acquisition of territory in the wake of a war of aggression. The war of the six days was a war of legitimate self-defense, and the President told me yesterday, yes, he does remember the slogans issued in those days to throw the Israelis into the sea, and so we defended ourselves in accordance with international law and practice. Thank you.

MARCH 1–10, 1978

AN EXCHANGE OF LETTERS

After the Ismailia summit, a meeting of the political committees established in Ismailia was scheduled in Jerusalem. But Egypt's delegation abruptly left before the conclusion of the conference. Egyptian foreign minister Muhammad Ibrahim Kamal interpreted Begin's toast remarks at the evening dinner as being insulting and undiplomatic although other observers thought Egypt was unable to agree to the compromise proposals being offered. In an attempt to restart the stalled negotiations following Egypt's unexplained retreat from the Jerusalem political conference session, Sadat wrote to Begin via the US ambassador to Egypt the following letter, which highlighted his difficulties with the process.

SECRET

Dear Mr. Prime Minister,

    I am sending you this message through our common friend, Roy Atherton,[5] who, in the name of the United States of America, is exerting valuable efforts to help us on the road towards a just and comprehensive settlement, in accordance with my concept that conditions should be created to establish good neighborly relations, in all the sense of the word, in our area. I think both parties should do whatever is needed to have good neighborly relations. This requires that no one treads on the other's land, sovereignty, honor or pride.

    Whereas we should be dealing with the substance of a comprehensive settlement, we are unfortunately still dealing with wording. Wording, in fact, will be easy if

---

5.   Alfred Leroy "Roy" Atherton Jr. (1921–2002) was an American diplomat who, at the time of the writing of this letter, was US assistant secretary of state for Near East affairs. He later became US ambassador to Egypt and served in that role from 1979 to 1983.

we agree on the substance regarding the withdrawal, the Palestinian problem and the security of all the parties.

Unfortunately, despite the Jerusalem and Ismailia meetings, and my talks in the U.S. and Europe, we still find ourselves in the same position that we were in prior to my visit to Jerusalem. What Israel has raised in the Military and Political Committees could have been raised in the Geneva Conference and bore no relationship to my new concept of peace as materialized in my initiative.

I am still committed to peace. I am not against reconvening the Political or the Military Committee, but we should get them out of the wrong direction they have taken and allow them to engage in the right dialogue. I am not seeking to impose conditions. But, for the meetings to be fruitful, and for the shuttling back and forth to be of positive use, there should be agreement on the main guidelines of a comprehensive settlement. I agree that the Atherton mission should continue. I am ready in principle to have the Military and Political Committees resume. But let us not convene and then let down the whole world.

Let us agree that Israel has need for security. And let us also agree that security should not be at the expense of land or sovereignty. This is a basic and elementary principle of today's world. Without acceptance of these principles, we will continue to move in circles and lose precious time.

On the matter of the Palestinian issue, which, as I said, is the core of the problem, Israel should not raise the issues in terms of land and sovereignty, or on the basis of the negation of the legitimate rights of the Palestinian people. A security requirement does indeed exist for Israel, which I fully recognized. To meet it, I am ready, in the interim period between signing an agreement and self-determination, to take my part in Gaza together with Israel, the Palestinians, and the U.N. to insure security. As to the West Bank, in my judgment, the

U.N. should initially take over as I have agreed with
King Hussein. Subsequently, however, a quadripartite
arrangement could be made, including the U.N., Israel,
King Hussein, and the Palestinians to insure security for
Israel during the interim period in the West Bank.

I recognize that security concerns would extend beyond
the interim period, and I am confident they will be met
satisfactorily in the negotiations.

The entire problem can be solved in a few days if we
agree on the elements of a settlement. My visit to Israel
has created new facts and conceptions. On the Egyptian
side, we no longer harbor any bitterness. We are going
ahead despite opposition by the rejectionists.

Regrettably, the Government of Israel has not yet
understood this. It still thinks only in terms of
strategic advantage and claiming [others'] land. But our
land is not something we can concede. Except for land and
sovereignty, I am ready to give everything in the nature
of peace as I have already proved by going to Jerusalem,
by inviting you to Ismailia, and by establishing direct
contacts at the Cairo Conference and in the Political and
Military Committees.

I have done this to give Israel a sense of security
which I realize it needed.

The rejectionists and the Soviet Union are active, but
we are facing them. Terrorism, like the murder of Youssef
El Sibai,[6] will not change our resolve to reach peace. But
you, Mr. Prime Minister, should know that you have given
them cards to play against my peace efforts:

You have misquoted my comments about the settlements,
claiming that I wished to burn them. The record shows
that I never used the term "burn." I simply said that
they should be removed and the airports could be plowed

---

6. Youssef el-Sebai, a confidant of Sadat, a literary figure and editor of *Al-Ahram*,
    was murdered by Palestinian terrorists in Nicosia, Cyprus, on February 18,
    1978.

under by Israel, as it has done in 1957, if it is concerned that they may be used as bases against it.

You have also publicly claimed that I went back on my word concerning the deployment of Egyptian military forces in Sinai. I told Gamassy in front of [Ezer] Weizman that I had promised you that my main forces will not exceed the passes. I never go back on my word.

Also, a few days before the Political Committee in Jerusalem, Radio Israel was reporting about settlements in Rafah, on Egyptian territory. It made it appear to the world that Israel was trying to create a fait accompli. And again now, while Roy Atherton is shuttling in the area in an effort to bridge the gap, the Council of Ministers of Israel has chosen this particular moment to declare in fact that it is pursuing the policy of establishing and expanding settlements, a policy that was described by the United States and by the whole world as an obstacle to peace.

My initiative was taken to facilitate all our efforts to achieve a settlement. It is regrettable that the Government of Israel does not seem to understand the intentions behind my initiative.

As for me, I have chosen my path. I will not let down the hundreds of millions in the world who have supported me. Otherwise, I would have declared to the world that there is no chance. I am not seeking to put mines on the road to peace, and the peace, and the peace initiative can continue. I have risked much in this initiative. The Soviet Union and others are working hard to prove I am wrong. But I have the courage to face them.

If you are ready for real peace, I am, as I have proved, ready too. I am ready, as the Americans say, for "big business" if you are too. In that case, old conceptions should be discarded, and I am ready to take my full share. If, on the contrary, old conceptions remain, we will be again in a vicious circle. I hope, for

Mar

1977

1979

1980

1981

the good for our peoples and the whole world, that we will be able to establish just and lasting peace.

Best regards,

Mohamed Anwar El Sadat

Begin replied as follows.

<u>SECRET</u>

Dear Mr. President,

I thank you for your letter of March 1, which our good friend Alfred Atherton handed to me personally.

The Assistant Secretary, to whom we are all grateful for his untiring efforts in the service of peace, has kindly undertaken to deliver to you this, my reply, during his next visit to Cairo.

Permit me, first, Mr. President, to dispose of misunderstandings concerning quotations and misquotations.

On January 8, 1978, I read in the press about "burning of settlements." That same evening, I made a public speech in which I reacted to the quotation as reported. However, it was only on January 13 that it was denied by an Egyptian official spokesman. I, of course, accepted the denial without question. It is a pity, indeed, that a full five days elapsed before the correction was announced.

During your visit to Jerusalem, which you made in kind response to my invitation, we held a private and friendly conversation. I remember every word of our dialogue which you summed up with a clear statement that your forces would not cross the Passes. Minutes later, I gave my Cabinet colleagues, waiting in the adjacent room in the King David Hotel, an account of our conversation and reported your statement verbatim.

As I told you in Ismailia, it was on the basis of this clear understanding that we built our peace plan and elaborated it in writing. We were, therefore, astonished on finding that the map subsequently presented by War Minister Gamassy to Defense Minister Weizman delineated a demilitarized zone of only 40 kilometers from the international boundary. This represents a difference of between 140–160 kilometers compared to what we had envisaged in our Jerusalem conversation. I did not say in the Knesset that you went back on your word. Quite the contrary: I called upon you, in keeping with your pledge, to instruct your military staff accordingly. I do so again in this personal message, Mr. President.

I feel bound to say, moreover, that it is I who was misquoted. In Jerusalem, I conducted an exchange with a group of Egyptian journalists in the course of which one of them made the statement that Egypt and yourself now recognize "Israel's right to exist and survive." I explained to the group that we have never asked for such recognition. Every nation, I said, has the same right to exist, be it large or small, strong or weak, near or far. Indeed, we were given our right to exist by the God of Abraham, Isaac and Jacob. We have paid a price for that right, higher perhaps than any other nation. It is inherent; it requires no recognition. What we do expect, however, on the basis of full reciprocity, is the recognition of our right to our land, sovereignty, independence, and to enjoy peace with our neighbors. This is the recognition that should be mutually established as a result of our negotiations.

Permit me, now, to pass on to other issues essential to our dialogue.

SECRET

Jerusalem, March 5, 1978

Dear Mr. President,

I thank you for your letter of March 1 which our good friend Alfred Atherton handed to me personally.

The Assistant Secretary, to whom we are all grateful for his untiring efforts in the service of peace, has kindly undertaken to deliver to you this, my reply, during his next visit to Cairo.

Permit me, first, Mr. President, to dispose of misunderstandings concerning quotations and misquotations.

On January 8, 1978, I read in the press about "burning of settlements." That same evening, I made a public speech in which I reacted to the quotation as reported. However, it was only on January 13 that it was denied by an Egyptian official spokesman. I, of course, accepted the denial without question. It is a pity, indeed, that a full five days elapsed before the correction was announced.

During your visit to Jerusalem, which you made in kind response to my invitation, we held a private and friendly conversation. I remember every word of our dialogue which you summed up with a clear statement that your forces would not cross the Passes. Minutes later, I gave my Cabinet colleagues, waiting in the adjacent room in the King David Hotel, an account of our conversation and reported your statement verbatim.

./2

no recognition. What we do expect, however, on the basis of full reciprocity, is the recognition of our right to our land, sovereignty, independence, and to enjoy peace with our neighbors. This is the recognition that should be mutually established as a result of our negotiations.

Permit me, now, to pass on to other issues essential to our dialogue.

./3

You complain that "we are unfortunately still dealing with wording." All of us remain engaged in this exercise because, Mr. President, your advisers propose to us "wording" which has one meaning: that the Government of Israel give a commitment of withdrawal to the lines preceding the Six Day War of defense. This is an old concept, going back to the autumn of 1967. As I said to you in Ismailia, Israel is not committed under resolution 242 to such a withdrawal, nor is it required to agree to such a precondition. In May and June 1967, we were threatened, Mr. President, with the destruction of our independence and, indeed, of our people. I remember well, when we last met, that you yourself recalled the slogan of those days: "Throw them into the sea." Israel defended itself.

As you know, it is the great rule of international law that in the wake of the use of the inherent right of national self-defense, territorial changes do take place in peace treaties. Were it otherwise, the whole map of Europe and the Far East should be changed radically.

I wish to reiterate again our acceptance, in accordance with resolution 242, of the principle of withdrawal, but not withdrawal to the lines of June 4, 1967. It is this wording, in principle, that we suggest to you in order that we might proceed together to make the substantive peace-making process possible.

In your letter, you continue to espouse the formation, after an interim period, of a Palestinian state in Judea, Samaria and the Gaza Strip. Mr. President, I have to say again, as I explained in Ismailia: such a state, in whatever form, would constitute a mortal danger to Israel. An interval of a few transient years will not eliminate the peril. No nation lives on borrowed time. The mortal danger must not be created.

In its proposals to you, the Government of Israel introduces a new approach and concept. We stand by our suggestion of complete administrative autonomy for the

Mar

Palestinian Arabs living in Judea, Samaria and the Gaza Strip; while security be assured for the Palestinian Jews. On hearing this from me in Ismailia your reaction – and again I remember your words vividly – was: "It is a step forward." Such a step can hardly, therefore, be characterized as "old" or as a step backward.

We also went very far in making a constructive proposal concerning our bilateral relations supported by security arrangements which, if fulfilled, will make it possible for Israel to assume the great risk – for the future – of withdrawing our armed forces to the international boundary. This, we are ready to negotiate for the sake of an agreement and the peace.

I am gratified to read in your letter of your wish to go on with the peace-making effort and that you are not against the resumption of the talks within the framework of the political and military committees which we agreed to establish during our good talks in Ismailia. I, therefore, suggest directly to you, Mr. President, that these negotiations be renewed. You told me in December, after having heard our proposals, that while we have difference of opinion, the Ismailia conference was successful and that discussion in the two committees would proceed on the basis of the Israeli proposals and Egyptian counter-proposals. Let us move forward through the resumption of the committees' talks by amicable negotiations within their framework.

Together, let us revive the spirit of the Jerusalem and the Ismailia meetings. It was a spirit of understanding, of goodwill and of open minds. This is the approach we need to reach an agreement and to build the peace for which we yearn.

Of course, we have our differences. We knew it before you came to Jerusalem, during our Knesset "debate," and in our subsequent exchanges. And yet, you properly summed up these initial meetings with the sentiment that we shall discuss our differences: we shall negotiate.

I suggest to you, Mr. President, that we resume the
negotiations as equal partners to a great undertaking:
the establishment of real peace in the Middle East.

> Best regards,
> Menachem Begin

Mar

Sadat continues the correspondence:

<u>SECRET</u>

Dear Mr. Prime Minister,

I have received your letter dated March 5, in answer
to my letter which the Assistant Secretary of State of
the U.S., Alfred Atherton, had delivered to you.

Let me first of all tell you that I agree with you that
the spirit of understanding, good will and open minds
should prevail in the contacts between us.

In fact, as I had already told you, conditions should
be created, through this spirit, for the establishment of
good neighbourly relations in the area, in every sense
of the word; thus old conceptions should be discarded
in order to allow us to reach a just, lasting and
comprehensive settlement.

Unfortunately, in your letter, you have insisted,
Mr. Prime Minister, on legalistic arguments that are not
only easily refutable, but which also seem to indicate
that the new spirit created by my peace initiative has
not found its way to the decisions and attitudes of the
Israeli Government.

When, for instance, you talk about the war of 1967,
you attribute to it a character of national self defense
on the part of Israel, which is contrary to historically
established facts, and, moreover, you build upon this,
to say the least, inaccurate assumption, consequences
which neither international law, nor the principles of
the charter of the UN can endorse. You are not unaware

that the principle of the inadmissibility of acquisition
of territory by war is a basic principle of the
international order which emerged from the tragedies of
the Second World War.

Again, when you refer to your positions, you insist
on retaining settlements on Arab land. This is a position
that has been clearly condemned by the whole world as
illegal and constituting an obstruction to peace.

I have recognized that problems of security must be
dealt with in a manner to be satisfactory to all parties.
I have clearly shown my readiness to meet with Israel's
security requirements in every way compatible with our
sovereignty. But the Government of Israel must also
clearly show that it does not consider that its security
requires trespassing on our land and our sovereignty. On
this no one can ever concede.

As to the Palestinian problem, which, let me remind
you, is considered by the whole world as the core and
crux of the conflict in our region, its solution should
be based on the respect of the legitimate rights of the
Palestinian people as recognized by the consensus of the
international community.

In an era where all the peoples of the world, however
small, claim and obtain their right to self-determination,
depriving a people of three million Palestinians of this
same right is not only contrary to law and justice, but
it is also an invitation to more strife and bloodshed.
This is what would, in your own terms, create a situation
of "mortal danger," of "borrowed time."

Mr. Prime Minister, we could endlessly engage in
legalistic debates on all the matters you raised.

We could also go back over and over again on the
question of "quotations and misquotations."

But, what I want to concentrate upon is the new spirit
and facts that have been created by my peace initiative.
The hundreds of millions of people in the world who have
supported it, saw in it the hope for a new era of peace.

We should not let these hundreds of millions down.

I never go back on my word.

I remain ready, as I have proved, for real peace if you feel you are ready too.

I remain ready to reconvene the Military and Political Committees. But if we do it now, without reaching, through the efforts of the United States, agreement on the main guidelines of a comprehensive settlement, the Committees will find themselves again in the vicious circle from which my visit to Jerusalem aimed at getting us out.

When negotiations resume, let it be clear that nobody wants to tread on others' land and sovereignty.

Let it be clear that the needs for security should be fully met in a way compatible with the desire to establish good neighbourly relations.

Let it be clear that no rights will be denied, that no claims contrary to international law and justice will be raised.

I am convinced that, given good will, clear vision, and a genuine determination not to remain prisoners of a past that has brought so much suffering to the peoples of our region, we can overcome all difficulties.

May God guide us towards a just and lasting peace.

Best regards,

Mohamed Anwar El Sadat

Mar

Part 3

From Camp David to the White House Lawn
September 1978–March 1979

SEPTEMBER 17, 1978

SPEECHES AT THE SIGNING
OF THE CAMP DAVID AGREEMENTS

The Camp David summit, which convened outside Washington September 5–17, 1978, was initiated by President Carter as a means of breaking a deadlock situation that had developed. In the months following the Ismailia summit, numerous meetings were held by all the principals. President Carter held meetings with President Sadat February 6–8, 1978, then with Begin March 21–22. In May, US-Israeli relations were strained when the US Senate approved arms sales to Egypt and Saudi Arabia (as well as to Israel, fulfilling a two-and-a-half-year-old commitment). Begin reacted to the US arms sale on May 16, saying, "The severity of the American Senate's decision…cannot be minimized," and protesting that "the conditions of peace are trying to be dictated to us."

US assistant secretary of state Harold H. Saunders remarked on June 12 that peace talks could resume after Israel gave its reply to the questions of the post-transitional West Bank arrangement for self-rule and a prior obligation in principle to withdraw from any West Bank and Gaza territory. Israel rejected assumed proposals of President Sadat that proposed conducting negotiations with preconditions such as withdrawal on June 25. US vice president Walter Mondale visited Jerusalem on July 2. The next day, Egypt published a Six-Point Peace Plan which was rejected by Israel although the government agreed to a tripartite meeting in London at the foreign ministers level proposed by Carter.

On July 23, Begin, after refusing Sadat's proposal that Israel hand over El Arish and the area around St. Catherine's Monastery, the traditional site of Mount Sinai, as gestures of goodwill, declared that "you don't get something for nothing" and that Israel would not hand over a "single grain of desert sand" without reciprocity. At the Leeds Castle Conference held near London July 17–20, Egypt rejected territorial compromise on its part while Israel expressed readiness to discuss, after a transition period, the question of sovereignty in Judea and Samaria ("the West Bank") and Gaza as well as territorial compromise. Against a background of personal negative attacks on

Begin, Secretary of State Vance delivered to Begin on August 5 the invitation to attend the Camp David Conference.

On his arrival in the United States on September 5, Prime Minister Begin said, among other remarks, "Twice I met the president of Egypt in a spirit of understanding and goodwill and common striving for peace: in Jerusalem and Ismailia. However, there is no doubt that this fifth meeting with President Carter and third with President Sadat is the most important, the most momentous of them all. My friends and colleagues, the foreign minister, the defense minister and I, and our friends and advisers, will make all endeavors possible to reach an agreement so that the peace process can continue and ultimately be crowned with peace treaties." Sadat and Begin and their advisors were secluded at Camp David for twelve days. The meetings at Camp David resulted in two documents, collectively known as the Camp David Accords. One was "A Framework for Peace in the Middle East" and the second was "A Framework for the Conclusion of a Peace Treaty between Egypt and Israel." The full and complete texts of the agreements and other related documents can be found in the appendix.

Following are extracts from the speeches made by President Carter, President Sadat and Prime Minister Begin at the signing ceremony of the Camp David agreements at the White House on September 17, 1978.

PRESIDENT CARTER

…We are privileged to witness tonight a significant achievement in the cause of peace, an achievement none thought possible a year ago, or even a month ago, an achievement that reflects the courage and wisdom of these two leaders.

Through thirteen long days at Camp David, we have seen them display determination and vision and flexibility which was needed to make this agreement come to pass. All of us owe them our gratitude and respect. They know that they will always have my personal admiration.

There are still great difficulties that remain and many hard issues to be settled. The questions that have brought warfare and bitterness to the Middle East for the last thirty years will not be settled overnight. But we should all recognize the substantial achievements that have been made.

One of the agreements that President Sadat and Prime Minister Begin are signing tonight is entitled "A Framework for Peace in the Middle East."

This framework concerns the principles and some specifics in the most substantive way which will govern a comprehensive peace settlement. It deals, specifically, with the future of the West Bank and Gaza and the need to resolve the Palestinian problem in all its aspects.... It also provides for Israeli forces to remain in specified locations during this period to protect Israel's security.

The Palestinians will have the right to participate in the determination of their own future, in negotiations which will resolve the final status of the West Bank and Gaza, and then to produce an Israeli-Jordanian peace treaty.

These negotiations will be based on all the provisions and all the principles of the United Nations Security Council Resolution 242. And it provides that Israel may live in peace within secure and recognized borders.

This great aspiration of Israel has been certified without constraint with the greatest degree of enthusiasm by President Sadat, the leader of one of the greatest nations on earth.

The other document is entitled "Framework for the Conclusion of a Peace Treaty" between Egypt and Israel.

It provides for the full exercise of Egyptian sovereignty over the Sinai. It calls for the full withdrawal of Israeli forces from the Sinai; and after an interim withdrawal which will be accomplished very quickly, the establishment of normal, peaceful relations between the two countries, including diplomatic relations....

There is one issue on which agreement has not been reached. Egypt stated that the agreement to remove Israeli settlements from Egyptian territory is a prerequisite to a peace treaty. Israel states that the issue of Israeli settlements should be resolved during the peace negotiations. That is a substantial difference.

Within the next two weeks, the Knesset will decide on the issue of these settlements....

During the last two weeks the members of all three delegations have spent endless hours, day and night, talking, negotiating, grappling with problems that have divided their people for thirty years.

Whenever there was a danger that human energy would fail, or patience would be exhausted, or goodwill would run out – and there were such moments – these two leaders and the able advisers in all delegations found the resources within them to keep the chances for peace alive.

I hope that the foresight and the wisdom that have made this session a success will guide these leaders and the leaders of all nations as they continue the process toward peace.

Thank you very much.

PRESIDENT SADAT

Dear President Carter, in this historic moment, I would like to express to you my heartfelt congratulations and appreciation. For long days and nights, you devoted your time and energy to the pursuit of peace. You have been most courageous when you took the gigantic step of convening this meeting. The challenge was great, and the risks were high, but so was your determination.

You made a commitment to be a full partner in the peace process. I am happy to say that you have honored your commitment.

The signing of the framework of the comprehensive peace settlement has a significance far beyond the event. It signals the emergence of a new peace initiative with the American nation in the heart of the entire process.

In the weeks ahead, important decisions have to be made if we are to proceed on the road to peace. We have to reaffirm the faith of the Palestinian people in the ideal of peace.

The continuation of your active role is indispensable. We need your help and the support of the American people. Let me seize this opportunity to thank each and every American for his genuine interest in the cause of people in the Middle East.

Dear friend, we came to Camp David with all the goodwill and faith we possessed, and we left Camp David a few minutes ago with a renewed sense of hope and inspiration. We are looking forward to the days ahead with an added determination to pursue the noble goal of peace.

Your able assistants spared no effort to bring out this happy conclusion. We appreciate the spirit and dedication. Our hosts at Camp David and the

State of Maryland were most generous and hospitable. To each one of them and to all those who are watching this great event, I say thank you.

Let us join in a prayer to God Almighty to guide our path. Let us pledge to make the spirit of Camp David a new chapter in the history of our nation.

Thank you, Mr. President.

PRIME MINISTER BEGIN

Mr. President of the United States, Mr. President of the Arab Republic of Egypt, Ladies and Gentlemen: The Camp David conference should be renamed. It was the Jimmy Carter Conference.

The President took an initiative most imaginative in our time and brought President Sadat and myself and our colleagues and friends and advisers together under one roof. In itself it was a great achievement.... As far as my historic experience is concerned, I think that he worked harder than our forefathers did in Egypt, building the pyramids.

Yes, indeed, he worked day and night, and so did we...

President Carter: Amen.

Prime Minister Begin: We worked day and night. We used to go to bed at Camp David between three and four o'clock in the morning, arise, as we are used to since our boyhood, at five or six, and continue working.

We had some difficult moments, as usually, there are some crises in negotiations; as usually, somebody gives a hint that perhaps he would like to pick up and go home. It is all usual.

Now when I came here to the Camp David conference, I said perhaps as a result of our work, one day people will, in every corner of the world, be able to say *"Habemus pacem"* in the spirit of these days. Can we say so tonight? Not yet. We still have to go the road until my friend President Sadat and I sign the peace treaties.

We promised each other that we shall do so within three months.

Mr. President, tonight, at this celebration of the great historic event, let us promise each other that we shall do it earlier than within three months.

Mr. President, you inscribed your name forever in the history of two ancient civilized peoples, the people of Egypt and the people of Israel.

Thank you, Mr. President.

I would like to say a few words about my friend, President Sadat. We met for the first time in our lives last November in Jerusalem. He came to us as a guest, a former enemy, and during our first meeting, we became friends.

In the Jewish teachings, there is a tradition that the greatest achievement of a human being is to turn his enemy into a friend, and this we do in reciprocity.

Since then, we had some difficult days. I am not going now to tell you the saga of those days. Everything belongs to the past. Today, I visited President Sadat in his cabin because in Camp David you don't have houses, you only have cabins. He then came to visit me. We shook hands. And, thank God, we again could have said to each other, "You are my friend."

And, indeed, we shall go on working and understanding, and with friendship and with goodwill. We will still have problems to solve. Camp David proved that any problem can be solved, if there is goodwill and understanding and some wisdom.

May I thank my own colleagues and friends, the foreign minister, the defense minister: Professor Barak who was the attorney general – now he is going to be his honor, the justice of the Supreme Court, the Israeli Brandeis; and [legal advisor to the State of Israel] Dr. [Meir] Rosenne; our wonderful ambassador to the United States, Mr. Simcha Dinitz; and all our friends, because without them, that achievement wouldn't have been possible.

I express my thanks to all the members of the American delegation, headed by the secretary of state, a man whom we love and respect. So I express my thanks to all the members of the Egyptian delegation who worked so hard together with us, headed by deputy prime minister Mr. Touhamy, for all they have done to achieve this moment. It is a great moment in the history of our nations and indeed of mankind.

I looked for a precedent: I didn't find it. It was a unique conference in the nineteenth century, perhaps.

Now, Ladies and Gentlemen, allow me to turn to my own people from the White House in my own native tongue.

[*In Hebrew.*] When you hear these words it will be morning in Israel, an early hour, and the sun will shine in the land of our fathers and sons.

Will we be able to come to you within a few days and to sing with you "We have brought peace unto you"? I can tell you this: we have made every possible human effort up to now in order that the day may come when each of us can say, peace has come to our people and our land.

Not only in this generation but also for generations to come. With the help of God, together, we will achieve this goal, and we will be blessed with good days of construction and brotherhood and understanding. May this be God's will.

[*In English.*] Thank you, Ladies and Gentlemen.

SEPTEMBER 20, 1978

BEGIN ADDRESSES JEWISH LEADERS IN NEW YORK

The following is a transcript of an address by the Hon. Menachem Begin on September 20, 1978 – only three days after the historic Camp David Accords were signed with Egypt.

The speech was given before an audience of about two thousand American Jewish leaders and guests of the Conference of Presidents of Major American Jewish Organizations in the grand ballroom of the Americana Hotel, New York.

This rare recording was found by Rabbi Avram J. Twersky of the Bronx, New York, from among his books and tapes. The discovery was made, ironically, only days after Begin's death in March 1992. The recording has since been presented to the Menachem Begin Heritage Center.

Mr. Chairman, the Ambassadors of Israel, Members of the dais, Ladies and Gentlemen, my Brethren:

We bring you from Camp David a peace agreement with security and with honor. [*Applause.*]

The framework we signed – concerning the bilateral relations between the State of Israel and Egypt – is actually a peace treaty. In that framework we have solved 98 percent of the issues, which will be included in the peace treaty.

There is one outstanding problem, and that concerns the settlements in northern and southern Sinai, which were built for the last ten years by my predecessors. I praise them for the decision to have built those settlements. It was no caprice and no attempt to take land from anybody else. They did it with prudence and understanding of the most vital issues of Israel's national security.

We want security not only for our generation, which suffered much and fought, and with God's help won the day. We care for our children and our children's children, for all generations to come, because after the destruction of our two Temples and two states, never again should there be a destruction of a Jewish state. [*Applause.*]

However, it became a problem in the negotiations for a peace treaty between us and Egypt. And I explained to the president of the United States that the foreign minister, the defense minister, and myself are not empowered and not entitled to give any commitment on this issue, because it is the policy which was approved by our democratic parliament that those settlements should stay. And therefore, the one thing we can do is to bring it back to Jerusalem, place it before our parliament, and let parliament decide.

We also took the serious decision on this issue to give the members of parliament a completely free vote – without any party discipline or any attempt of coercion. Every member of the 120 members of our Knesset will vote in accordance with his own conscience. It will be a free vote. But if it should be a free vote, we will not allow any foreign pressure to be exerted on the Knesset of Israel. [*Applause.*]

Nobody in the world is entitled to tell our 120 elected representatives in the legislature of Israel that if they do not vote as he would like, then there won't be negotiations for peace. That would mean illegitimate pressure on the consciences of our legislature. It is absolutely intolerable. What kind of a free vote would it be?

We shall abide by the decision of the Knesset – whatever it is. I am a servant of the Knesset – not its ruler. I have the honor to be a prime minister of a free and democratic state under a parliamentary regime. [*Applause.*]

But it won't be any reason not to start negotiations. Under any circumstances of outcome of the vote, because in any case, we suggest that that issue, too, should come up during the negotiations for peace treaties. And we have the experience at Camp David of twelve days and twelve nights that when you rack your brain, when you make an intellectual effort, any problem – even one that seems to be insoluble – can find a solution.

Therefore, the question will be brought before the Knesset during the next fortnight. Whatever the Knesset decides, we shall carry out. And we shall stand by the negotiations for the conclusion of the peace treaty between Israel and Egypt – the foundation for that peace treaty having been laid already at Camp David.

Concerning Judea, Samaria and the Gaza District:

We have also signed a very serious agreement.

Yes, it is based on our peace proposal. And at Camp David I could have heard from my friend, the president of the United States, a statement that made me both sad and happy, to the effect: "The world did not appreciate enough your peace proposal, brought to Washington and Ismailia in December, last year."

Admittedly, we had some difficult days, and even months, since March this year, until last month. But we are used to it. Everything which we lived through for the last forty years perhaps was a preparation for these days. To steel our character. To make sure that we do not bow to pressure. That we can also survive some name-calling. *"Meilah"* [So be it].

Now, on the basis of our peace plan, the agreement says that the Palestinian Arabs residing in Judea, Samaria and the Gaza District will have autonomy. Full autonomy. They will themselves select their administrative council. And eleven departments. And deal themselves with the daily affairs of their lives. We shall not interfere. They will have self-rule, as we believe it is just that they should have. And we, the Palestinian Jews, will have security. As we believe it is indispensable justice that they should enjoy it.

As a result, I hereby declare that the Israeli Defense Forces will stay in Judea, Samaria and the Gaza Strip to defend our people and to make sure that Jewish blood is not shed again by our implacable enemies. [*Applause.*]

And if anybody – if an unknown spokesman of the State Department ever made a declaration to the effect that the agreement means that our Defense Forces will stay in Judea, Samaria and the Gaza District only for five years, I hereby declare they will stay beyond five years. [*Applause.*]

About such a statement Churchill used to say that it is: "A terminological inexactitude." [*Applause.*]

Or, to put it simply, our Defense Forces will stay in Judea, Samaria and the Gaza District. There will be autonomy for our neighbors, there will be security for us, there will be peace for them – and for us. [*Applause.*]

This is the reason why, since the first Egyptian document that was produced during the talks between President Carter, President Sadat and myself, a problem arose which could have made the agreement impossible.

We were asked to sign a document, in which at least four times the words appeared: "the inadmissibility of the acquisition of territory of war." And unfortunately, those same words appeared also in the American document produced to us. We tried to plead with the Egyptians, and mainly, with our American friends. We explained to them that these words are taken from the preamble to Resolution 242 of the United Nations Security Council of November 1967. Under international law a preamble is not an integral part of the resolution itself. It does not have binding force. Therefore it stands separately as a doctrine. If it is a doctrine, it must mean a war of aggression. The aggressor must never get away with the spoils. But, if it is a war of legitimate national self-defense, this is the Golden Rule under international law, then territorial changes are not only permissible, but necessary. [*Applause.*]

Otherwise, every aggressor will not only commit, but also repeat, these aggressions. What is he going to lose? If he wins his aggressive war, he gets his spoils. If he loses, he gets back what he lost. This is simple *seichel* [Yiddish: intelligence] – not only law.

And as you do not add, we told our friends, the word "aggression," what does that preamble mean in relation and in connection with the Six-Day War, which was thrust upon us – as three Presidents of the United States of America wrote to us since the days of June 1967. We were then threatened with extinction. There were slogans in Cairo and in Damascus and in Rabat Ammon and in Baghdad to the effect: "Throw them into the sea! Cut them down! Kill them! Destroy them!" Military orders included a passage calling for the physical destruction of the civilian population of any town which the invading armies may conquer.

We faced another Holocaust, Ladies and Gentlemen. Surrounded on all sides by overwhelming forces. By thousands of Soviet-supplied tanks, hundreds of first-line combat planes, hundreds of thousands of soldiers.

With God's help, we repelled all of them. They did not win their night; we won the day. [*Applause.*]

And now you ask us to sign a document with those false and falsifying words: "inadmissibility of the acquisition of territory," as a result of such a war, of legitimate self-defense, of saving a nation surrounded and attacked and threatened with annihilation? All those arguments did not convince our friends. And time and again for eight days – since Wednesday – we refused. On behalf of the people of Israel, on behalf of the Jewish people, in the name of simple of human justice and dignity, above all, on behalf of truth, we refused to give this signature for those words. [*Sustained applause.*]

Ultimately, a talk took place between the President and myself on Wednesday night, the eighth day of our deliberations. I asked the President to lend me an attentive ear. I told him: "It is going to be, Mr. President, one of the most serious talks I have ever held with you since we met in July last year in the White House, and perhaps, I have ever held with anybody on earth."

And this is what I told him:

"Mr. President: Sinai. Do we ask for one square kilometer of Sinai? Didn't we produce a peace plan in accordance with which all the peninsula will go to Egypt? We take great risks. When we evacuate Sinai, ultimately, after two or three years, with all the security arrangements already agreed in the framework for peace, we still take great risks.

"In Ismailia I asked General Gamazi, the commander-in-chief of the Egyptian army, 'How much time will it take to move your army to the international boundary, as you have now already part of your army on this side of the Suez Canal?' He consulted with one of his officers and gave me the following sincere reply: 'Seven hours.'

"When we evacuate Sinai there won't be one Israeli soldier, or one Israeli tank, between that Egyptian army on this side of the Suez Canal, and on the other, to stop them. And in seven hours they can be on our southern border and threaten the civilian population of our country."

You may be quiet. It won't happen. If they try, *ich bin zey nit m'kaneh*. [Yiddish: I don't envy them. *Sustained applause.*]

However, this is the objective situation. Seven hours! Yes, it is a risk. I take it for the sake of peace. And we don't ask for ourselves even one square kilometer of territory of the Sinai.

"Judea and Samaria and the Gaza District: We suggest autonomy. We don't ask now for one square kilometer to be put under our sovereignty. Yes, Mr. President, we the Jewish people, as of right,[7] have a claim to sovereignty over Judea, Samaria and the Gaza District. [*Applause.*]

"There are some people who make a mockery of the Bible. Let them make a mockery of themselves. [*Applause.*]

"The Bible is a living document – eternally living document.

"We live on this Book, with this Book – forever.

"And my predecessor, of blessed memory, the late Mr. Ben-Gurion, aptly expressed himself when he said, 'Some people say that the British Mandate is our Bible. It is untrue,' he said. 'The Bible is our mandate!' [*Applause.*]

"Yes, Judea, Samaria and the Gaza Strip are integral parts of Eretz Yisrael – the land of our forefathers, which we have never forgotten during exile, when we were a persecuted minority, humiliated, killed, our blood shed, burned alive. We always remembered Zion, and Zion means Eretz Israel. It is our land as of right.

"Now, we don't ask even for one square kilometer. We leave the question of sovereignty open, because we want peace. Ours is the right and the claim. We know there are other claims. If they rival amongst themselves, if they collide with each other, we can't have an agreement, and then there won't be peace.

"Therefore we racked our brains and we wounded our hearts, and we found a way. Let the question of sovereignty be left open. And let us deal with the human beings. With the peoples on both sides. Let us give the Palestinian Arabs autonomy and the Palestinian Jews security, and we shall live together in human dignity, in equality of rights, in human progress. There will be justice. And we shall together advance. [*Applause.*]

"So, if we don't – in connection with the two subject matters which are now being negotiated at Camp David – ask even for one square kilometer, either in Sinai or in Judea, Samaria and the Gaza Strip, where is 'acquisition

---

7. "As of right" is a legal term meaning a legal right for which a party requires no specific approval from any court. Begin considered the decisions of the San Remo Convention of 1920 and the Supreme Council of the League of Nations in 1922 as being the international legal recognition of the Jewish people's right to reconstitute its national homeland in what was then known as "Palestine" extending over both sides of the Jordan River.

of territory'? What relevance have those words 'unjust' in connection with the Six-Day War to what we are doing at Camp David?"

I concluded this passage of my words to the president of the United States with a simple statement, taken, yes indeed, from the Bible.

And I told him: "Mr. President: Let my right hand forget its cunning before I sign such a document." [*Sustained applause.*]

Yesterday the president asked me to give him the Hebrew quotation of what I told him in King James's translation. I gave it to him. [*Audience laughter.*] I gave it to him.

And the original is: "*Tishkach yemini, im eshkachech Yerushalayim. Tidbak leshoni l'chiki im lo ezkereichi. Im lo a'aleh et Yerushalayim al rosh simchati.*"

The president got convinced. And then he went to President Sadat and convinced him that we cannot sign any document in which those irrelevant words will appear. Because, should we have signed them, that would be surrender to a subterfuge. They wanted us to give a commitment that we shall leave the Golan Heights – "inadmissibility of the acquisition of territory of war" – and we shall descend into the valley, ten meters from the Genazerath link to the east. And then the Syrians would shell with their Soviet-supplied artillery every moshav and every kibbutz in the valley. And this time even be able to reach Haifa.

It won't happen, Ladies and Gentlemen. [*Applause.*]

And they wanted us to give them a commitment a priori, before even one of the five years passes, that we shall relinquish, completely, Judea, Samaria and the Gaza district, and not only give up our paternal heritage, our inherent right, the Land of our prophets and of our kings, the Land of our fathers and of our children, but also the most vital demands of our national security.

Then we would be here, down in the valley. They would be here, up on the mountain. We would be nine miles from the seashore, in Hebrew in the double meaning of the expression "*kol ir v'em b'Yisrael*" [every city and suburb in Israel], would be in the range of the fire of the most implacable, most barbaric enemy of the Jewish people since the days of the Nazis.

Then there wouldn't be peace. There would be permanent bloodshed and ultimately a general war under the harshest conditions ever imagined by any human being.

Can such a situation be tolerated? Can such conditions be restored? Our parliament in the range of enemy's fire? Jerusalem taken into crossfire by Bethlehem in the south and by El Bira in the north? Every man, every woman, every Jewish child in direct danger of being maimed or killed? Could we agree, can we agree, to such injustice?

May I say to you a simple word: Never. [*Sustained applause.*]

And therefore, I couldn't have given a commitment about "inadmissibility," etc., taking into consideration our future, our security, the lives of our children.

Ultimately, that passage was deleted from the document and then we could go with our negotiations.

My brethren: We stand now at a crossroads. Not everything was solved. Much was achieved. We had difficult times. We were wronged, and some trembling knees started to tremble several months ago. There were some sunshine soldiers in our ranks, who left us at the first difficulties we faced. No recriminations.

Yes, it is written in our Torah about a man who has got a soft or a weak heart: Let him go home, and let him not influence other people with the softness or the weakness of his heart. No recriminations. But the lesson we have to draw, today as well: We have a great achievement. We want peace. We pray for it, we yearn for it.

When the people of Israel elected my colleagues and myself to serve them in the government, some people – there and here – immediately said: "That means war! The following day there will be war!"

What a mistaken concept.

Men who fought in the underground for liberation hate war. More than anything else in life, sometimes you have to fight, otherwise you will not be a human being. As it was proved in the forties in Europe. Only when the remnants took up some arms and fought, they became human beings. Until that time they were hunted animals. By cruel animals.

You fight for liberation. What news is it to you, American citizens? But a fighter for liberation hates war! And it is true that I dream about peace in Israel – between Israel and all her Arab neighbors – not since the seventeenth of May 1977. Not since June 1967. But since November 1947, because until then, five years passed when no Arab ever raised his hand on even one Jew, or vice versa. And we, from the Underground, fought for the liberation of Palestine, our land, to save our people from the danger of utter destruction and complete annihilation and to live with the Arab neighbors as I learned from my master and teacher Ze'ev Jabotinsky… [*interrupted by applause*] …in respect, in human dignity, in equality of rights, in autonomy.

We wanted peace for the last thirty-five years! It never came. Now we have a breakthrough. We may have peace. We hope it will come. There are still problems to be solved. Hurdles to be overcome. For those days – the good ones and the difficult ones – having learned the lesson what happened since March until last month.

This is my appeal to you. Always, under any circumstances, let us stand together. Always together. [*Sustained applause.*]

Then the difficult days will pass. Darkness will disappear, light will come, joy will arise, peace will be achieved, better days will come.

But as I spoke about those who got cold feet at the first difficulty, I would like to mention a few people… [*Sustained applause.*] …who stood with us in the most difficult days.

I only mention a few – the others whom I do not mention will forgive me because it could be a very long list and my time is limited.

Ladies and Gentlemen, I want to express our deep gratitude to Alex Schindler. [*Sustained applause.*]

He stood with us at the most difficult days. Never bowed his head and spoke to the mighty as a proud Jew.

I want to thank Ted Mann for his attitude. [*Applause.*]

I want to express our gratitude to a man whom I do not see. I don't know whether he is in the hall. To Rabbi [Fabian] Shoenfeld. A sage… [*interrupted by applause*] …who never flinched. [*Applause.*]

And I want to thank a man you all know – who is probably not here – of strong character. I want to thank Max Fisher.

And I want to express gratitude to all the others whom I cannot now mention by their names, who stood with us with civil courage. A great military French commander said: "To show civil courage is more difficult than military courage."

It is so.

Never doubted us. Never wrote letters to us or against us. Never tried to find favor with the mighty ones against the few – although not the weak ones. Those last nine months were quite an experience for all of us. And they taught us a lesson for all the years to come: Jews are a great people.

Tempered in suffering, experienced in resistance, proud with their heritage. And if they stand together, if there is "*achdut Yisrael v'ahavat Yisrael v'ahavat chinam*" [unity of Israel and love of Israel and unconditional love], no enemy will get the upper hand against them." [*Applause.*]

So today we shall rededicate ourselves to this goal. Let us do our duty. Let us rejoice in our achievements. I call upon you, when you go back to your *kehilot* [communities], that you should redouble and treble your efforts to solve the problem of intolerable poverty of 10 percent of the people of Israel.

May I issue a personal appeal to you – it is always on my conscience day and night, to know that 300,000 Jewish people live in the most abject conditions – a people who was commanded at the dawn of history: "*Tzedek, tzedek tirdof*" [Justice, justice, thou shalt pursue].

Make an effort so that after three years, with God's help, when I step down, I'll be able to say, "My friends and I brought peace to Israel and liquidated poverty in Israel."

NOVEMBER 21, 1978

AN ISRAELI GOVERNMENT COMMUNIQUÉ

US president Jimmy Carter invited Begin and Sadat for talks beginning October 12 at Blair House, the official diplomatic guest house of the president of the United States, aimed at breaking through the logjam in the negotiations. Sticking points included continued Israeli settlement in Judea, Samaria and Gaza and Egyptian demands for a target date for the autonomy plan implementation (giving Palestinian Arabs in these areas autonomy – though not sovereignty), as well as linkage between the Israel-Egypt treaty and the autonomy plan. On October 28, the Nobel Prize Committee announced its decision to award the 1978 Peace Prize to President Sadat and to Prime Minister Begin (but not to President Carter).

On November 19, a year after the Sadat visit, Begin declared before a Herut Party Central Committee meeting the Israeli government's readiness to sign the peace treaty with Egypt, "on condition that Egypt is prepared to do so." Begin defined his objections, saying: "The proposals submitted to us by the Egyptians are not acceptable to us; they contradict the Camp David agreement, which we are prepared to carry out as it stands." Two days later, the government formalized Begin's statements in the following official communiqué:

1. The Government of Israel is prepared to sign the Treaty of Peace with Egypt that was presented to it for consideration by the delegation of Israel to the peace negotiations, if Egypt is ready to act likewise.

2. The latest proposals submitted by the Government of Egypt are inconsistent with the Camp David agreements, and are unacceptable to Israel.

3. After the signing and ratification of the treaty of peace between Egypt and Israel, Israel is prepared to start negotiations in order to reach agreement on the implementation of the administrative autonomy in Judea, Samaria and the Gaza district in accordance with the provisions of the "Framework for Peace in the Middle East" agreed at Camp David.

NOV 30–DEC 4, 1978

AN EXCHANGE OF LETTERS

Following these developments, Begin received the following letter from Sadat:

```
The President
of the Arab Republic of Egypt

                              November 30, 1978

Dear Prime Minister Begin,
     I am addressing this letter to you with full awareness
of the historic responsibility we both share before our
```

peoples who gave us a solemn mandate to build a solid
structure for peace. We owe it to this generation and
the generations to come in both countries not to leave a
stone unturned in our pursuit of peace. The ideal is the
greatest one in the history of man and we have accepted
the challenge to translate it from a cherished hope into
a living reality.

You will recall that when I addressed the Israeli
people from the rostrum of the Knesset more than a year
ago, I said: "In the history of nations and peoples,
there come up certain moments when it becomes imperative
for those who are endowed with wisdom and vision to
penetrate beyond the past with all its complications
and residue to usher in an undaunted élan toward new
horizons". I believe that we are now witnessing one of
these moments. It is a moment of truth which requires
each one of us to take a new look at the situation and
reexamine his thinking and calculations. I trust that
you all know that when I undertook my sacred mission to
Jerusalem against all odds and in the face of the most
formidable complications, I was not trying to strike
a deal. I was and I am still determined to make peace.
If our commitment to that great cause is profound and
unwavering, then our task should transcend words and
legal formulations. Then also, the challenge before us
ceases to be a contest of oratory and scoring points here
and there. It becomes converted irreversibly to one of
winning the hearts and minds of our peoples and enabling
them to look beyond the unhappy past.

It was in this spirit that we entered into direct
negotiations with you in a sincere attempt to build new
bridges for the future. These negotiations reached their
high and low points as we went deeper into the core of
our complex problem. We have achieved some progress.
However, I feel that valuable time has frittered away in
futile arguments and discussions about issues of little
or no real significance. Apparently, some are still seized

with the notion that the solution could be reached at the expense of the other party. Still others remain captives to concepts like that of David and Goliath instead of being inspired by the brotherhood of Ismail and Isaac. Evidently, some old barriers do exist and it is our joint responsibility to break them. A few days ago, one of your colleagues chose to speak of the present state of affairs in terms which are in clear contradiction with the new spirit of peace. He said that Egypt must not forget that part of its territory is occupied and could remain occupied. We reject that logic and I am sure that the vast majority of the Israeli people [share] our view.

It might be appropriate to remind you of what we have offered to enable you to make the necessary decision for the establishment of peace. First and foremost, we proved our willingness to look seriously and sympathetically to your need to feel secure. Of course the need for security is mutual and not confined to you alone. Still, we lent an attentive ear to your concern for security in view of certain historical and psychological factors. This must not go unappreciated. Nor should it be misinterpreted or abused.

We offered you full recognition, not as a mere formality but as a dynamic process of coexistence that includes diplomatic relations, economic and cultural exchange for the mutual benefit of our two peoples and in fact for the good of the entire region. By conventional norms, this process can take place only after the completion of withdrawal. However, I accepted the request of our good friend President Carter to start the process after the completion of the interim withdrawal. I did so as a token of my full confidence in the future as well my faith in our peoples who are going to be the final arbiter.

We said, and still maintain, that we are most willing to establish with you normal relations that exist between good neighbors. No discriminatory barriers shall stand in the way of free movement of people or goods. Individuals

and groups will have an opportunity to know more about
one another and learn to live together in peace and
amity. You shall enjoy the benefits of the freedom of
passage through the Suez Canal and the Gulf of Aqaba.
Boycotts will be terminated. All of this is conceived
with the understanding that neither party is to seek any
special advantages or ask for the position of a favored
nation. This can not be forced upon two sides which are
terminating a state of war that lasted for over thirty
years. It could not be achieved by ignoring the facts
of our contemporary life. Only the natural development
and growth of our relations in the future can lead to
the intensification of exchange in the areas where the
interests of both parties meet. It is much better to
start on a solid basis and then proceed to add to the
structure a brick every day. This operation of peace
building will not be viewed or judged today or tomorrow,
but several years after. It is still my conviction that
the real peace process starts only after the signing.
Thus, what is important is to start now and on the right
foot. Once we [have] started, the door will be wide
open. We have not asked for any privileged position and I
assume that this is reciprocated on your part.

Let me make another point crystal clear to you in this
respect. When we express our readiness to offer you all
what I just mentioned, we are not doing so in return for
your commitment to withdraw from our territory. We think
that this is an obligation you bear under all accepted
norms of international law and contemporary international
relations. While we are changing the course of history,
we must not attempt to tamper with the law of nations. I
think I made it abundantly clear on every occasion that
we do not accept any bargaining over our sovereignty or
territory. Sooner or later, our land will be liberated.

The proper return here must be a genuine acceptance
on your part to coexist with your Arab neighbors. Your
relations with them should not be viewed in terms of

conquest or exploitation. Rather, it should be founded
on mutual respect and a firm belief in the equality among
nations. Coexistence with your Arab neighbors starts
with coexistence with the Palestinian people. This is
the message I have been trying to deliver to you since
I arrived in Jerusalem on November 19, 1977. In Camp
David, we reached agreement on a formula which we think
can bring about an equitable solution to the Palestinian
problem. If we value the ideal of peace highly, then
we should not at all detract from that formula. On the
contrary, we should add to it and give it every chance
for success. In my view, you should not attempt, or
appear to attempt, to evade your obligations under the
Camp David "Framework". Since we agreed that certain
steps shall take place in the immediate future to effect
a transfer of authority to the inhabitants of West Bank
and Gaza, I frankly see no reason why we should not agree
on a timetable for these steps. You have asked for a
timetable for such steps as the exchange of diplomatic
relations, the conclusion of an agreement on trade and
commerce, the conclusion of another agreement on cultural
exchange and the conclusion of a civil aviation agreement.
Is it not equally, if not more, important to fix a
timetable for the envisaged transformation in the West
and Gaza?

An argument has been advanced in this respect which
we do not find convincing. It is said that you do not want
to be bound to produce certain results which require the
cooperation of a reluctant party. My answer is that one
should not assume the wors[t] if we really believe in the
necessity and wisdom of the course we are taking. If the
implementation of any of these steps is hindered because
of reasons beyond your control, you will not be held
responsible for that. There is always an assumption of
rationality. Furthermore, I must tell you in all candor
that you are not doing much to encourage the moderate
elements among the Palestinians to cooperate. On the

contrary, much of your acts and words seem to be designed
to dissuade them from joining in with us. I need not list
to you any examples of these deeds and words for you are
quite aware of them. If the Palestinians are left with
the impression that the self-government plan, and not
the administrative autonomy as you call it, is a sham,
they will remain embittered and the voice of reason will
be drowned among them. As you well know, peoples never
abandon their cause in the face of neglect or force. You
might recall that your predecessor Ben-Gurion once said:
"forgive...but never forget". This admonition applies to
the Palestinians too.

The issue of "linkage" underwent much distortion
and confusion. Let me tell you that we are not seeking
that linkage as a means of shirking our commitments or
breaking our promises. If we make a commitment, we intend
to honor it fully regardless of the cost. Our record
speaks for itself in this respect. If we have any doubt
that we can honor a certain commitment, we shall not make
it in the first place.

We are talking about linkage because we are both
committed to work for a comprehensive peace settlement
not a separate agreement. If you go back to the days
of Camp David, you will remember that I told you on
September 7 that I am for permanent peace and not for
a separate agreement, a partial arrangement or another
disengagement. This attitude was clearly reflected in my
address to the Israeli people through the Knesset last
year, exactly as it is reflected in the outcome of our
deliberations. The "Framework for peace in the Middle
East" bears ample evidence to the nature of the peace we
are working for. If this is the case, why should it not
be spelled out and reaffirmed.

Dear Prime Minister Begin,

Parties often make mistakes in the course of
negotiations which is an arduous process. They think
that their task is to insist on their demands rightly

or wrongly, justly or unjustly. But if this attitude is
tolerated in negotiations for an armistice agreement,
it should not at all be adopted when nations are
making peace. I am not stating that to point a finger
of accusation at you. I am merely referring to two
unfortunate developments:

First: Your Delegation insisted on certain
unreasonable provisions that serve no useful
purpose. Certain concepts were blown out of
proportion or stretched beyond the tolerable
limit. This was the case with respect to the
proposed draft of Article 6.[8] What you are
entitled to is a commitment from us to discharge
our obligations in good faith as we hold you
responsible to do the same. It is inappropriate
for any of us to attempt to interfere with the way
the other party conducts its relations with third
countries. It is the responsibility of each party
to reconcile its commitments to various partners.

Much of the language used in your proposed
text in this respect is meaningless and self-
contradictory. One way of dealing with it could be
challenging the relevance of a certain provision
in application. But you know that this is not my
style. I always like to be clear and decisive for
I believe that I am doing the right thing for my
people and yours. I would like to set a model for
others to follow.

---

8. Article (Section) 6 refers to the issue of the Jewish communities. The original
proposed language stated, "After the signing of the framework and during the
negotiations, no new Israeli settlements will be established and there will be no
expansion of physical facilities in existing settlements." This became a matter
of contention, and misunderstanding, when Begin insisted he had agreed to a
"settlement freeze" that would last no longer than three months and would be
linked solely to the peace treaty negotiations with Egypt, not to the autonomy
talks. In addition, this matter would not be in the body of the treaty but in an
accompanying letter.

Second: Your delegation retracted its acceptance
of certain provisions or concepts after this
acceptance had been acted upon. It is not my
intention to get into a detailed account of what
happened in this respect. Suffice it to cite a few
examples:

a. withdrawing your proposal on the sub-phases of
   the interim withdrawal;
b. Going back on your offer to reduce the period
   of the interim withdrawal to six months;
c. Opposing, after consenting to, the formula of
   an exchange of letters on the West Bank and
   Gaza;
d. Opposing a tangible Egyptian presence in the
   Gaza Strip.
e. Reversing your previous position on the
   elimination of the arms race;
f. Insisting on deleting a paragraph from
   the preamble after having accepted it.
   That paragraph spoke of the necessity for
   maintaining the balanced and reciprocal
   implementation of the Parties' corresponding
   obligations.

Again, I am not stating the abovementioned for the
purpose of chastising your Government or attributing
malice to anyone. I am simply urging you and our
colleagues to reconsider your position and take a new
look at recent events as well as ways and means for
breaking the present impasse. I do not want to see a
resurgence of suspicion and ill-feeling as I am mainly
concerned for the future. I hope you will find it possible
to respond to this new initiative in the same spirit
which prompted me to write to you.

                              With best wishes,
                              Mohammed Anwar El-Sadat

Begin responded:

Jerusalem, December 4, 1978

Dear Mr. President,

I thank you for your kind communication delivered
to me on November 30 by the United States Ambassador in
Israel. I read its content with deep attention.

The Biblical reference you cite concerning the kinship
and brotherhood between our peoples is very moving. I
share its sentiment. May I say, however, that the
comparison between David and Goliath does not apply in
our time. We believe in the brotherhood and equality of
all nations.

Let us now turn from ancient to contemporary history.
To conclude, to sign, to ratify the peace treaty between
Egypt and Israel; to reach, if possible, appropriate
peace treaties with the other neighbors - Jordan, Syria
and Lebanon; to resolve the problem of the Palestinian
Arabs through the full autonomy of the Arab inhabitants
of Judea, Samaria and Gaza, together with genuine
security for Israel and her citizens - this, truly, is
history in the making. We wrote a page of it at Camp
David with the great and unforgettable assistance of our
good friend President Carter. Surely, we must persist
together to bring our efforts to fruition.

First, we should and can finalize the peace treaty
between our two countries. In the Camp David Framework we
agreed that:

> "In order to achieve peace between them, the
> parties agree to negotiate in good faith with a
> goal of concluding within three months from the
> signing of this Framework a peace treaty between
> them, while inviting the other parties to the
> conflict to proceed simultaneously to negotiate and
> conclude similar peace treaties with a view to
> achieving a comprehensive peace in the area."

This is our commitment. With respect to the peace treaty
between Egypt and Israel, it is an absolute commitment.
It is not predicated on any other factor, including
acceptance of the invitation as quoted above. Certainly,
we both seek a comprehensive peace settlement in the
Middle East. As you know, I have never suggested to you
to conclude a separate peace with Israel. The envisaged
peace treaty between our countries constitutes the first
indispensable step towards the broader settlement we seek.

In order to make this momentous prospect possible, the
Government of Israel a fortnight ago took the decision
that it was ready to sign the draft Egyptian-Israel
peace treaty as it stands. In so doing, the Government
expressed its willingness to forego two amendments to the
draft which it had held to throughout the negotiations.
Those amendments are important, but I will not dwell
on their significance now because of the action we took
in favor of what we hoped would lead to the immediate
achievement of our common goal.

As far as the text of the peace treaty is concerned,
it seems that the obstacle in the way of our two
Governments putting our signatures to it – a turning
point, indeed, not only in our mutual relations but for
the whole region – is your insistence on changing or
deleting sections of Article VI and, I am informed, also
Article IV. These Articles, as they read, were negotiated
and renegotiated by our delegations. They are vital and
indispensable.

In this context may I comment on your remark
about "legal formulations." To put it simply, everyone
tends to display a preference for his own formulation
while showing little sympathy for that of his partner.
Beginning with the paper you read to President Carter and
myself at Camp David and continuing through all the other
Egyptian draft documents, I have found numerous "legal
formulations." I say this without any recrimination. We
should both agree, surely, that this is in the nature

of things, for after all, we are dealing with political documents that should have proper international standing. Hence, by definition, they are formulated in judicial language.

The "legal formulation" to which you address yourself in seeking to change both the letter and substance of Article VI of the draft peace treaty is an immediate case in point. May I tell you that a number of the greatest authorities in international law share our view that under the circumstances this Article VI is absolutely vital to make our document a treaty of peace.

Therefore, should you, Mr. President, now give your approval to the text of the draft peace treaty as elaborated by our delegations, then no obstacle whatsoever exists to its signing within the specified three months, before the 17th of December 1978. This is the positive suggestion I make to you today.

On page nine of your letter you enumerated six points about which you express criticism of the attitudes of the Israeli delegation and Government. May I respond:

a) and b): It is true that your delegates and our delegates talked about the possibility of sub-phases in the interim withdrawal and the feasibility of reducing this withdrawal period to six months. Never did they reach an agreed protocol on these two subjects. In the natural course of discussion it was mentioned by the Israeli representatives as an idea, as a concept, or a possibility to be looked at.

And, indeed, as the negotiations proceeded, the Government of Israel considered the issue and decided that we could not undertake to reduce the interim withdrawal period to six months. We will fulfill completely our commitment under the Camp David Framework of the interim withdrawal within three to nine months. On the other hand, sub-phases will be considered, in accordance with the decisions of the Government, within the framework of a joint Egyptian-Israeli commission.

c): We have not objected to the concept of an exchange of letters concerning Judea, Samaria and Gaza.

d): We do, indeed, reject what you call "a tangible Egyptian presence in the Gaza Strip." Such a tangible or any other presence in Gaza is nowhere mentioned in the Camp David accord.

e) and f): In the course of the negotiations we objected to several of your proposals as you did to ours. Certain of our objections were approved by your delegation and vice versa. Such is the nature of free negotiations.

Respectfully, I must take exception to the sentence in your letter that reads:

"In my view you should not attempt, or appear to attempt, to evade your obligations under the Camp David 'Framework'".

We shall carry out our commitments fully under the Camp David agreement. We signed the Framework. Our signature is the commitment. We live by the famous rule: pacta sunt servanda.[9]

Permit me to illustrate this truth by referring to the matter of the autonomy in Judea, Samaria and Gaza. The Camp David Framework states:

"Egypt, Israel and Jordan will agree on the modalities for establishing the elected self-governing authority in the West Bank and Gaza."

---

9. Literally, "Promises must be kept." A legal principle that all agreements of the parties to a contract must be observed.

Had Israel sought to resort to "evasion" we could have declared that since Jordan – as one of the three above-mentioned parties – does not join now the negotiations, they should be held in abeyance. We have not said so. On the contrary, we have agreed that, notwithstanding the absence of Jordan, Egypt and Israel will conduct the negotiations with the aim of achieving an agreement. No further proof is necessary, if any, of Israel's sincere intentions towards its commitments.

Elsewhere in your letter you employ the phrase, "what you call administrative autonomy." You put it as a negation. This is unjustified.

At Camp David we agreed on autonomy, on full autonomy for the inhabitants of Judea, Samaria and Gaza. We did not agree on sovereignty. We did not agree on a "Palestinian state," nor on a nucleus for such a "state." As the text declares, we both clearly agreed on a freely elected "self-governing authority (administrative council). This is the commitment we have both underwritten.

As far as a timetable is concerned, it is of course not indicated at all in the Camp David agreement. Moreover, as I have already mentioned, we have to negotiate freely together with the aim of reaching an agreement in accordance with the Camp David Framework on the modalities, the powers, the responsibilities and other related matters concerning the administrative council and its election.

We, perforce, object to a timetable in connection with this matter. The example you give in your letter to determine the timetable for the exchange of diplomatic relations, for the conclusion of an agreement on trade and commerce, for the conclusion of another agreement on cultural exchange, or of a civil aviation accord – all these are proof of my thesis that a timetable cannot be applied to the matter of autonomy under the given circumstances. Each of the elements you mentioned are under the absolute control of the two sovereign states concerned, the states that sign the peace treaty and its specified annexes.

This is not the case with regard to the issues concerning the autonomy. As mattes presently stand very many, if not all the elements are beyond our control. To hold an election one needs an electorate and candidates. At present, we have neither and they cannot be forced. I could send you a collection of original, exact quotations by PLO men threatening every Palestinian Arab with death if he dares support or cooperate with the autonomy scheme in any way.

Recently, in Judea and Samaria, three meetings were held in which thousands participated. Words of incitement of the worst kind were voiced. We reacted with restraint although in other countries such inflammable incitement is either not tolerated or is punished. To my deep regret you, too, Mr. President, were violently attacked by, among others, the Mayor of Ramallah whose insulting words were uproariously applauded. Out of respect, I will not put his words into writing.

Suffice it to say, it is not a matter, as you put it to me, of Israel not being held responsible if developments beyond our control prevent certain desired results being realized. I am speaking of simple reason. All of us must learn from experience. Unwarranted charges may be made. It is our perfect right, a priori, to be in a position whereby we will not be required "to justify" ourselves.

Very soon, let me say one month, as agreed, after the exchange of the instruments of ratification of a peace treaty, it is Israel's desire to enter into negotiations with you (even without Jordan's participation) on all the issues relating to the election of the administrative council. We want the elections to be held as early as possible and we shall, of course, do all that we can to facilitate the necessary preparations. However, any attempt to fix a date before such preparations are made would not only be unreasonable but could also be very detrimental.

Dear President Sadat,

I entirely agree that both of us have taken upon ourselves an historic responsibility. In the course of our meetings and negotiations there have been good hours as well as some difficult ones. Were not the days in Jerusalem days of friendship and understanding? Did you not tell me that we should put our "cards" openly on the table, to speak with each other in complete candor? Did we not understand after our respective speeches from the rostrum of the Knesset that we have differences of opinion? Did I not tell you of my unshakeable faith in our people's right to return to the land of our forefathers and to live in it with our Arab neighbors together in peace and in understanding? Did I not sincerely suggest to you to put behind us, all the memories of the past – and each one of us can speak about *his* memories – and then together we declared: No more war, no more bloodshed – we shall negotiate?

In Ismailiya we brought you a peace plan. We reached several serious understandings just as we agreed, as is the nature of things, to differ on several issues. But we found common language and, again, we pledged to each other to continue the negotiations.

Then, suddenly, and I will admit I was taken totally by surprise, there came a turning point towards a non-desirable direction. I will not go into details because – and this is the all important thing – there came Camp David, the agreement, the evening at the White House, the joint reception by the Congress of the United States and the actual detailed negotiations on the peace treaty.

I feel it is the duty of both of us to overcome the remaining hurdles and strive to find the common language and understanding in order that we might, insofar as it

Dec

depends upon us, realize all that we have undertaken and put our signatures to.

In conclusion, therefore, I put to you two positive proposals - One: Let us sign the peace treaty as formulated on November 11, 1978. Two: Let us, a month after the exchange of the instruments of ratification, commence our free negotiations on all issues relating to the aforementioned elected administrative council.

I can but repeat what I told you on the phone when congratulating you on the Nobel Prize award: "...and the real prize is peace itself."

Let us give peace to our nations and joy to the world.

With best wishes.
Menachem Begin

DECEMBER 10, 1978

THE NOBEL PEACE PRIZE CEREMONY

The Nobel Peace Prize for 1978 was awarded jointly to Prime Minister Menachem Begin of Israel and President Anwar Sadat of Egypt at a ceremony held in Oslo on December 10, 1978. Unfortunately, President Sadat cancelled his appearance virtually at the last minute, and he sent his daughter Nona's father-in-law and confidant Sayed Marei to read his speech for him.

As Aase Lionaes, Chairman of the Norwegian Nobel Committee, said in her presentation speech, "Never has the Peace Prize expressed a greater or more audacious hope – a hope of peace for the people of Egypt, for the people of Israel, and for all the peoples of the strife-torn and war-ravaged Middle East." Following the presentation speech, Menachem Begin accepted his prize with these words:

MENACHEM BEGIN'S NOBEL LECTURE

Your Majesty, Your Royal Highnesses, Your Excellencies, Madame Chairlady and Members of the Nobel Prize Committee, Mr. Marei, representative of the President of Egypt, Ladies and Gentlemen.

I ask for permission first to pay tribute to Golda Meir, my predecessor, a great leader and prime minister, who strove with all her heart to achieve peace between Israel and her neighbors. Her blessed memory will live forever in the hearts of the Jewish people and of all peace-loving nations.

I have come from the Land of Israel, the land of Zion and Jerusalem, and here I stand, in humility and with pride, as a son of the Jewish people, as one of the generation of the Holocaust and redemption.

The ancient Jewish people gave the world the vision of eternal peace, of universal disarmament, of abolishing the teaching and learning of war. Two prophets, Yeshayahu ben Amotz and Micha Hamorashti, having foreseen the spiritual unity of man under God – with His word coming forth from Jerusalem – gave the nations of the world the following vision expressed in identical terms:

> And they shall beat their swords into plowshares and their spears
> into pruning hooks. Nation shall not lift up sword against nation;
> neither shall they learn war anymore.

We mortals who believe in Divine Providence, when recalling those sacred prophecies, ask ourselves not whether, but when is this vision going to become reality? We remember the past, even in this century alone – and we know. We look around – and see. Millions of men of all nations are under arms. Intercontinental missiles deposited in the bowels of the earth or lying on the beds of oceans can destroy man and everything he has built.

Not in Alfred Nobel's time, but in our own era, has mankind become capable of destroying itself and returning the earth to *tohu vavohu* [chaos and void]. Under such circumstances, should we, can we, keep our faith in an eternal peace that will one day reign over mankind? Yes, we should and we can. Perhaps that very capability of total destruction of our little planet – achieved for the first time in the annals of mankind – will one day, God willing, become the origin, the cause and the prime mover for the elimination of all instruments of destruction from the face of the earth and ultimate peace, prayed for and yearned for by previous generations, will become the portion of all nations. Despite the tragedies and disappointments of the past, we must never forsake that vision, that human dream, that unshakeable faith.

Peace is the beauty of life. It is sunshine. It is the smile of a child, the love of a mother, the joy of a father, the togetherness of a family. It is the advancement of man, the victory of a just cause, the triumph of truth. Peace is all of these and more and more.

But in my generation, Ladies and Gentlemen, there was a time indescribable. Six million Jews – men, women and children – a number larger than many a nation in Europe – were dragged to a wanton death and slaughtered methodically in the heart of the civilized continent.

It was not a sudden outburst of human or rather inhuman cruelty that from time to time has happened in the history of mankind; it was a systematic process of extermination which unfolded before the eyes of the whole world for more than six years. Those who were doomed, deprived of their human dignity, starved, humiliated, led away and ultimately turned into ashes, cried out for rescue – but in vain. Other than a few famous and unforgettable exceptions they were left alone to face the destroyer.

At such a time, unheard of since the first generation, the hour struck to rise and fight – for the dignity of man, for survival, for liberty, for every value of the human image a man has been endowed with by his Creator, for every known inalienable right he stands for and lives for. Indeed, there are days when to fight for a cause so absolutely just is the highest human command. Norway has known such days, and so have we. Only in honoring that command comes the regeneration of the concept of peace. You rise, you struggle, you make sacrifices to achieve and guarantee the prospect and hope of living in peace – for you and your people, for your children and their children.

Let it, however, be declared and known, stressed, and noted that fighters for freedom hate war. My friends and I learned this precept from Ze'ev Jabotinsky through his own example, and through the one he set for us from Giuseppe Garibaldi. Our brothers in spirit, wherever they dwell, learned it from *their* masters and teachers. This is our common maxim and belief – that if through your efforts and sacrifices you win liberty and with it the prospect of peace, then work for peace because there is no mission in life more sacred.

And so reborn Israel always strove for peace, yearned for it, made endless endeavors to achieve it. My colleagues and I have gone in the footsteps of our predecessors since the very first day we were called by our people to care for their future. We went any place, we looked for any avenue, we made any effort to bring about negotiations between Israel and its neighbors, negotiations without which peace remains an abstract desire.

We have labored long and hard to turn it into a reality – because of the blessings it holds for ourselves, our neighbors, the world. In peace, the Middle East, the ancient cradle of civilization, will become invigorated and transformed. Throughout its lands there will be freedom of movement of people, of ideas, of goods. Cooperation and development in agriculture will make the deserts blossom. Industry will bring the promise of a better life. Sources of water will be developed and the almost year-long sunshine will yet be harnessed for the common needs of all the nations. Yes, indeed, the Middle East, standing at the crossroads of the world, will become a peaceful center of international communication between East and West, North and South – a center of human advancement in every sphere of creative endeavor. This and more is what peace will bring to our region.

During the past year many efforts for peace were made and many significant events took place. The president of the Arab Republic of Egypt expressed his readiness to come to Jerusalem, the eternal capital of Israel, and to address our parliament, the Knesset. When that message reached me, I, without delay or hesitation, extended to President Sadat on behalf of Israel an invitation to visit our country.

I told him: You will be received with respect and cordiality. And indeed, so he was received, cordially and respectfully, by the people, by the parliament and by the government of our nation. We knew and learned that we have differences of opinion. But whenever we recall those days of Jerusalem we say, always, that they were shining, beautiful days of friendliness and understanding. It was in this same atmosphere that the meetings in Ismailia were conducted. In the spirit of the Nobel Prize tradition we gave to each other the most momentous pledge: No more war. No more bloodshed. We shall negotiate and reach agreement.

Admittedly, there were difficult times as well. Let nobody forget that we deal with a conflict of more than sixty years with its manifold tragedies. These, we must put behind us in order to establish friendship and make peace the beauty of our lives.

Many of the difficulties were overcome at Camp David where the president of the United States, Mr. Jimmy Carter, unforgettably invested unsparing effort, untiring energy and great devotion in the peacemaking process. There, despite all the differences, we found solutions for problems, agreed on issues and the Framework for Peace was signed. With its signature, there was rejoicing in our countries and throughout the world. The path leading to peace was paved.

The phase that followed was the natural arduous negotiations to elaborate and conclude a peace treaty as we promised each other to do at Camp David. The delegations of both countries worked hard and have, I believe, produced a draft document that can serve, if and when signed and ratified, as a good treaty of peace between countries that decided to put an end to hostility and war and begin a new era of understanding and cooperation. Such a treaty can serve as the first indispensable step along the road towards a comprehensive peace in our region.

If, because of all these efforts, President Sadat and I have been awarded the Nobel Peace Prize, let me from this rostrum again congratulate him – as I did in a direct conversation between Jerusalem and Cairo a few weeks ago on the morrow of the announcement.

Now, it is I who must express gratitude from the bottom of my heart for the great honor you do me. But, Ladies and Gentlemen, before doing so, permit me to remind us all that today is an important anniversary – the thirtieth anniversary of the adoption of the Universal Declaration of Human Rights. Let us always remember the magnificently written words of its first article. It expresses the essence of all the declarations of the rights of man and citizen written throughout history. It says:

> All human beings are born free and equal, in dignity and rights.
> They are endowed with reason and conscience and should act
> towards one another in a spirit of brotherhood.

Free women and men everywhere must wage an incessant campaign so that these human values become a generally recognized and practiced reality. We must regretfully admit that in various parts of the world this is not yet the case. Without those values and human rights the real peace of which we dream is jeopardized, for reasons self-understood, but which every man and woman of goodwill will accept.

I must remind my honored listeners of my brethren and the prisoners who are deprived of one of their most basic rights: to go home. I speak about people of great courage who deserve not only the respect but also the moral support of the free world. I speak about people who, even from the depths of their suffering, repeat the age-long prayer:

לשנה הבאה בירושלים.

[L'shanah haba'ah b'Yerushalayim.]
Next year in Jerusalem.

The preservation and protection of human rights are indispensable to give peace of nations and individuals its real meaning.

Allow me, now, to turn to you, Madame President of the Nobel Peace Prize Committee and to all its members and say, thank you. I thank you for the great distinction. It does not, however, belong to me; it belongs to my people – the ancient people and renascent nation that came back in love and devotion to the land of its ancestors after centuries of homelessness and persecution. This prestigious recognition is due to this people because they suffered so much, because they lost so many, because they love peace and want it with all their hearts for themselves and for their neighbors. On their behalf, I humbly accept the award and in their name I thank you from the bottom of my heart.

And may I express to His Majesty, the King, our deep gratitude for the gracious hospitality His Majesty, on this occasion, bestowed upon my wife and myself.

Your Majesty, Your Highnesses, Members of the Nobel Peace Prize Committee, Ladies and Gentlemen:

Seventy-seven years ago, the first Nobel Peace Prize was awarded. Jean Henri Dunant was its recipient. On December 10, 1901, the president of the Norwegian parliament said:

> The Norwegian people have always demanded that their independence be respected. They have always been ready to defend it. But at the same time they have always had a keen desire and need for peace.

May I, Ladies and Gentlemen, on behalf of the people of Israel, respectfully subscribe to these true and noble words.

Thank you.

ANWAR EL-SADAT'S NOBEL LECTURE

Sadat's speech was read by his envoy, Sayed Marei. From Nobel Lectures, Peace 1971–1980, *editor-in-charge Tore Frängsmyr, editor Irwin Abrams (Singapore: World Scientific Publishing, 1997).*

Your Majesty, Your Royal Highnesses, Mr. Prime Minister of Israel, Madame Chairman and Members of the Nobel Peace Prize Committee, Excellencies, Distinguished Guests, Ladies and Gentlemen:

السلام عليكم

[Assalaamu aleikum.]

Peace be upon you.

This is the traditional way in which, every day, we greet one another. It reflects our deepest feelings and hopes. We always say it and we mean it.

Your Majesty, Ladies and Gentlemen:

The decision of the Nobel Prize Committee to bestow upon me the Peace Award has been received by the people of Egypt not only as an honor, but also as a confirmation of the universal recognition of our relentless efforts to achieve peace in an area in which God has chosen to bring to mankind, through Moses, Jesus and Mohamed, His message of wisdom and Light.

Your Majesty, Ladies and Gentlemen,

Recognition is due to a man of the highest integrity: President Jimmy Carter, whose signal efforts to overcome obstacles in the way of peace deserve our keenest appreciation.

The road to peace is one which, throughout its history which coincides with the dawn of human civilization, the people of Egypt have considered as befitting their genius, and their vocation. No people on earth have been more steadfastly faithful to the cause of peace, and none more attached to the principles of justice which constitute the cornerstone of any real and lasting peace.

Do I need to remind such an august and distinguished gathering, that the first recorded peace treaty in history was concluded more than three thousand years ago between Ramses the Great and Hattusillis, Prince of the Hittites, who resolved to establish "good peace and good brotherhood"?

And since then, through the ages, even when wars appeared as a necessary evil the real genius of Egypt has been one of peace…and its ambition has been to build not to destroy, to create not to annihilate, to coexist not to eliminate. Thus, the land of Egypt has always been cherished by God Almighty: Moses lived there, Jesus fled to it from injustice and foreign domination, and the Holy Koran has blessed it. And Islam, which is the religion of justice, equality and moral values, has added new dimensions to the eternal spirit of Egypt.

We have always realized that the qualities of chivalry, courage, faith and discipline that were characteristic of a romantic concept of war, should, in an era where war has become only synonymous with devastation to all, be a means of enriching life, not generating death.

It is in this spirit that Alfred Nobel created the prize which bears his name and which is aimed at encouraging mankind to follow the path of peace, development, progress and prosperity.

Ladies and Gentlemen,

It is in the light of all this, that I embarked a year ago upon my initiative aimed at restoring peace in an area where man received the words of God.

Through me it was the eternal Egypt that was expressing itself: Let us put an end to wars, let us reshape life on the solid basis of equity and truth. And it is this call, which reflected the will of the Egyptian people, of the great majority of the Arab and Israeli peoples, and indeed of millions of men, women and children around the world that you are today honoring. And these hundreds of millions will judge to what extent every responsible leader in the Middle East has responded to the hopes of mankind.

We have now come, in the peace process, to a moment of truth which requires each one of us to take a new look at the situation. I trust that you all know that when I made my historic trip to Jerusalem my aim was not to strike a deal as some politicians do.

I made my trip because I am convinced that we owe it to this generation and the generations to come, not to leave a stone unturned in our pursuit of peace. The ideal is the greatest one in the history of man, and we have accepted the challenge to translate it from a cherished hope into a living reality, and to win through vision and imagination the hearts and minds of our peoples and enable them to look beyond the unhappy past.

Let me remind you of what I said in the Knesset, more than one year ago. I said:

Let me tell you truthfully: Today we have a good chance for peace, an opportunity that cannot be repeated, if we are really serious in the quest of peace. If we throw or fritter away this chance, the curse of mankind and the curse of history will befall the one who plots against it.

I would like now, on this most solemn and moving occasion, to pledge again that we in Egypt – with the future rather than the past in mind – are determined to pursue in good faith, as we have always done, the road to peace, and to leave no avenue unexplored to reach this cherished goal, and to reconcile the sons of Ismail and the sons of Isaac. In renewing this pledge, which I hope that the other parties will also adhere to, I again repeat what I said in the Knesset more than a year ago:

> Any life lost in war is the life of a human being, irrespective of whether it is an Arab or an Israeli.
>
> The wife who becomes widowed is a human being, entitled to live in a happy family, Arab or Israeli.
>
> Innocent children, deprived of paternal care and sympathy, are all our children, whether they live on Arab or Israeli soil, and we owe them the biggest responsibility of providing them with a happy present and bright future.
>
> For the sake of all this, for the sake of protecting the lives of all our sons and brothers;
>
> for our societies to produce in security and confidence;
>
> for the development of man, his well-being and his right to share in an honorable life;
>
> for our responsibility toward the coming generations;
>
> for the smile of every child born on our land.

This is our conception of peace which I repeat today…the Day of Human Rights.

In the light of this let me share with you our conception of peace:

First, the true essence of peace, which ensures its stability and durability, is justice. Any peace not built on justice and on the recognition of the rights of the peoples would be a structure of sand which would crumble under the first blow.

The peace process comprises a beginning and steps towards an end. In reaching this end the process must achieve its projected goal. That goal is to bring security to the peoples of the area, and the Palestinians in particular, restoring to them all their right to a life of liberty and dignity. We are moving steadily towards this goal for all the peoples of the region. This is what I stand for. This is the letter and the spirit of Camp David.

Second, peace is indivisible. To endure, it should be comprehensive and involve all the parties in the conflict.

Third, peace and prosperity in our area are closely linked and interrelated. Our efforts should aim at achieving both, because it is as important to save man from death by destructive weapons as it is not to abandon him to the evils of want and misery. And war is no cure for the problems of our area. And last, but not least, peace is a dynamic construction to which all should contribute, each adding a new brick. It goes far beyond a formal agreement or treaty, it transcends a word here or there. That is why it required politicians who enjoy vision and imagination and who, beyond the present, look towards the future.

It is with this conviction, deeply rooted in our history and our faith, that the people of Egypt have embarked upon a major effort to achieve peace in the Middle East, an area of paramount importance to the whole world. We will spare no effort, we will not tire or despair, we will not lose faith, and we are confident that, in the end, our aim will be achieved.

I will ask you all to join me in a prayer that the day may soon come when peace will prevail, on the basis of justice and the recognition of the rights of all the peoples to shape their own life, to determine their own future, and to contribute to building a world of prosperity for all mankind.

MARCH 21, 1979

BEGIN ADDRESSES THE KNESSET ON THE PEACE TREATY

The Nobel Peace Prize was followed by another three months of difficult negotiations. On December 15, 1978, Israel's cabinet announced that Egyptian demands, brought to Jerusalem by Secretary Vance from Cairo and supported by the US, were rejected by the cabinet as being "inconsistent with the Camp David framework," as were the "attitude and interpretation of the US government" with regard to the Egyptian proposals. Israel, blamed for the stalemate, with Carter expressing frustration two days earlier, formally and publicly protested.

On December 23, Foreign Minister Dayan, Egypt's prime minister and foreign minister Mustapha Khalil and Secretary of State Vance met in Brussels. During the last two weeks of January 1979, Alfred Atherton was engaged in shuttle diplomacy between Cairo and Jerusalem. Over February 20–26, another Camp David summit at the ministerial level was convened with Foreign Minister Dayan at the head of the Israeli delegation. No agreement on the disputed points was achieved and Carter contemplated a head-of-government-level meeting. Begin at first declined the invitation but arrived in Washington on March 1 when the plan was changed and only "personal talks" between Carter and Begin would be conducted.

After five days of almost acrimonious discussions, Carter announced he was flying to Cairo and Jerusalem on March 7. On March 12, Carter addressed the Knesset after addressing Egypt's People's Assembly on March 10. In Cairo again on his way back to Washington, Carter got Sadat to agree to Israeli proposals, including no linkage and no mention of Israeli settlements in the treaty and its annexes.

For two days, the Knesset deliberated the final version of the Israel-Egypt Peace treaty. The vote was ninety-five in favor, eighteen against, two abstentions and three not participating in the vote. Here are excerpts from Prime Minister Begin's closing statement on March 21:

I should like to begin first of all by indicating the importance of this debate. This is one of the great moments in our parliament. Generally, as in any democratic house of representatives, the days are prosaic ones. But there comes a day, a night, a moment, when all the glory and the splendor of a democratic parliament are visible to the entire nation, to the entire world. This is the night, these are the two days, this is the moment. There is no imposing, no coercion: this morning, too, the Knesset will vote according to its own will and the free decisions of its factions – and there are factions whose members will vote each according to his own awareness and his decision.

The decision will be a fateful one, of immense significance, and, it may be said without an exaggeration – historic. For we stand, as we believe, at a turning point at least in the relations between two Middle East nations, out of the hope that this will be a basis and a watershed between ourselves and the others. We have been privileged to witness a major moment in our national parliamentary life. How fortunate are we to have been privileged to attain this hour.

I thought about whether I should engage in polemics with those Members who expressed their opposition to the peace treaty, or with those who stated things – whether at my expense or that of the Government – which are not correct, which are even offensive. I arrived at the conclusion that it would be best if I refrained from such polemics. I shall be silent, and leave things as they were stated, without replying. But if there was an iota of a certain feeling – which I shall not call by its proper name – in certain statements, I shall recommend to those who expressed them to read, or perhaps to peruse once again, Psalm 29.

I have come to offer one reply this morning – not to a member of the Knesset, but to Dr. Khalil, the prime minister of Egypt – in which I had responded to his earlier remarks. I should like to note that had Dr. Khalil not declared three things – the Old City of Jerusalem will be severed from Israel, Israel will return to the lines of 4 June 1967, a Palestinian state will be established in Judea, Samaria and Gaza – I would not have expressed our view on those three points from this rostrum, for a simple reason: what I said is to me self-evident. There is no need to state it in our house of representatives. The great majority – as every man and woman in Israel knows – supports my stand on those three points.

But the prime minister of Egypt need not imagine that he can unilaterally, on the brink of the signing of the peace treaty, do hurt to the profoundest feelings of the Jewish people, wherever it may be. Jerusalem. A return to the lines of June 4, 1967 – which themselves invite war and bloodshed. And the proof: experience. Or the establishment of a Palestinian state, namely: creation of danger to the very survival of the Jewish state, one of the wondrous miracles of human history. Dr. Khalil should not imagine that he can thus injure our feelings and we will say, "Nothing has happened, the atmosphere is excellent," and be silent.

Following my reaction he claimed my remarks had befouled the atmosphere. Not so: it was your remarks, Dr. Khalil, which befouled the atmosphere. And I only reacted to your remarks, as you in fact compelled me to do. It cannot be claimed that an injury to our nation spoils things and the reaction to it is what creates an uncomfortable atmosphere. One or the other: either everyone keeps silent, or everyone speaks out. I hope that this will serve as a lesson for the coming days. I am once more ready to propose to my comrade, the prime minister of Egypt, a verbal ceasefire: let us wait. We are about to sign a peace treaty, with goodwill, in trust. We want to honor every word to which we have signed and below which we will place our signature. Do not injure our people's feelings. You ought to know what Jerusalem means to this people. Do not injure our people's feelings. Do not say to it that a new danger will arise over it. Then I will not have to respond from the rostrum of this free parliament, and we shall all be able to go to Washington and sign as free men the most important document ever written and signed by authorized representatives of the Jewish state and an Arab state....

Toubi: [*Interjection by MK Tewfiq Toubi, of the Democratic Front for Peace and Equality.*] Mr. Prime Minister, I want to ask you: Why is it an injury to the feelings of the people to say that the Palestinian Arab people also has the right to establish its own independent state? After all, in 1947, they danced in the streets of Tel Aviv – they danced for joy over the decision to establish two states!

Begin: Mr. Toubi, you have asked now honorably, and I shall reply to you honorably. When they danced in 1947, the Jews did not dance because Jerusalem was taken from them, and Bethlehem-Judea. Rather, they rejoiced that they would have their own state. After nineteen hundred years of wandering throughout the world, of going to the stake, of murder, of persecution, of ghettos, and, in the last generation, of the destruction of a third of their people. Therefore we, who were still in the underground, did not dance; we said we would not join the dancing, because our homeland had been thus partitioned – that is what we said; so that we are in touch with the spirit of our people.

Because suddenly – true, following a war of independence of great historic value and of great numbers of victims – they attained the day on which they knew they would have their own government, their own parliament – the Jews – their own army to defend them so that a Jew would never again be dragged to the gas chamber, so that a little Jewish child would never again be hanged until he was dead. This was what the rejoicing was all about. Restoration of our days as of old[10] with national independence.

I ask you, as an Arab – and you know that I have respected the great Arab nation from my earliest days, and its contribution to human civilization – look at what happened. Consider the phenomenon yourself: the Arab states all around, and our Arab neighbors in Palestine – did they accept that decision, or did they decide to drown it in blood? We all remember the declarations made then: "The Jews will be annihilated!" Therefore we were advised not to declare our independence, and for that reason there were differences of opinion within all the parties. But we did establish our state. And then do you know what happened, Knesset Member Tewfiq Toubi? In order to maintain our independence in a small portion of the land, we sacrificed one percent of our population – in today's terms that would be thirty thousand killed. Can you imagine what would befall this nation if it sacrificed thirty thousand of its sons? That was what happened in 1948.

Shamir: [*Interjection by MK Moshe Shamir, of the Likud.*] And today in this treaty, you are compelling the Knesset to agree that monuments will be set up to the Egyptian murderers of 1948, at Negba and at Yad Mordechai, on Israeli soil! The Knesset will today approve this!

Begin: I want to tell you, here before the entire nation, that on this issue, too, our views differ. I want to say, as a Jew and a Jewish fighter, that I see no fault, but rather a sign of honor for this nation, if we build a monument to a soldier of another nation who fell in fair battle. No fault! The opposite! No fault, but a badge of honor for our nation.

Mr. Speaker,[11]

The autonomy idea: certainly it is possible to terrify us, to criticize it, reject it, even scorn it. All that is possible. But the fact is – and today we may say this out of full awareness – that this

---

10. The reference is to wording from Lamentations 5:21.
11. Yitzhak Shamir was then Speaker of the Knesset.

idea was the key to the attainment of the peace treaty with Egypt. Without it we would not have made it. This may not be a reason to show any special fondness for the idea, but the fact is that even my colleagues from the Alignment, my honorable opponents, are today making a motion which contains their own plan, as they worked it out, for an autonomy regime. This means something. Because at one time the idea was totally rejected, out of hand. Today the entire House realizes that this was an important idea, a positive idea, and the only way we were able to enter into a peace treaty with Egypt.

True: I shall again state, before the entire nation, that we will have a year of struggle, perhaps a difficult year – both domestically and externally, perhaps. Various voices may be heard. I say that we wholeheartedly want to implement this idea, and to enable our Arab neighbors to run their affairs by means of an institution which they themselves will effect in free, democratic, secret elections, each voter with his ballot, on a day which should be a great one for them and for us, too. For the first time they will go to the polls as free people, without fear – we shall ensure that they will not be afraid – if they so wish, and elect their own representatives. And their representatives will run their daily affairs for them, in all spheres of life.

Wilner: [*Interjection by MK Meir Wilner, of the Democratic Front for Peace and Equality.*] Excuse me, Mr. Prime Minister, what you are doing now in the West Bank shows what kind of freedom there will be. The entire matter of the autonomy regime is just a ruse to get Sadat to agree to continuation of the occupation.

Begin: Mr. Wilner, if so, then wait until Sadat comes here, and make this interjection to him. For it is directed against Sadat. What do you want from me? I do not agree that this is a ruse for Sadat – that you learned from *Pravda* – but when I was in the USSR I heard them say, right across the entire Soviet Union: "In *Pravda* there is no *izvestia*, and in *Izvestia* there is no *pravda*."[12]

---

12. *Izvestia* and *Pravda* were the two primary propaganda organs in the Former Soviet Union (*Pravda* was the mouthpiece for the Communist Party, and *Iz-*

The simple truth is that President Sadat looked for no ruse. And we may well have an argument with him [over this issue]. What I said remains valid. But I must add that we deceived no one: from the outset we said that this autonomy regime would be established and would be maintained, provided there is security for Israel, in Judea, Samaria and Gaza and from them. That is a *conditio sine qua non*. That is what we said to the president of the United States, and to President Sadat, on every public opportunity, in all the conferences and meetings: a *sine qua non*. The two are interdependent. So here, too, I would ask that people give it a chance. Let's try it. Let us try to see if we can live together in this tiny land: the entire width from the Jordan to the sea is seventy kilometers, forty miles. Where are there many such small countries on the face of the earth?

And precisely to partition it, with a border running through it – that is the solution of genius! And the border shall become a bloody one. How do I know this? From the teacher of teachers: and his name is Experience. And not to learn from the experience of nineteen years?! We shall not try to evade the directive of this special teacher.

Therefore in what have we sinned that we want to provide the possibility of trying to live together? What do you say is happening in the "West Bank" – as you term it – Mr. Wilner?[13] What would you like? That our soldiers should move about and be stoned, when every stone can not only wound but kill? Well, we want to live in peace!

Mr. Speaker,

The autonomy idea opened the possibility of signing a peace treaty with Egypt. We want to implement it, with the *sine qua non*

---

vestia for the government). *Izvestia* means "news." *Pravda* means "truth." So the expression means, "In *Pravda* there is no news, and in *Izvestia* there is no truth." The expression was alternately rendered, "*Nye pravda v'Pravdye, i nye izvestia v'Izvestiye* (There's no truth in *Pravda*, and no news in *Izvestia*)."

13. "West Bank" has been the term favored by those who feel that the portion of Israel that abuts the Jordan River is more properly attached to the country that lies on the other side of the water, while Jewish nationalists prefer the traditional names for the area, which formed two regions of the historical Land of Israel: Judea and Samaria.

Mar

1977

1978

1979

1980

1981

that there is no more border, all live together in peace, in mutual respect, in understanding, in liberty, without injury to either side. You will see how beautiful will the Land of Israel be under such conditions. Let us make the attempt to build it thus.

If only they had listened to us in 1948, when all the organizations – the Haganah, the IZL and the LEHI[14] – called on our neighbors to stop the bloodshed: come, our Arab neighbors, let us live together, let us build the land together, in eternal splendor. This is what we wanted already thirty and more years ago. But nothing helped: five wars were waged against us.

Mr. Speaker,

If the Knesset in another few minutes approves the Treaty of Peace with its annexes and its accompanying letter, the way will be paved to hold in Washington – next Monday, probably – the first ceremony of the signing of this peace treaty by President Sadat, by myself and also by the president of the US. I hope that a week later, either in the following order or vice versa, that perhaps President Sadat will be in the Knesset and the two of us will sit on either side of you and we will sign the peace treaty with all the members of the Knesset witnessing that the peace treaty has been signed. And I will go to Cairo – how did President Sadat put it? "In the heart of the capital of Egypt" – where the two of us will sign the peace treaty. How do I know this? I wish to inform the House that I received yesterday a personal message from President Sadat, who wanted to let me know that he asserts that every word that President Carter said to me on Saturday night, in a private conversation, concerning these three ceremonies, is correct – and President Sadat added that he would honor every word, as stated by President Carter to you. So I do not yet know the date – nor can

---

14. The Haganah, or "the Defense," was a Jewish paramilitary organization in Mandate Palestine, which later formed the seeds of the Israeli army, the Israel Defense Forces. The IZL, Irgun Zvai Leumi (National Military Organization, also known by the pronouncing of its Hebrew initials as Etzel), which Menachem Begin headed, was a resistance organization dedicated to opposing the British regime in Palestine. LEHI, Lohamei Herut Israel (Fighters for the Freedom of Israel, also called the Stern Group or the Stern Gang after its founder Avraham Stern), was a more militant breakaway group from the IZL.

I promise that this is how it will in fact be – but I trust President Sadat's statement concerning the honoring of this commitment.

I want to stress: there was one Knesset member who had some rather mocking things to say about these three ceremonies. I want to say to him – and to everyone – that great psychological importance attaches to this, which is also political importance. That all the peoples of the Middle East may see that the authorized representative of Egypt, the spokesman for Israel are sitting together and signing the treaty, both in Jerusalem and in Cairo: this, too, will be a cornerstone in the building of normal relations. So this is what we proposed, and I am happy to inform the Knesset that the suggestion was accepted by both the president of the United States and the president of Egypt.

Mr. Speaker,

At this late hour we are concluding this great debate which will be remembered for many days in the annals of our people, for it was very serious, very profound, painful – but nonetheless of major importance.

I ask your leave, Mr. Speaker, to send from here, with the concurrence of all the members of the House, greetings to the president of Egypt. Because with his courage – and courage was needed in the face of the pack of wolves all around, from Damascus to Baghdad! – he decided to come and talk peace with Israel. And we invited him, and returned peace unto him. I send from here the greetings of the representatives of the people of Israel to the great Egyptian people. Five times have our sons met on the battlefield. Each of them did his duty: every soldier in every army who is sent to the battlefield just does his duty. So we have no grudges. We are not living in the past. We want to build a new future. We send greetings to the Egyptian people in anticipation of the new relations which are to arise between it and ourselves.

Mr. Speaker,

I shall now say a few totally personal words. I want to tell my old friends in this House which is my second home – that half my life I have spent in this House. What is my innermost feeling? True: it is good that we have attained such a moment. There is concern for the future, as there must be. There is also apprehension in the

Mar

heart, totally natural. But despite and with all this we feel in our heart that we have reached a certain turning point. May it be one which is entirely positive – for us, for the Egyptian people, for other peoples around us. For with all our heart and all our soul, all of us together want to attain the goal than which there is none simpler, or more human: Peace.

And with God's help, may we be able to return from the signing and say to the people: "We have brought peace unto you."[15]

MARCH 26, 1979

SIGNING THE PEACE TREATY ON THE WHITE HOUSE LAWN

The difficult negotiations were concluded and the historic peace treaty between Israel and Egypt was signed on the lawn of the White House on March 26, 1979, at which time the following addresses were delivered.

PRESIDENT CARTER

During the past thirty years, Israel and Egypt have waged war. But for the past sixteen months, these same two great nations have waged peace.

Today we celebrate a victory, not of a bloody military campaign, but of an inspiring peace campaign. Two leaders who loom large in the history of nations, President Anwar Sadat and Prime Minister Menachem Begin, have conducted this campaign with all the courage, tenacity, brilliance and inspiration of any generals who have ever led men and machines onto the field of battle.

At the end of this campaign, the soil of the two lands is not drenched with young blood. The countrysides of both lands are free from the litter and the carnage of a wasteful war.

Mothers in Egypt and Israel are not weeping today for their children fallen in senseless battle. The dedication and determination of these two world statesmen have borne fruit. Peace has come to Israel and to Egypt.

I honor these two leaders and their government officials who have hammered out this peace treaty which we have just signed. But most of all,

---

15. *Hevenu shalom alechem*, "We have brought peace unto you," is a popular Jewish folk song.

I honor the people of these two lands whose yearning for peace kept alive the negotiations which today culminate in this glorious event.

PRESIDENT SADAT

President Carter, dear friends. This is certainly one of the happiest moments in my life. It is a historic turning point of great significance for all peace-loving nations. Those among us who are endowed with vision cannot fail to comprehend the dimension of our sacred mission. The Egyptian people with their heritage and unique awareness of history have realized from the very beginning the meaning and value of this endeavor. In all the steps I took I was not performing a personal mission. I was merely expressing the will of a nation. I am proud of my people and of belonging to them.

Today a new dawn is emerging out of the darkness of the past. A new chapter is being opened in the history of coexistence among nations, one that is worthy of our spiritual values and civilization. Never before have men encountered such a complex dispute which is highly charged with emotions. Never before did men need that much courage and imagination to confront a single challenge. Never before had any cause generated that much interest in all four corners of the globe.

Men and women of good will have labored day and night to bring about this happy moment. Egyptians and Israelis alike pursued their sacred goal undeterred by difficulties and complications. Hundreds of dedicated individuals on both sides have given generously of their thought and effort to translate the cherished dream into a living reality. But the man who performed the miracle was President Carter. Without any exaggeration, what he did constitutes one of the greatest achievements of our time. He devoted his skill, hard work and above all his firm belief in the ultimate triumph of good against evil to ensure the success of our mission. To me he has been the best companion and partner along the road to peace.

With his deep sense of justice and genuine commitment to human rights we were able to surmount the most difficult obstacles. There came certain moments when hope was eroding and retreating in the face of pride. However, President Carter remained unshaken in his confidence and determination.

Happily he was armed with the blessing of God and the support of his people. For that, we are grateful to each and every American who contributed in his own way to the success of our endeavor. We are also heartened by the understanding of hundreds of thousands of Israelis who remained unwavering in their commitment to peace. The continuation of this spirit is vital to the coronation of our efforts.

We realize that difficult times [lie] ahead. The signing of these documents marks only the beginning of peace. But it is an indispensable start. Other steps remain to be taken without delay or procrastination. Much will depend upon the success of these steps. We are all committed to pursue our efforts until the fruits of the comprehensive settlement we agreed upon are shared by all parties to the conflict.

President Carter once said that the United States is committed without reservation to seeing the peace process through until all parties to the Arab-Israeli conflict are at peace. We value such a pledge from a leader who raised the banner of morality and ethics as a substitute for power politics and opportunism. The steps we took in the recent past will serve Arab vital interests. The liberation of Arab land and the reinstitution of Arab authority in the West Bank and Gaza would certainly enhance our common strategic interests. While we take the initiative to protect these interests, we remain faithful to our Arab commitment with our culture and creed.

Let there be no more war or bloodshed between Arabs and the Israelis. Let there be no more suffering or denial of rights. Let there be no more despair or loss of faith. Let no mother lament the loss of her child. Let no young man waste his life on a conflict from which no one benefits. Let us work together until the day comes when they beat their swords into plowshares and their spears into pruning hooks; and God does call to the abode of peace; He does guide whom He pleases to His way. Thank you.

PRIME MINISTER BEGIN

Mr. President of the United States of America, Mr. President of the Arab Republic of Egypt, Mr. Vice-President, Mr. Speaker of the House of Representatives, Mr. Speaker of the Knesset, Members of the Cabinet of the United States of Egypt, of Israel, Members of the Congress, and the Knesset, Your Excellencies, Chairman of the Board of Governors of the Jewish Agency, Chairman of the Executive of the Zionist Organization, Distinguished Guests, Ladies and Gentlemen:

"I have come from the land of Israel, the land of Zion and Jerusalem, and here I stand, in humility and with pride, as a son of the Jewish people, as one of the generation of the Holocaust and redemption. The ancient Jewish people gave the world the vision of eternal peace, of universal disarmament, of abolishing the teaching and learning of war. Two prophets, Yeshayahu ben Amotz and Micha Hamorashti, having foreseen the spiritual unity of man under God – with His word coming forth from Jerusalem – gave the nations of the world the following vision expressed in identical terms.

"And they shall beat their swords into plowshares and their spears into pruning hooks. Nation shall not lift up sword against nation; neither shall they learn war anymore.

"…Despite the tragedies and disappointments of the past, we must never forsake that vision, that human dream, that unshakeable faith. Peace is the beauty of life. It is sunshine. It is the smile of a child, the love of a mother, the joy of a father, the togetherness of a family. It is the advancement of man, the victory of a just cause, the triumph of truth. Peace is all of these and more and more."

These are words I uttered in Oslo on December 10, 1978, while receiving the second half of the Nobel Peace Prize – the first half went, and rightly so, to President Sadat – and I took the liberty to repeat them here, on this momentous, historic occasion.

It is a great day in the annals of two ancient nations, Egypt and Israel, whose sons met in our generation five times on the battlefield, fighting and failing. Let us turn our hearts to our heroes and pay tribute to their eternal memory; it is thanks to them that we could have reached this day.

However, let us not forget that in ancient times our two nations met also in alliance. Now we make peace, the cornerstone of cooperation and friendship.

It is a great day in your life, Mr. President of the United States. You have worked so hard, so insistently, so consistently, for this goal; and your labors and your devotion bore God-blessed fruit.

It is, of course, a great day in your life, Mr. President of the Arab Republic of Egypt. In the face of adversity and hostility you have demonstrated the human value that can change history: civil courage. A great field commander once said: civil courage is sometimes more difficult to show than military courage. You showed both. But now is the time, for all of us, to show civil courage in order to proclaim to our peoples, and to others: no more war, no more bloodshed, no more bereavement – peace unto you, Shalom, Salaam – forever.

And it is, Ladies and Gentlemen, the third greatest day in my life. The first was May the fourteenth, 1948, when our flag was hoisted, our independence in our ancestors' land was proclaimed after one thousand eight hundred and seventy-eight years of dispersion, persecution, and physical destruction. We fought for our liberation alone – and won the day. That was spring; such a spring we can never have again.

The second day was when Jerusalem became one city, and our brave, perhaps hardened soldiers, the parachutists, embraced with tears and kissed the ancient stones of the remnants of the Western Wall destined to protect the chosen place of God's glory. Our hearts wept with them – in remembrance.

> *Omdot hayu ragleinu b'sha'arayich, Yerushalayim, Yerushalayim habnuya k'ir shechubrah lah yachdav.* ("When our feet stood within thy gates, O Jerusalem, O Jerusalem built as a city that is compact together." Psalm 122)

This is the third day in my life. I have signed a treaty of peace with our neighbor, with Egypt. The heart is full and overflowing. God gave me the strength to survive the horrors of Nazism and of a Stalinite concentration camp, to persevere, to endure, not to waver in or flinch from my duty, to accept abuse from foreigners and, what is more painful, from my own people, and from my close friends. This effort too bore some fruit.

Therefore, it is the proper place and appropriate time to bring back to memory the song and prayer of thanksgiving I learned as a child in the home of a father and mother that don't exist anymore, because they were among the six million people, their sacred blood, which reddened the rivers of Europe from the Rhine to the Danube, from the Bug to the Volga – because, only because they were born Jews, and because they didn't have a country of their own, neither a valiant Jewish army to defend them, and because nobody, nobody came to their rescue, although they cried out: save us, de profundis, from the depths of the pit and agony; that is the song of degrees written two millennia and five hundred years ago when our forefathers returned from their first exile to Jerusalem, to Zion.

[At this point Prime Minister Begin put a black kippa (skullcap) on his head and said:]

> *Shir hama'alot b'shuv Adonai, et shivat Zion hayinu k'cholmim. Az yimalei s'chok pinu ulshoneinu rinah. Az yomru vagoyim higdil Adonai la'asot im eileh, higdil Adonai la'asot imanu hayinu s'meichim. Shuvah Adonai et sh'viteinu ka'afikim banegev. Hazorim b'dimah b'rinah yiktzoru. Haloch yeilech uvachoh nosei meshech hazara bo yavo v'rinah nosei alumotav.[16]*

I will not translate. Every man, whether Jew or Christian or Muslim, can read it in his own language. It is Psalm 126.

Mar

---

16. "A song of stepping up. When God caused the return to Zion, we were like dreamers. At that time, our mouths filled with laughter, and our tongues with song. Then, among the nations was said, 'The Lord has done great things for them.' Indeed, God did do great things for us; we were joyous. Cause the return of those who should return, as the dry river beds in the south. Those who sow in tears will reap in happiness. He who goes out weeping, carrying seed for sowing, will certainly joyfully come again, carrying his sheaves." (Translation by Yisrael Medad.)

THE WASHINGTON HILTON

Mr. President of the United States of America, Mr. President of the Arab Republic of Egypt, Mr. Vice President, Mr. Speaker of the House of Representatives, Mr. Speaker of the Knesset, Members of the Cabinets of the United States of Egypt of Israel, Members of the Congress, and the Knesset, Your Excellencies, Chairman of the Board of Governors of the Jewish Agency, Chairman of the Executive of the Zionist Organization, Distinguished Guests, Ladies and Gentlemen.

" I have come from the land of Israel, the land of Zion and Jerusalem, and here I ~~stand~~ am, in humility and with pride, as a son of the Jewish people, as one of the generation of the Holocaust and Redemption. The ancient Jewish people gave the world the vision of eternal peace, of universal disarmament, of abolishing the teaching and learning of war. Two prophets, Yeshayahu Ben Amotz and Micha Hamorashti having foreseen the spiritual unity of man under God — with His word coming forth

from Jerusalem — gave the nations of the world the following vision expressed

Begin's handwritten draft of the speech he gave on the White House lawn
upon signing the Israel-Egypt peace treaty, written on Washington Hilton stationery

In identical terms:

"And they shall beat their swords into ploughshares and their
spears into pruning hooks. Nation shall not lift up sword against nation,
neither shall they learn war any more."

Despite the tragedies and disappointments of the past we must never
forsake that vision, that human dream, that unshakable faith. Peace
is the beauty of life, It is sunshine It is the smile of a child,
the love of a mother, the joy of a father, the togetherness of a family.
It is the advancement of man, the victory of a just cause, the triumph of
truth. Peace is all of these and now, and more."

These are words I uttered in Oslo, on December 10th 1978 while
receiving the second half of the nobel peace prize — the first half went,
and rightly so, to President Sadat — and I took the liberty to repeat
them here, on this momentous, historic occasion.

Connecticut Avenue at Columbia Road, N.W.   Washington, D.C. 20009   202/483-3000

THE WASHINGTON HILTON

It is a great day in the annals of two ancient ~~people~~ nations, Egypt and Israel, whose sons met in ~~our~~ ~~the~~ precedentor five times on the battlefield fighting and falling. Let us turn our hearts to our heroes and pay tribute to their eternal memory; it is thanks to them that we could have reached this day. However, let us not forget that in ancient times our two nations met also in ~~friendship and even~~ alliance. Now we make peace, the corner-stone of cooperation and friendship.

It is a great day in your life, dear President of the United States. You have worked so hard, so insistently, so consistently, for this goal, and your labours and your devotion bore God-blessed fruit. ~~Presid~~ Our friend, President Sadat said that you are the "unknown soldier" of the peace-making effort. I agree, but ~~this~~ as usually, with ~~and~~ an amendment. A soldier in the service of peace you are, you are, dear President, even, horrible dictu,

THE WASHINGTON HILTON

an intransigeant fighter for peace for Out [struck] Jimmy Carter the

President of the United States is not completely unknown. And so is

his effort, which will be remembered by generations to come.

It is, of course, a proud day in your life, Mr. President of the

Arab Republic of Egypt. In the face of adversity and hostility you have

demonstrated ~~their~~ the human value that can change history; civil courage. A great

field—commander once said: civil courage is sometimes more difficult

to show than military courage. You showed both. But now it is

time, for all of us, to show civil courage in order to proclaim

to our peoples, and to others: no more war, no more bloodshed,

no more bereavement — peace unto you, ~~[struck]~~ shalom, salaam —

for ever.

And it is, ladies and gentlemen, the third greatest day in my

THE WASHINGTON HILTON

life. The first was May 14th 1948 when our flag was hoisted, our independence in our ancestors' land was proclaimed, after 1878 years of dispersion, persecution, and physical destruction. We fought for our liberation - belong - and won the day. That was spring, such a spring we can never have again.

The second day was when Jerusalem became our city, and our brave, perhaps most hardened soldiers the parachutists embraced with tears and kissed the ancient stones of the remnants of the wall destined to protect the chosen place of God's glory. Our hearts wept with them — in remembrance.

בשנת ת/ש/ח הוכרזה עצמאות במולדת אבותינו

This is the third day in my life. I have signed a treaty of peace, with our neighbors, with Egypt. The heart is full and overflowing.

to survive the horrors of decision and of a definite concentration camp
and some other dangers.

THE WASHINGTON HILTON

God gave me the strength to persevere, to endure, ~~and~~ not to ~~waver~~ waver in
from my duty
or flinch, to accept abuse from foreigners, and, what is more painful,
from my own people, and ~~helas~~, from my ~~close~~ friends. This effort
too ~~has~~ cost some friend.

Therefore it it the proper place, and appropriate time, to bring back
to ~~my~~ memory the song and prayer of thanksgiving I learned, as a child, in the
the home of ~~my~~ father and mother, that doesn't exist, any more,
because they were among the six million people, men, women and children,
who sanctified the Lord's name with their sacred blood, which reddened
~~all~~ the rivers of Europe from the Rhein to the Danube, from the
Bug ~~to~~ to the Volga — because, only because they ~~been~~ were Jews,
and because they didn't have a country of their own, neither a valiant
Jewish Army to defend them, and because, nobody, nobody came to

their rescue, although they cried out: save us, save us, O the
[Pharaoh?], from the depths of the pit and agony; that is the
song of degrees written two millennia and five hundred years ago
when our ~~the~~ forefathers returned from their ~~fir~~ first exile to
Jerusalem, to Zion:

[Hebrew text, handwritten]

THE WASHINGTON HILTON

I will not tremble. Every man, whether Jew or Christian or Muslim, can read it in his own language. It is just ~~Psalt~~ Psalm ~~126~~ one hundred twenty six.

Part 4

Constructing Peace
April 1979–April 1982

MAY 26, 1979

SADAT SPEAKS IN BEERSHEBA

On April 2–3, Begin visited Cairo and held talks with Sadat. It was agreed that El Arish, the major city of the northern Sinai, would be transferred to Egypt on May 25, eight months ahead of the original date scheduled for the return. This was the second time Israel was returning El Arish to Egypt, having captured and returned it previously in the 1956–1957 Sinai Campaign. The official transfer was made on April 25. On that day, Interior Minister Yosef Burg, Defense Minister Kamal Hassan Ali and Secretary of State Cyrus Vance were present at the opening of talks in Beersheba to define conditions for the autonomy plan, to establish administrative autonomy for the Palestinian Arab residents of Judea, Samaria and Gaza.

On May 26, Prime Minister Begin flew to El Arish and met with President Sadat in the newly Egyptian city. Then the two of them flew to Beersheba for additional events. The Jerusalem Post, *reporting on the El Arish event, described an emotional meeting of veterans of all the wars between Israel and Egypt, presided over by Sadat and Begin. The two groups of disabled soldiers met warily. The ice was broken when a blind Israeli soldier in a wheelchair approached a disabled Egyptian soldier, who took his hand, and then the soldiers began to embrace and to weep, the years of animosity dissolving in the heady relief of the new status quo: peace.*

From El Arish, President Sadat and Prime Minister Begin traveled to Beersheba. Sadat spoke in response to warm welcoming remarks made by Israeli president Yitzhak Navon.

President Navon, Dear Friends:

I was greatly moved by your warm reception. The genuine feeling of friendship between our two peoples is the best guarantee for a secure and happy future for every Arab and Israeli. Together we will revive the tradition of brotherhood and compassion between our peoples.

Our meeting today is a living symbol of the historic change that is taking place in our area. It signals the actual inauguration of peace and coexistence. Now that we have ended the state of war between our two countries, as part of a comprehensive settlement that will eventually include all parties to the conflict, we are moving without any hesitation to open the channels of communication and exchange. The potential is great. The future holds a tremendous promise. We are determined to give this march towards peace every chance for success and fulfillment. There will be no barriers between our peoples, no more anxiety or insecurity, no more suffering or suspicion.

And if I am to comment on what President Navon has stated in Arabic,[17] let me tell you this in all candor. When I made my initiative, in November '77, and in the Knesset I have addressed you, the Israeli people, through the Knesset – I have told you my position, my people's position. I have asked that let us start a new page. I was genuine in every word I said: you must have felt this – and I am genuine until this moment.

When President Navon said that you have given us Sinai, let me say this: we have fought together, and today our disabled from both countries have met together, and we have given a solemn [assurance] that there will be no more war and that the security issue should be met with. I am happy that what I promised you in Jerusalem in November '77, that there will be no more war after the October War, and that the security issue should be met for both sides – I am very happy and proud because God helped me, with Premier Begin, to achieve this.

But in the same speech before the Knesset I have insisted that land will not make security. The land of the others, as your land is sacred to you, the land of the others is sacred to them. That's what I told you in the Knesset.

---

17. President Navon had addressed the crowd in Arabic.

What we have achieved, really, through the spirit of the initiative of '77, is something that no one in the whole world could have imagined or believed that it will take place. But I didn't come to the Knesset to ask for my land – as I told you in the Knesset. On the contrary, I came to the Knesset and I addressed you, the Israeli people, to tell you that: Let us start a new era of love instead of hatred, with friendship instead of enmity. Let us write a new chapter, let us put a foundation for a new order in this world, for those who want to solve their problems should follow after that. By God, we have succeeded in this.

But never let us go back to what has taken place in the past. As I told you, me and my people, we are genuine for peace. But also we are genuine for our land, for everything on our land – for oil – for everything that is in Sinai or on our land. As I told you, the land of the others will not provide security. Only friendship, brotherhood, friendly relations, good-neighborhood relations – all this will provide peace. What we need really is a new era. Let us not mention the past at all. Let us not mention who was right and who was wrong, but let us look to the future through love, friendship....

It is not that you have given us the land. It is the new era of under-standing, friendship, the respect of both of us to others' land, to others' sovereignty, the complete trial to build every day – even every moment – a new momentum between our two peoples, who have got their civiliza-tion very deep-rooted in history.

As I said, no more anxiety or insecurity. No more suffering or suspicion. Blessed are the peacemakers. May God Almighty grant us the strength and vision needed to complete our task and fulfill our mission.

Thank you very much.

SADAT RECEIVES AN HONORARY DEGREE

Later that day, both Sadat and Begin spoke in the presence of Secretary of State Vance at Ben-Gurion University, on the occasion of the awarding of an honorary degree to President Sadat.

PRESIDENT SADAT

Dear Friends:

For centuries Arabs and Jews have lived together in peace and fraternity. A common descent, from Abraham, a similar religious belief, and a shared cultural heritage have bound us in our pursuit of happiness and fulfillment.

In the dawn of Islam our great prophet, Muhammad, signed a charter which stipulated that the Jews who live among us shall have an equal right with our own people to our assistance and good offices. The Jews of the various branches domiciled in Yathrib (the pre-Islamic name of Medina) shall form, with the Muslims, one composite nation; they shall practice their religion as freely as the Muslims.

This spirit of amity and friendship proved to be a profound and lasting one. Maimonides chose to write his great works in Arabic. Some have linked his writings with those of Al-Farrabi. Our region never witnessed the communal conflicts that existed between Jews and non-Jews in other parts of the world. It is the responsibility of those among us who are endowed with vision to revive such spirit today.

The challenge before us is not one of scoring a point here or there. Rather it is how to build a viable structure for peace for your generation and for the generations to come. Fanaticism and self-righteousness are no answer to the complex problems of today. The answer is tolerance, compassion and magnanimity.

We will be judged not by the hard positions we took but by the wounds we heal, the souls we saved and the suffering we eliminated.

We have taken the first step towards a comprehensive peace in the Middle East. It was a giant step, measured by the accumulated obstacles and psychological barriers that existed in the past. Yet it is meant to be followed up and completed.

This is an awesome task that requires all the goodwill and cooperation we can muster. Events of the recent past have shattered away old concepts of security based on territorial expansion and denial of national rights. The real key to security is genuine acceptance without reservation. I have no doubt that you will demonstrate in the months ahead a veritable willingness to live in peace with all your neighbors, including the Palestinian people.

Let us pledge ourselves to the cause of peace and brotherhood. Let no man, Arab or Jew, waste his precious life on war and destruction. Let us join together in a solemn prayer to God Almighty to turn our souls from hatred and prejudice. Let us devote our energy and resources to improve the quality of life for every man, woman and child.

Thank you very much.

PRIME MINISTER BEGIN

Mr. President of the Arab Republic of Egypt, Mr. Vice-President, Chairman of the Board of Governors of the Ben-Gurion University, Rector of the University, Members of the Egyptian and Israeli Cabinets, Mr. Speaker of the Knesset, Mr. President of the Supreme Court and its Justices, Our masters and teachers, the Chief Rabbis of Eretz Israel, Chairman of the Zionist Executive, Their Excellencies, Their Eminences, Chief of Staff, Leader of the Opposition in the Knesset, Members of our Parliament, Professors, Students, Honorable Guests, Ladies and Gentlemen:

We signed, duly ratified, and brought into effect the treaty of peace between our two ancient nations. It is, no doubt, a turning point in the history of Egypt and Israel, in the annals of the region in which our nations were born, established their kingdoms and civilizations, contributed great values to the culture of mankind, were oppressed and subjugated, fought for their liberties, regained their independence. In the case of the Jewish people I have to add a unique phenomenon: of return to the land given to our people by God and liberated and rebuilt by valiant men.

For thirty-one years, since we reconstituted the national home for the Jewish people, Israel, a state of war existed between our two countries. It had great, painful bearing on the lives and development of our peoples, on their social structure, on their economic situation. The flight time between our main airports is only forty-five minutes, as we – President Sadat and I, and our colleagues – are going to prove later in the day, but for almost two generations this small geographical distance was an impassable infinity. Our young fighting men met five times on the battlefield with unavoidable mutually inflicted severe losses of life and limb.

Now, this state of war, in the wake of the exchange of the ratification documents, is terminated and peace and good neighborliness are established between us (with open borders to be peacefully crossed, in both directions, by our citizens). Practical steps have already been taken of normalization, which is much more than the opposite of a state of war – which indeed is the essence of peace. A boat flying the Israeli flag has sailed from Suez and passed the Suez Canal to Port Said, while good-hearted Egyptian citizens cheered its crew. The canal will continue to be open to all Israeli ships. El Arish was peacefully and amicably transferred to Egyptian sovereignty.

I am convinced that both countries are determined to carry out faithfully all their commitments under the peace treaty concerning withdrawal in stages of forces, demilitarization – which must ensure that the Sinai Desert will never again become a *place d'armes*, or a route for attack – and the establishment of completely normal and friendly relations as befits two nations which freely decided to put an end to the state of war and live, side by side, as good neighbors. I believe I can say that today, both President Sadat and I send from this ancient city of Abraham our thanks and greetings to the president of the United States, Mr. Jimmy Carter, who rendered to us historic services in bringing about this great achievement.

At Camp David, with the help of President Carter, we reached an additional agreement which we signed in Washington on the seventeenth of September. On behalf of the government of Israel I wish to declare that we shall carry out all the stipulations of that agreement too, in letter and in spirit. Good faith should prevail amongst us. Israel has already given, decisively, proof of her good faith. For in the Camp David Agreement it is written that Israel, Jordan and Egypt will negotiate the modalities, powers and responsibilities of the self-governing authority (Administrative Council) to be freely elected by the Palestinian Arabs, inhabitants of Judea, Samaria and the Gaza District.

We have invited, both in written and spoken word, the Jordanian government to participate in the negotiations. It refused. As peace is involved,

I will not hesitate to repeat our invitation. But until today King Hussein's refusal is a fact of life. Had we acted by the letter itself we could have said: let us wait with the start of the negotiations to provide full autonomy for the inhabitants of Judea, Samaria and Gaza District until Jordan agrees to join us in the talks. But we do not say so. Notwithstanding the fact that Jordan refused to participate, we are prepared to negotiate and have already started to negotiate with an Egyptian delegation with the purpose to do our best to reach an agreement.

The constructive idea of autonomy is ours. At Camp David it was accepted by both the American and the Egyptian delegations It is a progressive, noble idea. The Arab inhabitants of Judea, Samaria and the Gaza District will elect their own Administrative Council, which will deal with all the aspects of their daily lives, without interference. We shall reserve security, which under the circumstances of the destructive, inhuman, bloodthirsty rampage by the genocidal so-called PLO is an absolute inescapable necessity of life, already recognized by every man of goodwill. Thus Jews and Arabs will live in Eretz Israel together, in peace, in security, in human dignity, in common advancement.

The negativists, the enemies of peace, claim that Egypt and Israel signed a "separate" peace treaty. We did not. We consider and believe that, by the signing of the treaty between Egypt and Israel, we made the first but indeed the decisive step toward a comprehensive peace settlement in our region – the first step, to be followed, in the future, with God's help, by peace treaties with other neighbors of Israel. This is our goal, this is what we are striving for. Such is the purpose we are determined to work for. And if the others are willing, so it shall be, and the Middle East, the cradle of human civilization, will again become the source of human progress.[18]

May

---

18. The Ministry of Foreign Affairs has the word "progress" here; another source records instead "pride."

PRESS CONFERENCE ON RETURNING FROM ALEXANDRIA

The second session of the autonomy talks was held in Alexandria on June 11 and 12. A third round of talks was held in Herzliya on June 25, 1979, and was attended by the prime minister of Egypt, Dr. Mustafa Khalil, at the head of the Egyptian delegation. On July 12, 1979, Begin and Sadat met in Alexandria. The following are excerpts from the press conference given by Prime Minister Begin on his return.

The two days I spent in Alexandria together with my friends are good days in my life. All those mutual visits by President Sadat and his advisers to our country and by my friends and myself to Egypt are a process of building the reality of peace. I have never agreed to the statement made by the German chancellor on the eve of the First World War that a treaty is a scrap of paper. A treaty of peace is a serious document but it is of course a framework with many articles and passages and sentences. This framework should be filled up with reality. Now what we have done through those mutual visits is to build the reality of peace.

My impression about the people in Alexandria: I passed the streets of Alexandria nearly half a dozen times – five or six times – and every time thousands of men, women and children lined up the streets and received us cheering, waving, etc. It was really heartwarming. President Sadat remembers, as he told me, he will always remember, the reception accorded to him in Beersheba. And the reception given to me in Alexandria was very like that accorded to the president of the Arab Republic of Egypt in our town. So the reception was wonderful and I am very grateful to President Sadat, the Vice-President, and the Prime Minister for the wonderful hospitality they bestowed upon me. Now we had two talks between President Sadat and myself. The first day it lasted more than an hour, the second nearly two hours. During our first talk we tackled practical problems; one of them is the rebuilding of the railroad line directly between Cairo and Lydda, which existed, as you know, until the War of 1948. Now it is partly still in existence and partly destroyed.... President Sadat and I agreed that this is a practical idea and we should find a way to rebuild that railway....

...And other issues we tackled – such as open borders. There will be more visitors now of either country to the other. I was in the synagogue of Alexandria; several people came to see me with tears in their eyes and said: "We have relatives in Israel, we would like to visit them." I brought it up in my conversation with President Sadat... and he was gracious enough to agree to enable every Egyptian citizen, a Jew, to come to our country and visit his family. This will happen very soon; even today, a family will come to visit their mother whom they didn't see for twenty-five years, by the personal approval of the President. It's a great gesture.

Yesterday, we had a different talk. Yesterday we raised the basic issues concerning the mutual relations between our two countries and also the situation in the Middle East. There were issues in which we were in complete agreement; there were some problems on which we agreed to differ. We didn't hide anything from each other. We opened our hearts to each other and therefore both of us, President Sadat and I, said openly and publicly that we consider yesterday's talk between us as the most important between us for the last two years and one of the most important of our lives....

We will continue with the peace-making process. As I said in the press conference in Alexandria, "Now both of us understand, President Sadat and I, that peace between Israel and Egypt is real and forever." And so this is the importance of the visit to Alexandria. As you know, I invited President Sadat to pay me a visit; he immediately agreed. And as I visited him at a Mediterranean port, he will pay me a visit also to a Mediterranean port in Israel, in Haifa....

And so, mutually, in understanding, we continue building the reality of peace.

SEPTEMBER 4, 1979

SADAT SPEAKS UPON
ARRIVAL AT HAIFA PORT

Following a warm welcome speech by Israeli president Yitzhak Navon, President Anwar El-Sadat gave a statement at his arrival at Haifa Port on September 4, 1979. No one knew it yet, but this third visit to Israel was to be Sadat's last.

President Navon, Premier Begin, Dear Friends:

It is with hope and confidence that we visit Haifa in another step in our holy pursuit for peace.

It is also quite significant that our meeting is taking place in the city which is the living symbol of coexistence and fraternity between Arabs and Jews. For centuries those cousins lived side by side in peace and harmony, worshipping God and tilling the land for their common good.

We are here to consolidate the gains we achieved along the road to peace. I would like you to know that every Egyptian is determined to make peace a living reality that expresses itself in all the walks of life.

Never again will there be bloodshed and suffering. Never again would human life be wasted in futile conflict from which no one benefits.

We are also equally determined to spread the umbrella of peace to include the Palestinian people. This is a moral commitment to which we will remain faithful at all times.

Dear Friends, the challenge might be great, but the promise is greater. We are committed to meet the challenge. In the interest of every man, woman and child in the region we will pursue our goal with all vigor and devotion. This is God's commandment and it is also our own choice.

May God Almighty guide our steps and lighten our way. May He grant us the strength we need to overcome all obstacles and the wisdom to heed His words: "May God summon under the canopy of peace all those who wish it, with the help of God."

…AND AT A DINNER IN HIS HONOR

Later that evening President Sadat made additional remarks at a dinner in his honor.

…To my satisfaction and happiness, a new sense of mutual trust is emerging across the border. This is a revival of the great heritage of our forefathers and spiritual teachers. For this feeling to continue, it has to be cemented and fortified by our behavior with one another every day. It should be reflected in the way we think of each other, the manner in which we formulate our policy and interpret the other party's moves. We should make a major effort to erase what remains in the minds of some of us from the unhappy past. Persisting barriers should be broken and eliminated, through hard work by both sides.

We are here to work for that goal and we are determined by God's will to succeed. We approach our task with a sense of history and optimism. As you have always noticed, I am an optimist by nature. I pay no attention to the voices of defeat and pessimism. I am never deterred by the size of the challenge. That is what men are for.

For [the] answer to the challenge before us is neither despair nor fanaticism. It is broad-mindedness and understanding.

Above all, we should never lose sight of our goal. We did not take the giant steps we took to reach a tactical accommodation with Israel. We did so to bring peace to every home in the area and to put an end, once and [for] all, to the causes of war and conflict. We took that difficult road to restore the fraternity and affinity that have always existed between Arabs and Jews. Thus, it is a historical mistake to think of what someone gave and what the other got. Rather, we should think and move in terms of what we all can do to make the Middle East a zone of happiness and fulfillment. Each and every one of us should invest his potential to insure the creation of a better tomorrow for this generation and the generation to come.

First and foremost, we should all realize that the only durable peace is the comprehensive peace. Any misconception of this point would be a gross mistake whose price no one can afford. It is with this in mind that we shape our determination to pave the way for a just settlement to the Palestinian problem, which is [the] heart and core of the entire conflict. The realization of the legitimate rights of the Palestinian people is not incompatible with

Sep

Israel's interests. It is the only guarantee for coexistence. It is a prerequisite to a world of harmony and tranquility for all of us.

Dear Friends, we came here with a message of friendship and amity from forty-one million Egyptians. We brought with us all the goodwill men can possess. I am certain that our endeavor will be fruitful. This is the dictate of reason and the wave of the future. None of us will be judged in the annals of history by the arguments he made or the demands he presented. We all shall be judged by the suffering we ended and the wounds we healed....

SEPTEMBER 5, 1979

JOINT PRESS CONFERENCE IN HAIFA

At the outset of a joint press conference with Sadat in Haifa on September 5, 1979, both Prime Minister Begin and President Sadat gave opening statements.

PRIME MINISTER BEGIN'S OPENING REMARKS

I would like to express my full agreement with the statement made by the President, that the cordiality of the meetings between our peoples is a reflection of the warmth and the friendship between ourselves. Yes, indeed, the President saw the people of Israel in Jerusalem, Beersheba and Haifa; I saw the people of Egypt in Cairo and Alexandria; both of us saw the people en masse, waving, cheering and expressing their deep wish for peace between our nations for cooperation, for friendship, and this is the blessing of the good days.

The Camp David Agreement was signed...almost a year ago, and since then great events took place and we made real progress. I am grateful to the President for his invitation...we shall in the next few weeks determine both the place and the time of our next private meeting. Our colleagues in the negotiating teams in the meantime will do their very important work. Now we reached in principle agreement, the President said, about the controlling process of the peace treaty in Sinai during the period of the next months – two and a half years – on a bilateral basis, but other details will be dealt with by the Ministers of Egypt and of Israel together with our American friends.

Secondly, we reached in principle an agreement on the oil issue, and on the quantity which will be supplied, or sold, by Egypt to Israel – and again there are several details which will be open for negotiations between the competent ministers. Israel decided to turn over Santa Katerina to Egypt before the nineteenth of November because of the symbolic importance of this date connected with the visit of President Sadat to Jerusalem nearly two years ago. But we also decided that all the arrangements which were predetermined in the wake of normalization should be in force, namely: the tourism will continue during the intervening weeks, both through the use of the airfield, in the air and on the land – and so it will continue also after the period of normalization, and there will be from this point of view no change. And this is very important also for the peacemaking process: the continuation of the normalization.

Thank you very much, Ladies and Gentlemen, for your attention.

PRESIDENT SADAT'S OPENING REMARKS

My Dear Friend the Prime Minister, Ladies and Gentlemen:

Let me seize this opportunity to express my gratitude to my friend Prime Minister Begin, who gave me the opportunity to meet with the population of Haifa, Jews and Arabs. I was very keen, really, to visit this town – I never visited it before – and in all candor, I am indebted to the population here, Jews and Arabs, for the very warm welcome they accorded to me. And I think it is accorded mainly to the Egyptian people, who share with the Israeli people here and everywhere all the intentions to keep the momentum for the peace process and to reach a comprehensive peace settlement once and for all for all those who live in this region.

As I told yesterday in my speech immediately after I arrived, in the last two years we have really made a great achievement: no one can believe that in such a short time – two years, November '77 and now we are in September '79 – all this big event could have taken place and changed the course of history. And as I told the Haifa population, that we have succeeded to fulfill what we have agreed upon in Jerusalem, the Prime Minister and me, that the October War is the end of the wars.

We have achieved also the understanding and friendship which enable us to sit together and continue and persevere for the achievement of the comprehensive peace settlement. The Camp David Agreements and the Treaty of Peace between Egypt and Israel both are a very solid cornerstone for the comprehensive peace settlement in this area. It is only a matter of time when everyone will join: I have no doubt of this. As I said in Alexandria, I have no differences, in the sense of differences between me and Premier Begin, or between Egypt and Premier Begin. My main aim was to continue the process of normalization, meeting with the Israeli people in Haifa after I met with them in Jerusalem and in Beersheba, and to continue the discussions for the achievement of the comprehensive settlement, namely, in this precise moment, the full autonomy that we have agreed upon in Camp David, including Jerusalem.

Yesterday and today we have really made a very intensive discussion about all the issues. There has been an issue of the United Nations force, or the observers, which the Soviet Union raised. Well, we decided, Premier Begin and me, to take the whole matter in our hands, both of us, through a temporary agreement, until we meet with our friends in America and reach a permanent agreement to solve this. The Soviet veto will never stop or end the peace process: on the contrary, it will give it more momentum.

There are other matters that we have discussed and agreed upon, and certain matters that we have discussed and disagreed upon – and we think that like this we have taken in our hands the matter of the United Nations forces and observers issues. We think also that we shall continue together, and with our friends in the United States, to meet on the various levels – either it is summit level between Premier Begin and me, or the ministerial level, to continue the discussions and to solve and bridge the differences between us in the fields where there are differences between us.

I seize this opportunity to invite Premier Begin to come and sit with me in Egypt so that we can continue what we have agreed upon. That we shall meet on all levels in the future until we reach an agreement upon the full autonomy, including Jerusalem, and all the issues for the future and for the achievement of comprehensive peace in the area.

Thank you very much.

A DINNER PARTY IN HAIFA

PRIME MINISTER BEGIN'S SPEECH

At a state dinner in President Sadat's honor, Prime Minister Begin addressed the assembled guests, followed by remarks from the guest of honor.

Mr. President of the Arab Republic of Egypt, Mrs. Sadat, Members of the Egyptian and Israeli cabinets, Mr. Speaker of the Knesset, our Parliamentary Colleagues, Dear Friends, Ladies and Gentlemen:

In extending a heartfelt welcome to my dear friend President Sadat, to his gracious lady, to their lovely daughter, to all our Egyptian friends, may I say that this visit to our beautiful ancient and rebuilt city and harbor of Haifa is a noble response by the President and his entourage to my visit to another beautiful and ancient Mediterranean port and city – famous Alexandria. These mutual visits, paid in the spirit of understanding and friendship, continue to make the peace we concluded a living reality. We all hope that so it will be in the future.

Admittedly, it is an unusual time, characterized by a paradox. Ladies and Gentlemen, peace is being attacked. Unusually, and in other times, war was being condemned as a tragic, horrifying phenomenon, causing unspeakable suffering to human beings, orphaning of children, bereavement of families, destruction of moral and other values. War was always deemed to be a disaster to all those involved in it and to others as well. There was even a brave, alas, a fruitless attempt by Briand and Kellog to outlaw war forever as an instrument of national policy.

Now what is happening before our eyes? Now peace, not war, is condemned. In international conference halls, by official communiqués, by various spokesmen. The object of all these negative statements is the peace treaty Egypt and Israel have concluded, signed and ratified and duly brought into effect. Consider: what did these nations [Egypt and Israel] do? They put an end to the state of war that lasted for thirty-one years. They pledged not to raise arms against each other, to cooperate in friendship with each other in all spheres of human interest and activity. What a damaging action. What a horrible, new reality? This is perhaps the most

Sep 9

amazing paradox of our days. What has always been a praiseworthy cause for joy and rejoicing has become, in certain circles, a cause for alarm. I believe, Mr. President, that our answer to all this is simple: We are patient. We did our duty. Our nations and their representatives took a momentous decision to bring peace, yes, a general, comprehensive peace settlement, to the war-torn Middle East. It is a good, God-blessed decision. No words of wrathful, artificial condemnations can change its real nature. We shall not be discouraged. We shall proceed with our efforts. We signed a great, international document, a peace treaty. We will carry it out in good faith, in cooperation, in understanding, in friendship, for the good of our peoples and of the region and of the world.

At Camp David we reached a second agreement concerning the full autonomy for the Palestinian Arabs in Judea, Samaria and the Gaza district. It is also a good, positive progressive agreement, to which we should be faithful. In this agreement, there are constructive clarities, not what some call ambiguities. If we base the negotiations between our competent teams headed by Prime Minister Dr. Khalil and Interior Minister Dr. Burg on the clear stipulations of the Camp David agreement, we can, as we both wrote to President Carter, during a year, reach an agreement on the outstanding issues and set another example of how understanding between nations can be achieved and how they can live together in peace, in security, in human dignity, in common advancement. On this issue, too, let us not pay attention to the negativists, to those who condemn agreement instead of war, and let us proceed with our efforts in complete faithfulness to what we agreed upon and signed. The time will come when others will see the justice of our intentions and actions.

I raise my glass to his Excellency, the President of the Arab Republic of Egypt, to all our guests, to peace, to our friendship, to the cooperation, prosperity and happiness of our two ancient nations.

PRESIDENT SADAT'S SPEECH

Prime Minister Begin, Mrs. Begin, Dear Friends:

Once again we meet in an atmosphere of amity and friendship. Once again, we lay a new brick on the foundation of peace. Once again we see a smile on every face and find joy in every heart. This is the essence of peace. This is the only road to the future.

We are determined to take that road no matter what the obstacles might be. We made a firm commitment to our peoples and all the nations of the world to pursue the noble goal of peace and reconciliation. This is not merely a line of policy. It is a sacred mission that started the day I visited Jerusalem. It is an irreversible stream which is engraved in the minds and hearts of million of people of good will everywhere.

To be sure, that road is not full of roses. It is an uphill struggle against formidable odds. But so was the road of the prophets and great reformers throughout history. Let us derive from their shining record the wisdom and vision necessary to find our way. Let us vow to overcome all obstacles and remove all barriers. We have effectively confronted many difficulties in the past. There is no reason why we cannot do the same in the months ahead. Reconciliation between Israel and the Palestinian people is the shortest cut to a new era of peace and happiness. We share a responsibility to see that process in motion. You have your legitimate concern. Similarly, they have their legitimate rights and aspirations. We want these ends to meet.

I have dealt with Prime Minister Begin since I launched my initiative. We have experienced agreement and disagreement on several issues: however, we remained always faithful to our goal of reaching a comprehensive peace that covers every nation in the area. We all realize that in the absence of such a comprehensive settlement, tension and instability will build up every say. This is a price none of us can afford.

In our meetings yesterday and today, we discussed many points that bear directly on the Palestinian question. We will pursue our dialogue until we reach agreement. We both know that time is of the essence. We will solve the remaining problems through resort to reason and mutual understanding. We are not trying to resolve the entire question. We are only helping the Palestinian people to take the first step forward. Subsequently, they will speak for themselves. This is their inherent right.

Dear friends, let us join together in a solemn prayer to God Almighty to enlighten our minds and purge our hearts. Let us sow the seeds of love in every corner in our region. Let there be no more suffering, no more violence, no more destruction. God willing, we shall succeed.

PRESIDENT SADAT SPEAKS TO ISRAELI JOURNALISTS

During his Haifa visit, President Sadat honored Israeli journalists with an extended question-and-answer session. Following are excerpts.

Q: Many Israelis are worried in case you retire from your post. What guarantees do we have that we will have another Egyptian president who will pursue your attitude, and that we will not lose Sinai and peace together?

Sadat: Let me tell you this: Lots of your people, our friends in Israel, have visited Egypt. Egypt is not a one-man country. We are a democracy, and you have to come and see by your own eyes, there on the spot.… In the last plebiscite, on the treaty, five thousand only said "no" out of forty-one million people.… We are a state, we have a government, we are a state of institutions, we are a democracy – you have to come and see by your own eyes. But don't ever repeat these words, "lose Sinai and lose peace." Don't ever repeat this. I shall not agree to it.

Q: In a recent interview in the German weekly *Der Spiegel*, the president of Syria, Assad, strongly attacked your Middle Eastern policy and yourself personally. Would you like to comment on your position personally and the position of your country in the Arab world?

Sadat: Let me tell you this: I have done my best. Before I visited Jerusalem I visited Damascus. Forty-eight hours before I arrived in Jerusalem I was in Damascus. I had a long session of five hours of talks with Assad at his home, and I tried to convince him – but the man couldn't understand or does not want to understand. For many reasons, this is something in the Arab family, no need to tell. They chose to sever their relations with Egypt immediately after we signed the treaty in Washington. What is the situation now? What is the situation of Egypt and what is the situation of the others who have severed their relations with us?

Egypt is achieving every day, not only in the area but in the whole world, achievements. One day before I arrived here I opened with the Foreign Minister of Germany one of the giant plants for fertilizers. Before that, we had El Arish on the twenty-fifth of May. After that, we shall be having our oil in October, Mount Sinai after then, the first phase of withdrawal. In the same time we are conducting the negotiations between us and Israel and the United States for the full autonomy for the Palestinians. What is in the other camp? There is a plot in Iraq and he has to remove his president and kill his very intimate friends and to see them by himself shot – Sadam Hussein. In Syria the situation is deteriorating, they are much nearer to you here, I can see the borders from the balcony here, than it is from Egypt – everything is deteriorating, especially after this Lebanese fiasco. What is happening between Morocco, Algeria, Libya. What is happening there on the Gulf? What is taking place there in Saudi Arabia even – the king left to Switzerland and they speak about some changes there also. In the middle of this you will find Egypt: the island of peace, island of love, island of democracy – and if you don't believe this, just come and see by your own eyes on the spot. At one time I said this: "Let me see what the Arabs can do without Egypt and what Egypt can do without the Arabs." I think this situation will be cleared by the end of this year.

Q: Last night in the last sentence of your speech in the dinner, you asked us to salute the peace between Israel and Egypt. What will it demand for you to envision not only a situation of no more war, but a real peace and cooperation?

Sadat: Believe me, I am open – because this [process] is not a tactical step, this is peace.... I envisage open borders, friendship.... If you ask me about peace, I'm not at all worried about the details in the oil problem or so…it will continue to flow. There are differences: this is a matter for the ministers to decide.

But let me tell you this: When I look to the future, for instance, I am planning to begin the Nile water to Sinai – Sinai will not be any more isolated like it was before, and you know that the tunnel that we built under the canal will be ready by next summer.

After the tunnel is completed, I am planning to bring the sweet Nile water – this is the sweetest of the four big rivers in the whole world – to Sinai. Well, why not send you some of this sweet water to the Negev desert as good neighbors – the water has already arrived in Sinai when I transfer it from the Nile to Sinai, and Sinai is on the borders with the Negev: why not? Lots of possibilities, lots of hopes.

And in the same time, let me assure you, the decision of war and peace in Egypt, as you well know: there will be no war after the October War, this is a fact.

Q: As you said, the conditions in Lebanon, Syria and Iraq are most unstable. There has been for years now unrest, fighting, bloodshed…

Sadat: Iran also, add Iran.

Q: …civil war. There is serious danger that similar conditions could develop in the future also in the West Bank. Would you agree, Mr. President, that for that reason for essential security reasons for Israel – Israel should also be in the future in charge of security in the West Bank, also during the autonomy period?

Sadat: During the autonomy period – what we called in Camp David the transitional period, the five years – the Israeli forces will withdraw to the security locations in the Western Bank and the Gaza. I am of the idea that, let us not cross the bridge until we reach it. Let the Western Bank and the Gaza have the full autonomy, and after three years we will be sitting together, and let me hope that King Hussein resumes his responsibility, like I resumed my responsibility towards Gaza, and sits with us – and until then, I don't think anything will harm Israel or will harm the security of Israel. But, on the other side, you remember when I visited Jerusalem two years before, I said I recognize two facts: one is that there should not be war after the October War – and thank God we have fulfilled this, once and forever. The second issue that I said was that there is a security issue to be met with for both sides. Let us sit together round a table, as civilized people, and discuss this security issue. Until this moment, this is my view. Whatever comes, I don't think any one of you, or in my country, could have imagined that in two years, after two years I'm sitting now relaxed like this here, and hailed by the whole population of Haifa in such warm feelings that I felt that I shall always feel that I am indebted to those people in Haifa here, Jews and Arabs. So let us take it step by step. But I'm not at all ignoring the security issue, but let us always take every step when the proper time comes.

Q: What is the most important achievement in this visit?

Sadat: Well, the most important achievement in my view is that we have cemented our agreements in Camp David and the treaty between Egypt and Israel, and we are ready together – Menachem Begin and me – to face whatever comes. And for instance, this issue of the United Nations forces: well, we decided together to take the whole thing in our hands, we need not go and convince the Soviet Union or any other one, we take the matter in our hands, and we shall be working out the details for the supervision of the security issue in Sinai until we have agreed upon a temporary agreement to be concluded between us with our friends the Americans also, so that we can continue to face our obligations of Camp David and the treaty as well.

Q: With all your beliefs in the strategic moves for peace, there is some linkage with the autonomy. How do you foresee the necessary progress on the autonomy talks in order not to impede the broader peace process?

Sadat: In the first hand, let me tell you this: our work is dedicated for a comprehensive peace settlement. It started with my initiative in the Knesset in my speech there, it continued in Camp David, and on the signing of the treaty. There are lots of details in this matter of full autonomy, as I said yesterday, heaps of reports we shall be receiving about, for instance, the elections. How could the elections be done, and so-and-so, and we have to decide upon it, Begin and me. But let me tell you this, in candor: we shouldn't jump over this period and say that the future of Palestine will be so, the Palestinians will be so-and-so. No. They are not with us, and we can't decide anything behind their backs. Let us have them. The only thing that your colleagues asked me is this: let us stand fast together and agree together after differences – we have

Sep

1977

1978

1979

1980

1981

differences, we have fields of differences, fields of agreements, this is quite natural as human beings. But let us stick together to the cornerstone of the whole comprehensive settlement, that is Camp David and the Egyptian-Israeli treaty. Everything after that will be solved easily. But if we reach the moment when we face any conflict between us – difference of opinion, yes, it is natural – but conflict, I don't think we shall have any conflict between us again....

Q: We all have to go home now and write an article summing up your visit. What would you write if you had to write it instead of us?

Sadat: Thank God I am not a journalist anymore, thank God. It's a very difficult job for me. If you ask me my idea, I would say this: I don't know if it is by coincidence – I wonder if it is only coincidence – that a few days before I arrived here, we found – my archaeologists found – the very famous city Ayon, where Joseph lived, married and studied, and where Plato also studied. We have found the house of the priests. My archaeologists now are doing their best to locate the house of Joseph. I have told my friend Yadin yesterday to come and join efforts with my archaeologists. But let me tell you this: when we find the house where Joseph lived, married and brought his two sons and studied also – and it was three thousand years before, when it was the capital of the culture all over the world, because as I told you, Plato was there, and was examined before they accepted him in Ayon. This Ayon we found fifteen kilometers from Cairo, in a place called Mattariya. Whenever we find the house of Joseph, and my archaeologists say they have found the location of the houses of all the priests there – and his father-in-law was a priest – and they told me they will be trying to locate Joseph's house...well, as I told you, I wonder if it is by coincidence or anything else that this happened a few days before. But write this: whenever we find the house of Moses, I shall refuse any Israeli claim of territory.

SEPTEMBER 6, 1979

SPEECHES ON SADAT'S DEPARTURE FROM HAIFA

PRIME MINISTER BEGIN

The next day, September 6, Sadat departed from Israel from Ben-Gurion Airport and both Begin and Sadat made public statements. Although Begin spoke warmly of future visits, this would in fact be the last time Sadat set foot on Israeli soil.

Mr. President of the Arab Republic of Egypt, Mrs. Sadat, Mr. President of the State of Israel, Mrs. Navon, Ladies and Gentlemen:

Mr. President, on behalf of the people and government of Israel, I have the honor to express our gratitude to you and to your gracious lady for the visit you paid to our people and country.

This was a momentous visit and it gave positive result. Again, it was proved that the warmth of the hearts of our people, as that of the Egyptian people, brings them, with every visit you pay to Israel and I pay to Egypt, nearer and closer.

We had very serious discussion. During this visit again close, intimate friendship was established between the representatives of our two countries, which in our time is a treasure to be guarded, cherished.

And so you end a three-day visit to Israel. I do believe that the city of Haifa and its people, both Jews and Arabs, the mayor and all of us, did their best to make your stay enjoyable. Our president and his gracious lady took part in the reception in Haifa, and we all remember the wonderful words he uttered in greeting you on behalf of all the people of Israel.

These were three good days for our country and for the great human ideal of peace. When we look around the world we can see that it is in turmoil. Not only our region around, but in many parts of the world there is hatred and bloodshed, and we want to build a corner which will serve as an example to other nations of tranquility, of goodwill, cooperation, of understanding. We did lay the foundation for these great human values already. The time that passed was not in vain. We made efforts. Our colleagues did their best. And therefore we…lived to see the great day when we put our signatures on a document called "Treaty of Peace between Egypt and Israel" – a turning point in the annals of the Middle East.

And then we want to continue with the Framework we agreed upon at Camp David, to be faithful to it. I do believe with all my heart that difficulties will be put aside if all of us are faithful to agreements we reached and decided to bring them into fruition. We, all of us, are grateful to you and to your gracious lady for the days we spent together. There will be more visits. You will come again to us, representatives of Israel will visit your ancient country, and so the peace we concluded will be more and more reality in life itself. And when the years pass, we are absolutely convinced – all over the world it will be said that in this foundation we built a strong and beautiful edifice. It is peace not only between our countries, it is real peace between our nations.

Mr. President, Godspeed to you and to your lady on your way back home. We do not say today goodbye but *au revoir*.

PRESIDENT SADAT

We came to Haifa with a message of love and friendship. We leave today with a renewed sense of hope and confidence in the future. The sentiments expressed by every Israeli throughout our visit were overwhelming. I interpret this not only as a message to the Egyptian people, but also as a vote of confidence to the prospects of peace.

It was equally heartening to find a clear realization of the true nature of the peace we are working to achieve. It is a comprehensive peace that encompasses every aspect of the dispute. What we have accomplished constitutes a giant step of unparalleled dimensions, but it remains a first step that should be cemented and fortified by other important steps. Each and every one of us bears the historic responsibility of translating this commitment into a living reality.

The talks I held with my friend, Prime Minister Begin, were constructive. They were conducted in the spirit of Jerusalem and Camp David. We were both aware of the vital necessity to make progress on the Palestinian question soon. We are determined to pursue this goal in the months ahead with all vigor and in full awareness of our mission. I am very pleased with the ever-growing friendship between our people. Very soon, our relations will reach a new era for our common benefit. This driving spirit must be invested to spread the blessings of peace to every corner in our region. In this task, we need the cooperation and understanding of every person of good will. This is how the course of history is changed. This is how a better world is built. And to this goal we remain faithful forever.

NOVEMBER 18, 1979

THE SECOND ANNIVERSARY OF SADAT'S TRIP TO JERUSALEM

Upon the second anniversary of Sadat's trip to Jerusalem, Begin sent him the following letter.

Jerusalem, November 18, 1979

Dear Friend,

Please accept my heartfelt congratulations on the occasion of the second anniversary of your historic visit to Jerusalem.

I shall always cherish the moment when I heard the statement you made before the Egyptian People's Assembly declaring your "readiness to come to Jerusalem and address the Knesset." Without hesitation I immediately extended to you a respectful and cordial invitation to visit our country and to speak freely to our people and the world from the rostrum of Israel's Parliament. Those were great days for all of us; they captured the attention of all nations and the feeling was abroad that something unusual was unfolding in the Middle East.

As I had assured you in my written invitation, the people of Israel did, indeed, receive you with high respect and warm cordiality. You met with my colleagues and with the representatives of all our political parties and, in our own private conversations, we successfully paved the way for future contacts.

Both of us well recall the stations we subsequently passed: Ismailiya, Camp David, Washington, Cairo, El-Arish-Beersheba, Alexandria-Haifa. Admittedly, there were difficult hours along the way. But, ultimately, with the great contribution of our friend President Jimmy Carter, we reached the common ground and signed the Camp David Framework for Peace in its two parts and the Treaty of Peace between Egypt and Israel which we all consider to be the first and decisive step towards a comprehensive and general peace settlement in the Middle East.

From the warmth of the receptions accorded to us in each other's countries and by virtue of the steps undertaken towards normalization we have learned to transform the Treaty into a living reality of peace, friendship and cooperation. In stating this I cannot but make mention, with the deepest feeling, that meeting we witnessed together at El-Arish between the soldiers, the war invalids of Egypt and Israel who said to each other and to us: "No more war." What a unique, moving scene that was.

We shall of course continue, my friend, with our peace efforts, faithfully carrying out the Camp David agreement including the full autonomy for the Palestinian Arabs, inhabitants of Judea, Samaria and the Gaza District. We will, I know, also continue to assist each other and prove to other nations, near and far, large and small, that we can live together in peace, in security, in cooperation and in mutual friendship.

It is in this spirit that I send to you on this memorable day my sincere congratulations and warmest best wishes.

Sincerely,
Menachem Begin

JANUARY 10, 1980

PRESS CONFERENCE IN ASWAN

Prime Minister Begin spent January 8, 9 and 10, 1980, in the southern Egyptian city of Aswan meeting with President Sadat and other officials. Among other things the talks resulted in practical agreements about the opening of respective embassies as well as the establishment of mail, phone and shipping arrangements. On January 10, at the conclusion of the talks, Begin and Sadat held a joint press conference.

PRESIDENT SADAT

We need more meetings to solve these differences. I myself, I thought that we can in this visit reach a directive for our ministers, but still we have our differences upon key issues. But upon the normalization, let me tell you this: the normalization shall be carried out according to the Camp David [Accords], by word and spirit also. For sure I would have liked that we could have made much progress, but we still have time; we still have another four months to agree upon the autonomy and upon what I have already raised – the Jerusalem question.

We have come now immediately after we visited a location where the real fight between man and nature for building the prosperity for my people here – I have shown my friend our efforts to reclaim the land and our hopes for the future to build prosperity, especially after we have laid, together with our friend President Carter, the cornerstone for peace – comprehensive peace in the area.

Let me seize this opportunity and ask my dear friend Prime Minister Begin to convey to the President of Israel and to the people of Israel all the very best wishes of my people for achievements and prosperity – and mine also.

Thank you very much.

PRIME MINISTER BEGIN

Mr. President, Ladies and Gentlemen of the press:

I wish to express my deep gratitude to my dear friend President Sadat for his invitation. We had very important and interesting political talks

about the area, the latest events and our bilateral problems. The President
also enabled me to see – my family, my colleagues and myself – the marvels
of the ancient Egyptian civilization, also the modern technology of the
two dams at Aswan. And just before we arrived at this airfield, we have
seen reclamation of the desert for the first time in history, and I was deeply
impressed by the work done – with brains and energy and devotion – which
of course will continue, and the desert will blossom.

As the President said – and I agree with him – we have reached an
important agreement, and we had our differences of opinion. The agreement concerns the efforts to bring into effect normalization of the relations
between Egypt and Israel, in accordance with the peace treaty signed by us,
and by President Carter as a witness, between Egypt and Israel. In detail,
as I may say, with the agreement of the President: on Sunday an Egyptian
delegation will visit Israel, an Israeli delegation will visit Egypt, in order
to find the proper buildings for the embassies and consulates and for the
ambassadors, so that we can, in accordance with the peace treaty, upon
reaching the interim withdrawal line, establish normal diplomatic and
cultural relations; whereas a month later, the ambassadors will come to
the respective countries.

Secondly, there will be established points of crossing on land – at the
suggestion of the President, by our Joint Military Committee – so that
normal transport can start and continue between the two countries on land
and sea and in the air. As the President told me at El Arish – and President
Sadat is a man of his word – from that date, it will be the twenty-sixth of
January, the national airlines of both countries will start flights to each of
the two countries. Postal services, telecommunications, telephone connec-
tions, etc., will be established on that date.

We should recognize the importance of this agreement. Of course, it
is a result of the peace which we reached and the treat which we signed,
and we honored [with] our signatures; as we have done since April the
twenty-sixth until this very day – as we shall do in the future.

We also reviewed the situation in the area, and we paid special attention to the very tragic and unfortunate events in the intolerable invasion
of Afghanistan by the Soviet Union. We have found that we have the same
opinion. Yes, differences of opinion were left. The President mentioned
Jerusalem – on this issue we differ, as we already told you on other occasions.
The President made a suggestion to me, which has two parts.

First: that we reach an agreement on the full autonomy for the Palestinian Arabs – in our language, in Judea-Samaria; in the President's language, in the West Bank; and in the Gaza district – but that we implement it first in the Gaza district. This suggestion I will bring to my colleagues in the cabinet for consideration, because I am duty bound to bring it before my colleagues, members of the government of Israel, and consult with them. And after we take a decision, I will appropriately inform the President.

And now, may I invite my dear friend, President Sadat, to visit Israel, because now it is his turn – it's a kind of shuttle policy, in the most positive sense. And I do hope that the President will accept and soon will be our guest, and we shall receive him again, as I promised him before he came for the first time to Jerusalem – this is our ninth personal meeting since then – with great respect and deep cordiality. Thank you, Mr. President. Thank you, Ladies and Gentlemen.

EXCERPTS OF THE QUESTIONS FROM THE PRESS

Q: Both to Mr. President and Mr. Prime Minister: Could you elaborate on the considerations involved in the Gaza Strip first approach, and the autonomy talks?

Sadat: Well, as the Prime Minister stated, it was a proposal from my side, because I quite agree with the Prime Minister's statement, that I have put this proposal: first let us agree on the full autonomy for both sides, the Western Bank and the Gaza Strip, but let us start the implementation in Gaza. And this is because there is a certain responsibility attached to this problem: Gaza was under the Egyptian administration before '67, and we feel it is our duty, according to the full autonomy, to end the occupation and let them enjoy the full autonomy. This is what is behind my proposal.

Begin: I will leave out all the motives, on which there can be, again, different opinions. I only stated – and the President agreed with me – the very fact that the President made to me such a suggestion, in two parts: first, let us agree on the autonomy in Judea-Samaria and the Gaza district, and then the implementation will start in the Gaza district. This is a very serious problem to us, also from the point of view of the Camp David agreements. From our point of view, it's not foreign land, as Judea and Samaria is not foreign land. People called the land Palestine; historically it was called Eretz Israel. And, therefore, we have a deep interest in it and we have to consider very carefully any propositions – especially as it is a new idea, which I would not say contradicts the Camp David agreement, but is not written in the agreement. Even such a change can only come into being when it is being agreed by both sides. And, therefore, the Cabinet of Israel will have very carefully to consider the suggestion of the President.

MARCH 17–24, 1980

LETTERS AFTER ASWAN

This meeting was followed by a series of letters that were exchanged between the two leaders.

March 17, 1980

Dear Prime Minister Begin,

In our last meeting in Aswan, we pledged to do everything possible to ensure the success of the efforts we have been exerting along the road to a comprehensive and lasting peace. I need not reiterate, here, the factors which make it imperative for all of us to reach that goal without delay. Strategic considerations, both regional and global, render the continuation of the present situation most detrimental to the cause of peace and stability. This makes it all the more important to make real progress every day in the negotiations on the establishment of the self-governing authority for the West Bank and the Gaza Strip. That is also why we agreed to step in, when the need arises, and give the necessary directives to our delegations to the negotiations.

It is with this in mind that I am writing to you today. I have been following very closely the course of

the negotiations with hope and faith. I firmly believe
that both our peoples are firmly committed to the cause
of peace. It is my clear conviction, also, that they
are aware of the necessity for reinforcing the historic
step we took on the road to peace. That is precisely why
we have been exercising patience and restraint even in
the face of several discouraging and alarming signs. We
had hoped that, in the course of the negotiations, a
way would be found to give the process the shot in the
arm it badly needs. However, I must tell you, in all
candor, that I am deeply concerned over the present state
of affairs. Enough time has passed without making any
tangible progress on major substantive issues of special
significance. Several months were spent merely on defining
the positions of the parties and identifying the areas
of agreement and disagreement. On the other hand, we
noticed that certain attempts have been made to depart
from the Camp David formula and treat it lightly. All
this has been taking place despite our positive policy of
taking every conceivable action to bolster the bridges of
confidence between our peoples and eliminate any remaining
barriers. We have been faithful not only to the letter
of the peace accords, but also to the spirit of Camp
David and my mission to Jerusalem. With all the good will
nations can command, we accepted the early implementation
of the provisions on normalization.

Nevertheless, we see no signs of any meaningful
progress in the negotiations. The twenty-sixth of
May is approaching in a matter of a few weeks. If the
negotiations fail to produce the necessary progress to
keep the process alive, the consequences will be very
grave indeed. Many people will question the wisdom of
continuing the talks. On the other hand, the violation
of the fixed date, be it a target date or a deadline,
might give the impression that the talks have become
open-ended since no other date is fixed. All this will
expose us to charges and suspicions of procrastinating

or lacking the sense of urgency which is required under the circumstances. The door will be wide open before any other efforts to seek a solution to the problem. It would be quite difficult for us to oppose such efforts or prevent any move within the United Nations for the purpose of establishing new terms of reference. On the other hand, this will give credence to the allegations that the peace accords we signed constitute a separate peace arrangement. We reject this categorically. As I told you in our first meeting in Camp David, I would never accept a separate or partial agreement. I need not emphasize this any further.

Likewise, the success of our endeavor [necessitates] that you refrain from taking any action or making any statement that might poison the atmosphere or exacerbate the situation. Certain actions taken by your government lately have not been sensitive to the delicate stage of the negotiations. Statements made by Israeli officials lately have not been helpful, to say the least. This is not likely to generate the kind of response we would like to see on the part of the Palestinian people in the West Bank and the Gaza Strip, whose cooperation is vital to the success of our mission.

In the coming few days, our representatives will be meeting to pursue their discussion. These talks will provide an indication of the manner in which the negotiations are developing. It is essential that they address themselves seriously to the major issues of substance with full awareness of the consequences of success and failure. It is also essential to set up a Committee that would be entrusted with the task of discussing the issue of security for it is obvious that such issue is adversely interfering with many aspects of the negotiations. Hence, a real attempt to define it and clarify it would be a good step in the right direction. If the Committee on security starts its function promptly and in a positive manner, it will provide a hopeful sign that would contribute to the creation of a more favorable atmosphere.

I am certain that you will take these thoughts as seriously as I am taking them. We both have a stake in strengthening the structure of peace by every feasible means. Accordingly, I expect to hear from you positively.

With best wishes for good health and contentment,

Jihan joins me in extending our best wishes to Mrs. Begin and the family

Mohamed Anwar El-Sadat

President Sadat replied:

Jerusalem, March 24, 1980

Dear President Sadat,

Thank you for your letter of March 17, 1980, which I read with great attention.

May I, in the first place, reiterate that Israel never intended to sign a separate peace treaty with Egypt. I said so on many occasions, in your presence and in your absence alike, privately and publicly, in my country and abroad.

We want peace with all our neighbours and we want to solve, positively, the problem of the Palestinian Arabs, inhabitants of Judea, Samaria and the Gaza District. That is why we, both, invited Syria and Jordan to join the peace-making process and envisaged the participation of Palestinian Arabs in the Egyptian delegation. However, it is a sad fact that King Hussein and President Assad continue vehemently to oppose the Camp David agreement; that they refused and are still refusing to join our common effort. His refusal is surely not the fault of Israel or of Egypt or of anybody else.

The same question applies to the Palestinian Arabs. We would, of course, exclude from any such delegation

members of the P.L.O. which is bent on the destruction of
Israel, proclaims a genocidal aim and genocidal methods,
but we would wholeheartedly welcome a representation
of the Palestinian Arabs in the Egyptian delegation
to participate in the negotiations concerning the full
autonomy for the inhabitants of Judea, Samaria and the
Gaza District. However, no such representatives appeared
with the Egyptian delegation at the conference table.
Again,
I ask, can Israel or anybody else be blamed for their
absence?

Following the signing of the Egyptian-Israeli peace
treaty a year ago, we opened and continued our bilateral
negotiations, thus proving the good faith which Israel
has shown all along the way. Theoretically speaking, we
could have said: "As no Palestinian Arab representatives
participate, let us delay our negotiations until they do."
It never occurred to us to make such a proposal and thus
postpone our autonomy negotiations for an unknown period.
We entered into these negotiations with the determination
to make a common effort with you and reach a compete
agreement in terms of the Camp David accord.

In the joint letter which you and I addressed to
President Carter on March 26, 1979, the very day we
signed our peace treaty, we stated as follows: "Egypt
and Israel set for themselves the goal of completing the
negotiations within one year so that elections will be
held as expeditiously as possible after agreement has
been reached between the parties."

With all my heart I wish that this goal will be
achieved, but I must stress that it is neither a target
date nor a deadline, as can be proved by the appropriate
minutes of the negotiations preceding the finalization of
the text.

We still do not have to lose hope that until the date
mentioned above we may reach an agreement provided all

parties faithfully adhere to, and carry out, the Camp David framework.

The Israel delegation cannot be blamed for any deviation from the Camp David agreement or for any proposal which may be deemed to contradict it. But it is my duty to inform you that several proposals made by the Egyptian delegations do not follow the clear definitions of the accord. To prove this thesis I will give several examples:

1. The Egyptian delegation suggested officially that the self-governing authority be composed of an Assembly from which an executive council will emanate as well as a judicial authority.

   I am certain you agree with me that such an arrangement is not to be found in the text of the Camp David agreement. In our deliberations at Camp David we agreed to write "self-governing authority (administrative council)." We repeated that formulation in our joint letter to President Carter. We should use the Camp David language as President Carter one day said in my presence to his advisers. It is not a so-called matter of substance. An Assembly, an executive and a judiciary would mean, in fact, a Palestinian state, all but in name.

   To this we could not agree; this we cannot accept. We spoke quite a number of times about what it would involve for us, our security and our future and for others as well. I agree with you completely that in our considerations we should take into account both regional and global developments as all of us face common dangers.

2. Jerusalem: We, of course, talked many times about this sensitive issue. President Carter recently made a statement to the effect that Jerusalem should remain undivided, with free access for

Mar

all religions to their holy shrines. This is
exactly the situation as it prevails now and it
is guaranteed by law forever. Jerusalem is not
mentioned at all in the Camp David accord. I know
that you wrote a letter about it to President
Carter; so did I. The President of the United
States then wrote a letter to me. If we stand by
our letter, where do we commit any breach of the
Camp David agreement?

3. You mentioned the problem of security. Certainly,
    it is all-important to us, with the P.L.O. on the
    rampage, "promising" us lately a hot summer. We
    both know what it means in human lives. But, at
    Camp David, we decided that after a withdrawal
    of Israeli forces – which we will, of course,
    carry out – "the remaining Israeli forces will
    be redeployed into specified security locations."
    However, the Egyptian delegation recently
    submitted a proposal that those remaining forces
    will have to ask and receive permission from the
    self-governing authority to carry out a move.
    Such an idea was not even mentioned in the Camp
    David agreement.

    But here, too, I have to emphasize that
    this is not a legalistic problem. The issue is
    decisive. How many people may be killed until
    permission is granted and what may happen if it
    is refused?

Having given these few examples, I would like to
reiterate my deep wish to reach an agreement with you on
the issues of the full autonomy for the inhabitants of
Judea, Samaria and the Gaza District, if possible, before
the end of May. We can do so, I repeat, if we are all
determined to carry out what we agreed upon at Camp David.
Let us continue with our efforts; they can be crowned
with success.

My wife joins me in sending to you and Madame Jihan
and the family our warmest regards,

With my best wishes

Yours sincerely,
Menachem Begin

MAY 18-20, 1980

LETTERS AHEAD OF THE NINTH ROUND OF AUTONOMY TALKS

The ninth round of the autonomy talks were convened in Herzliya, Israel, on May 1, 1980. To many, it seemed obvious that the talks had been deadlocked. The US was supportive of a demand for a settlement "freeze" and was still unable to cajole Jordan to engage in negotiations for peace. The Arabs of Judea, Samaria and Gaza were not willing to cooperate in the autonomy talks and a target date of May 26 seemed unattainable. Sadat and Begin commenced another round of correspondence. Here is Sadat's letter to Begin from May 18, 1980.

Dear Prime Minister Begin,

In our meetings and correspondence alike we pledged
to do everything possible in order to facilitate the
process of reaching agreement on the establishment of a
self-governing authority with full autonomy for the West
Bank and Gaza. We discussed in length the necessity of
making tangible and adequate progress in the autonomy
negotiations in the light of our joint commitment to work
for a comprehensive peace settlement of which all the
parties benefit. In our meeting at Aswan, I emphasized to
you the need for issuing new directives to our delegation
with a view to accelerate the pace of progress and
overcome the existing problems. Subsequently, we held
separate talks with President Carter in Washington to
stimulate movement in this direction.

However, I must tell you in all candor that I was
disappointed by the lack of meaningful progress despite
the intensification of the talks. You would recall that I
drew your attention to the geopolitical considerations
which make it imperative for both of us to set our
priorities in such a manner that would enhance the
prospects for reaching agreement. Despite our difference
of opinions on several issues of substance, it has always
been my conviction that it should not be that difficult
to reach agreement so long as we are working in the
context of a transitional arrangement and not that of a
final settlement. We are not working in a vacuum either.
We have the "Framework for Peace in the Middle East"
which outlined a viable formula for that transitional
arrangement.

Under these circumstances, it would not be advisable
for any party to undermine the process through the
imposition of any preconditions or the taking of any
actions that threaten the essence of the negotiations
or purport to confront the other party with a new fait
accompli which might jeopardize the rights or positions
of the parties. Thus we were pleased when the head of
the Israeli delegation, Dr. Josef Burg, in response to
a letter from Dr. Moustafa Khalil, stated on May 5 that
you subscribe to the notion that no preconditions should
be set for the negotiations and that the autonomy talks
should be guided by the principles and provisions of the
Camp David Framework.

In this spirit, we did not give much weight to certain
statements issued by Israeli officials on matters which
are related to the negotiations. We took this as a way
of taking a negotiating position in public for obvious
political reasons however, a regrettable development
took place in the past few days when certain negative
moves were initiated that would result in poisoning the
atmosphere of the negotiations and make it very unlikely
to reach agreement. I am referring specifically to the

move which is being considered by the Knesset to turn
the annexation of East Jerusalem into Basic Law. You
are quite aware of our position on Jerusalem. While
we are not calling for a division of the City or the
introduction of any barriers between its different
sectors, we insist on achieving it without territorial
annexation or violating the rights and interests of 800
million Muslims. It is true that we are familiar with
your view on this issue and we are not asking you to
forfeit your right to state your views in the course
of the negotiations. But it is a different matter to
take certain actions through your political institution
for the purpose of co-opting the outcome of the talks.
These actions seem to be designed to render these issues,
however crucial, not negotiable or useless to discuss.
Instead of stemming these attempts on the basis that they
adversely interfere with the peace process and create a
situation which is hard to keep under control, it appears
that the Israeli Government is encouraging or even
endorsing such moves.

Another case in point is your position on the
settlement issue. As that matter was being brought up
for discussion in the negotiating chambers, an Israeli
official revealed your plans to intensify settlement
activities and establish new settlements in the coming
five years, i.e., for the duration of the transitional
period. I trust that you agree with me that such plans
are incompatible with the spirit of negotiations. It
is an attempt to predetermine the outcome of the talks
through taking advantage of your military occupation of
the West Bank and the Gaza Strip. It is for this reason
that Minister Kamal Hassan Ali wrote to Dr. Burg during
the Herzliya talks about that particular issue.

On the other hand, at a time when you were expected
to carry out the confidence building measures which we
discussed several times and provided you with a list
thereof as early as October 13, 1978, we witnessed

an unfortunate escalation of action taken by Israeli
authorities against the inhabitants of the West Bank and
Gaza.

How can we possibly win them over and enlist their
support for the peace process in the midst of these
actions?

Dear Premier Begin,

I believe that we have a historic opportunity to make
a breakthrough that would bring about the reconciliation
between Israelis and Palestinians. I also believe that,
with good will and open minds we can make this cherished
hope a living reality. With this in mind, I am urging
you to effect the necessary change of attitude that would
make it possible for us to resume negotiations. I leave
it to your discretion and judgment to choose the ways and
means for introducing such a change.

With best wishes,
Sincerely,
Mohamed Anwar El-Sadat

Begin replied two days later.

TOP SECRET

Jerusalem, May 20, 1980

Dear President Sadat,

I thank you for your message of May 18 which I
received through our Ambassador Dr. [Eliyahu] Ben-Elissar.

I read the text of your communication carefully
but I feel bound to state that I still am at a loss
to understand why the autonomy negotiations have been
unilaterally postponed by being twice suspended. On
May 7, at the end of their Herzliya talks the members
of the three negotiating teams together affirmed that
they would reconvene in Cairo on May 12 for continued
intensified negotiations as agreed upon in Washington

between President Carter and ourselves. Next day, without any prior notification, I received through the American Ambassador an announcement that the planned talks have been postponed because of your own wish to reflect.

In the course of your address to your Parliament on May 14 you announced that at the personal request of President Carter you decided to renew the talks although you did not propose a date for their resumption. On the following day we were once more all taken by surprise by the announcement that the negotiations were again postponed or suspended.

In your letter to me, Mr. President, you dwell on several causes for your action.

One refers to a bill presented to the Knesset concerning Jerusalem as the capital of Israel in its entirely. Permit me to share with you the exact translation of the three paragraphs of the bill:

1. The capital of Israel is Jerusalem.

2. The entirety and unity of Jerusalem, in its boundaries as drawn after the Six Day War, will not be
   infringed.

3. The permanent seat of the President of the State,
   the Knesset, the Government and the Supreme Court
   is Jerusalem (as, in fact, it now is).

On September 17, 1978, I addressed a letter to President Carter as follows:

"I have the honor to inform you, Mr. President,
that on June 28, 1967, Israel's Parliament (the
Knesset) promulgated and adopted a law to the
effect: 'the Government is empowered by a decree
to apply the law, the jurisdiction and the administration of the State to any part of Eretz Israel
(Land of Israel – Palestine) as stated in that
decree.

"On the basis of this law, the Government of
Israel decreed in July 1967, that Jerusalem is
one city indivisible, the capital of the State of
Israel."

There is no difference whatsoever between the contents
of my letter to President Carter and the recent private
Knesset bill which elicited a virtual universal parliamentary consensus. In this connection you will recall,
dear Mr. President, that during one of our friendly meetings in Egypt, I personally read to you the letter I had
written at the time to Mr. Carter which was published
together with all the documents pertaining to the Camp
David agreement. The talks between our delegations were
not interrupted; on the contrary we resolved, time and
again, to continue them.

On the other hand, it is my duty to draw your
attention to the resolution concerning Jerusalem adopted
by the Egyptian Parliament on April 1, 1980. Manifestly
untenable in the eyes of Israel the resolution states,
inter alia:

"The Council reiterates and emphasizes that all
the Israeli measures undertaken in the city with
a view to changing its identity, its demographic
composition and geographic structure are unlaw-
ful acts, are null and void and are totally non-
binding."

However, Israel did not, because of that resolution, suspend the negotiations.

The second point you make concerns the statement by
my colleague, the Minister of Agriculture, at one of the
sessions of the negotiating teams. Surely, the statement
in question cannot be construed as a reason for the
suspension of the talks. Our position on settlements in
Judea, Samaria and the Gaza District is certainly well-
known to you as is that on Jerusalem: it is the exercise

of our inherent right and an integral part of our national security.

It is a feature of the negotiating process for either party to state its position on any issue. In this connection may I respectfully remind you that General Ali, during the last Herzliya session, made a statement on security issues which was totally unacceptable to us and in absolute contradiction to the provisions of the Camp David agreement. However, we did not, because of that statement, suspend the negotiations.

In Judea and Samaria horrible atrocities were perpetrated by members of the PLO. Seven men were ambushed and killed and seventeen men and women wounded. The latest crime was an attack on worshippers returning from prayer services. It is our unbounded duty to seek out the murderers and act to prevent a recurrence of these and other atrocities. Certainly, the authorities of any state would not do otherwise.

It is our hope that peaceful conditions will be restored and it is to this end that we labor. We have never given up that hope of Jews and Arabs living side-by-side together in peace and understanding as we agreed at Camp David.

You mention "atmosphere". Were I to dwell on this matter quotations from the Egyptian Press would cover a large part of my letter, including poisonous attacks on me personally. But I prefer not to do so. We have to overcome the differences and continue with our peace efforts as we have in the past.

Dear Mr. President, as the suspension of negotiations was twice an Egyptian decision it is proper that Egypt should suggest a date for their resumption to be agreed upon and determined by all participants. Let us hope that with a common effort the negotiations will be brought to a successful conclusion.

Yours sincerely,
Menachem Begin

May

AUGUST 2–27, 1980

LETTERS FOLLOWING BEGIN'S HOSPITALIZATION

In July Prime Minister Begin suffered a mild heart attack and was hospital-ized for several weeks. (His first heart attack was in 1977; heart failure would ultimately be the cause of his death in 1992.) President Sadat wished Begin well but resumed their challenging discussion in a letter on August 2, 1980.

Dear Prime Minister Begin,

I hope that you have fully recovered and regained your health as you assume the awesome responsibilities you bear at this crucial point. It is the duty of each one of us to cope with a multitude of problems in the light of the current state of affairs, both regionally and globally. We have no choice but to confront these problems with vision and courage. None of us can be unmindful of or indifferent to events around us and their far reaching consequences.

Above all, we have the task of completing the work we have done on the road to peace. I am sure that I need not remind you that, in our various meetings in Egypt, Israel and at Camp David, we made a firm commitment to work tirelessly for a comprehensive peace settlement in the Middle East. Many were those who were skeptical about the prospect for such as a comprehensive peace for reasons you are certainly familiar with. However, I remained firm in my determination to pursue the noble cause of peace regardless of the enormity of the effort needed to accomplish the mission. Through determination and perseverance, we were able to achieve last year what was considered impossible by any measure. On the other hand, much remains to be done if we are to continue the peace march for the good of all the peoples of the area

including the people of Israel most certainly and, in
fact, for the good of all nations of the world. With this
in mind, we vowed, in the letter we exchanged on March 26,
1979, to negotiate "continuously and in good faith" in
order to conclude the negotiations on the establishment
of the self-governing authority with full autonomy for
the West Bank and Gaza at the earliest possible date.

As I pointed out time and again in the course of
our talks, the making of meaningful progress in this
regard is in the best interest of the Israeli people as
much as it is in the best interest of the Palestinians.
It would be a grave mistake of untold proportions to
waste this opportunity to set in motion the process
of reconciliation and harmonious coexistence between
Israelis and Palestinians. It is imperative to start
this process without delay so that we might finally put
an end to violence and fiction in the holy land while the
opportunity exists, for it might not arise again in the
foreseeable future.

As you well know, negotiating in good faith requires
a certain operational behaviour on the part of the
participants. First and foremost, they are under an
obligation to apply self-restraint and refrain from
taking any action which is incompatible with the spirit
of negotiations or which is likely to undermine the peace
process in one way or the other. No issue should be
considered, or rendered, not negotiable. No party should
attempt to confront the other with a fait accompli by
taking measures which purport to prejudice the outcome
of the negotiations or predetermine it unilaterally. Nor
should any party set precondition irrespective of his
claims. In essence, the negotiating process is one which
enables the parties to settle their differences and
reach agreement on controversial issues in a collective
manner and through an approach based on mutuality and
reciprocity and not through unilateral action. It is
inconsistent with this fundamental principle that any

Aug 1980

party attempts to determine a given aspect of the dispute
unilaterally and outside the area of meaningful exchange
of views. It is true that such unilateral actions have
no legal validity whatsoever vis-a-vis other parties, but
they certainly poison the atmosphere of the negotiations
and produce a most unfavorable reaction to the process
within the circles whose cooperation is vital to the
success of our endeavor.

Let us view together what took place in the recent
past with the objective of assessing the situation in
clear terms and discussing how best we can serve our
cause:

1. We started the current negotiations last year
    with the goal of reaching agreement before May
    26, 1980. That target was not met for reasons
    on which I am not going to dwell. Nevertheless,
    we decided to continue negotiating in view of
    the seriousness of the issues involved and our
    keen desire to give you ample time to make the
    necessary adjustments in your position.

2. We took this attitude despite the fact that
    what is involved, at this stage, is merely a
    transitional arrangement and not a final settlement
    to the Palestinian problem. We are simply opening
    the door for such a settlement through setting
    up a transitional regime for a limited period in
    order to enable the Palestinians to assume their
    share of the responsibility.

3. To our disappointment and to the surprise of many
    of Israel's friends, events did not take the
    course which was likely to bring us closer to
    an agreement. On the contrary, provocative and
    negative actions have been taken unjustifiably
    and in open defiance to the process and its
    very essence. All along, we were hoping that

the factors which prompted you to take this
negative attitude would subside and give way to
a more positive and responsive approach. To my
regret, these hopes have not materialized and the
situation continued to deteriorate.

4. I am referring here to the actions which are
being taken with respect to Jerusalem and
the settlements, together with the repressive
measures taken in the West Bank and Gaza.

5. At this point, it might be useful to refresh
your memory with respect to Jerusalem. You would
recall that this issue was the first one I raised
with you and your colleagues since I started
the peace initiative. Throughout our talks, I
emphasized to you the centrality that issue
occupies in the minds and hearts of 800 Million
Muslims and a greater number of Christians. I
pointed [out] to you on several occasions in
the clearest terms that a breakthrough in it is
certain to give our peace drive more momentum
than any other single action.

6. You would remember that in our meeting in
El-Areesh in May 1979, I told you that there was
a historic opportunity for us to proceed without
delay towards the comprehensive settlement as
we started the successful implementation of the
Egyptian–Israeli Peace Treaty.

7. You would also recall that in that meeting and
subsequent ones in Alexandria, Haifa and Aswan, I
concentrated on the issue of Jerusalem and told
you that if it is a matter of vital interest to
18 million Jews all over the World, it is equally
vital and sensitive to 800 million Muslims. It is
impossible to ignore this fact and be insensitive
to this spiritual and cultural interest. Many

1
9
7
7

1
9
7
8

1
9
7
9

Aug 1
9
8
0

1
9
8
1

Muslims throughout the globe are inclined to judge Israel's intentions by its behaviour on this question. Why loose [*sic*] their confidence and that of many others while we have a viable and attractive alternative? As I told you, I believe that it is not the most difficult issue and that it should be possible to find a solution that respects the rights and satisfies the aspirations of both sides.

8. We are aware of the fact that an overall agreement on the status of Jerusalem can be deferred to the stage of negotiating the final settlement. However, it is also a fact that the issue of Jerusalem is overlapping with many issues which are subject to review at present. Thus, it was natural that it was raised in various meetings both at the plenary level and those of committees, notably the Legal Committee and the Elections Committee.

9. Some might argue that all the actions you have taken with respect to Jerusalem by the various branches of your Government represent no more than a negotiating position that should not be taken seriously, especially in light of the fact that they are of no legal validity. However, we can not ignore the following facts:

    a. That such measures form a flagrant violation of Security Council Resolution 242 to which we are both committed to observe and implement.

        I need not elaborate on these legal matters, but it is clear that recent Israeli actions represent a territorial expansion and an acquisition of territory by war, an act which is explicitly prohibited under the

provisions of Resolution 242. It might be
worth mentioning that your Government has
declared on recent occasions that it will
neither tolerate nor accept any tampering
with the resolution.

b. Furthermore, such actions run contrary to the
letter and spirit of Camp David. It violates
the letter of the "Framework for Peace in the
Middle East" insofar as it is a breach of
Resolution 242 which is undoubtedly the legal
base for the Accord. As to the spirit of Camp
David, I believe that we vowed to settle
all our differences together in a spirit of
reconciliation and not by unilateral acts.
It was clearly understood, as we signed the
Accords, that none of us will resort to the
imposition of a fait accompli on the other.

c. It goes without saying, also, that these
actions contradict the provisions of the
Fourth Geneva Convention which prohibits the
annexation of occupied territories.

10. When I mentioned to you my belief that it is
not impossible to find a happy solution to the
question of Jerusalem, I stated before the
entire World that such a solution should not
result in dividing the city or the setting up
of barriers that could curtail the freedom of
movement or worship. I outlined a formula which
would set a shining model for coexistence and
good neighborliness among Muslims, Christians
and Jews. In essence, that formula calls for the
restoration of Arab legal and historic rights
in the city while keeping it united for all
practical purposes.

Aug

1977

1978

1979

1980

1981

11. In all candor, I feel that the ideas I presented
    and publicized in this respect have not been
    given due consideration on your part. I have
    not received any objective reaction or comment
    on the proposed formula which safeguards the
    interests of all those concerned, thus rendering
    an invaluable service to the cause of peace
    and a monumental contribution to the process of
    reconciliation between Arabs and Jews.

12. Your Government has also adopted a negative and
    counter-productive policy with respect to another
    sensitive issue, namely that of the settlements.
    I need not elaborate on the universal rejection
    and condemnation of this policy; both on legal,
    moral and political grounds. I am not here to
    enumerate the serious consequences of such policy.
    Suffice it to reiterate what I stated before, that
    these settlements in the West Bank and Gaza are
    illegal and a real obstacle to peace. Therefore
    they must be removed, be them old or new.

13. I am certain that you remember that I talked to
    you about the settlements in Aswan. I advised
    you, then, not to fight that lost cause because
    anything that you do in this respect is doomed to
    failure.

14. You would also recall that I offered to provide
    you with water that could reach Jerusalem,
    passing through the Negev, in order to make
    it easy for you to build new quarters for your
    settlers on your own land. You misunderstood
    the idea behind my offer when you said that the
    national aspirations of your people are not for
    sale. I never had this in mind as I told you. I
    was merely cooperating with you in order that we

might find a way out to the satisfaction of both sides.

Although the removal of illegal settlements should not hinge upon any incentive, I am willing to go that far to solve that problem as another Egyptian contribution to peace.

I know that you do not need anyone to find a way out for you. But it is always helpful to find certain openings which one was not aware of. At times, our Arab brothers need such a way out due to certain complications in their position. This is a burden I bear as the President of the Egyptian people who have been destined to be at the vanguard of events and developments in the entire region. This is the legacy of our past and the promise of our future.

15. We reached an understanding with you that Israel will take a number of confidence building measures without delay and prior to the beginning of the transitional period. The purpose of such measures was defined among us as: alleviating the suffering of the Palestinians and improving the atmosphere in the West Bank and Gaza as a prelude to the election of the self-governing authority. We spoke specifically about a group of actions that were listed in a memorandum presented to you on October 13, 1978 during the Blair House talks. It is obvious that the conditions in the West Bank and the Gaza Strip have not improved ever since. To the contrary, they witnessed a marked deterioration. Is this the way to win the support and confidence of those who are addressed by the Camp David "Framework"?

16. Our position has been both clear and unwavering since I initiated the peace process with my

Aug

mission to Jerusalem. It might be useful, however,
to repeat it as follows:

First: We remain wholeheartedly committed to
    peace. To us, it is a sacred and strategic
    goal. We will continue to work for it even
    if this entails doubling our efforts in this
    respect.

Second: We will adhere to the letter and spirit
    of Camp David and call for a strict observance
    of all the commitments under these historic
    documents.

Third: We remain prepared to help our partners
    in the peace process and provide them with
    solutions and [a] way out even when they fail
    to see the realities of the situations and the
    wisdom of this or that act. We apply to Israel
    here the same rule we have been applying to our
    Arab brothers.

Fourth: We firmly believe that all matters will be
    settled at the end, because this is the desire
    of all peoples of the area and the world. No
    one can turn the clock back or put the region
    again in the darkness of war and devastation.

Fifth: We reject all measure or actions taken by
    Israel unilaterally and against the universal
    consensus with respect to Jerusalem and the
    settlements. These actions are null and void
    completely.

Sixth: The historic and legal rights of the Arabs
    and Muslims should be respected while keeping
    different functions in the city united. Freedom
    of worship and movement should be guaranteed.

Seventh: Israel should desist from all settlement
    activities. Settlements built in the West

Bank and Gaza should be removed together with settlements in other occupied territories.

<u>Eighth</u>: No nation, certainly not Egypt or Israel, can determine the future of the Palestinian people. This is their God-given right of which they can not be deprived under all circumstances. Egypt will oppose any encroachment on that right.

<u>Ninth</u>: If we reach agreement on the establishment of the SGA,[19] we are prepared to begin its implementation in the Gaza Strip as a first step to be followed by implementation in the West Bank.

Dear Prime Minister Begin,

I am certain that you know, deep in your heart, that it is virtually impossible to continue the negotiations if the present attitude continues. Hence, in the spirit of my journey to Jerusalem and the Camp David Peace Accords, I urge you to take the remedial action which is necessary for the removal of the obstacles which have been placed on the road to peace in the past few months. I leave it to you to choose the appropriate ways and means for achieving that. If we fail to remove those obstacles in due time, we will be reducing the vital process of negotiations to a meaningless exercise in futility which would be a disservice to our cherished ideal of peace. I am sure that none of us wants to or can do that. I hope to receive a positive reply from you so that the negotiations could proceed in a promising atmosphere and as soon as possible.

With best wishes to you and Mrs. Begin,
Mohammed Anwar El-Sadat

Aug

---

19. Self-Governing Authority.

Begin responded on August 4, 1980.

Jerusalem, August 4, 1980

Dear President Sadat,

I thank you for your letter dated August 2, 1980, which I studied carefully yesterday evening.

Thank God, my health is good. May I tell you something of my thoughts during the illness which suddenly befell me. My good doctors put me under a machine, made in Israel, unique in its sophistication, which you saw in Haifa, and which we even export to the United States. After nearly two hours of ordeal they had a photo of my heart. The Professor decided to show it to me.

So what is the human heart? Simply, it is a pump. And I thought, God Almighty, as long as this pump is working, a human being feels, thinks, speaks, writes, loves his family, smiles, weeps, enjoys life, gets angry, gives friendship, wins friendship, prays, dreams, remembers, forgets, forgives, influences other people, is influenced by other people - lives. But when this pump stops - no more! What a wonder in the Cosmos is this frailty of the human body, without which the mind, too, becomes still, helpless or hapless.

Therefore, it is the clear duty of every man who is called upon to serve his people, his country, humanity, a just cause - he is duty-bound to do his best as long as the heart pumps.

I agree with you wholeheartedly that there is no nobler task than to work for peace, yes indeed, a comprehensive peace between all nations and, notably, between our nations which originate from and live in our region, known as the Middle East.

You will, I hope, forgive me for this quasi-philosophical introduction. It is relevant. Both our nations yearn for peace. I believe that both of us, too, want peace. It is in this spirit that for the sake of sincerity and clarity, I must make several remarks

concerning your detailed letter. Because, whenever you
mention our meetings at Camp David, in Alexandria, in
Aswan, etc., you always remind me of what you told me;
but what about my response? You will agree with me that
in none of our meetings was there a monologue either by
you or by me. We conducted always a dialogue. You spoke;
I responded. I spoke; you answered. Let us, therefore,
refresh our memories.

1.   You write in your paragraph 14:

   "You would also recall that I offered (in
   El-Arish) to provide you with water that could
   reach Jerusalem, passing through the Negev... You
   misunderstood the idea behind my offer when you
   said that the national aspirations of your people
   are not for sale."
   I believe, Mr. President, that when you
   recreate by memory our short dialogue in El-Arish,
   you will agree with me that:

   a.   You suggested to me bringing water from the
        Nile to the Negev; in that conversation
        you never mentioned bringing the water to
        Jerusalem.

   b.   I never said that the national aspirations
        of my people are not for sale. That would be
        gross language and I never used such language
        in our talks. You took the initiative and
        made to me a double proposal. You said: We
        must act with vision. I am prepared to let
        you have water from the Nile to irrigate
        the Negev; and let us solve the problem of
        Jerusalem, because if we solve this problem,
        we will have solved everything.

   I then responded:
      "Mr. President, water from the Nile to the
   Negev - a good idea, indeed a great vision,

Aug

but we must always distinguish between moral historical values, and such is Jerusalem, and material achievements. Let us separate the two issues: Jerusalem on the one hand, and water from the Nile to the Negev on the other hand."

2.   I will, of course, come back to the issue of Jerusalem, but I would like now to respond to another point in your letter, on which you dwell rather extensively: Good faith, goodwill, mutual understanding, promoting peace and cooperation.
    These are the facts:

a.   Your Minister of State for Foreign Affairs, Dr. Boutrus Ghali, pays visits to African countries and repeatedly influences their governments not to renew diplomatic relations with Israel. Is not this unilateral action a clear breach of the Egyptian-Israeli peace treaty, annex III, Article 5, Section 3, which stipulates:

> "The parties shall seek to foster mutual understanding and tolerance and will, accordingly, abstain from hostile propaganda against each other."

This, certainly, is hostile propaganda in third countries which used to say that they cannot renew diplomatic relations with Israel as long as there is a state of war between it and an African state (Egypt). But now there is peace between Egypt and Israel. A peace treaty was signed between us and duly ratified. Why, then, this unilateral act of hostility towards Israel?

b.   If the Egyptian delegate to the United Nations Emergency General Assembly votes for the most hostile anti-Israel resolution since that other abominable resolution was adopted in the Assembly equating Zionism – one of the most humane, national liberation movements in history – with racism (of which we, the Jews, have been and are the first victims), is not this a unilateral act of hostility contrary to our peace treaty?

c. The Egyptian delegate voted for a resolution demanding that by November 15, Israel withdraws from Judea, Samaria (my language), the Gaza District, the Golan Heights and Jerusalem. Is not this a flagrant contradiction of the Camp David agreement? There it is written: "A withdrawal of Israeli armed forces will take place and there will be a redeployment of the remaining Israeli forces into specified security locations" – this, following the election of the self-governing authority (administrative council). It is also written in the Camp David agreement: "All necessary measures will be taken and provisions made to assure the security of Israel and its neighbours during the transitional period and beyond."

"The transitional period," as agreed between Egypt, the United States and Israel, is five years; "beyond" is indefinite. "The remaining forces" mean army units which remain (in Judea, Samaria and the Gaza District). Yet your delegate voted in the United Nations in favour of an "ultimatum" to Israel to commence evacuation of these territories in less than five months.

d. The Egyptian delegate made a speech at the United Nations in which he said, inter alia:

Aug

i.   Israel should withdraw to the pre-June
     5, 1967 lines, whether on the West Bank,
     including East Jerusalem and the Gaza
     Strip. Where, Mr. President, is this
     written in the Camp David agreement?
     The quotations mentioned above tell us
     of stipulations that are completely
     different.

ii. Israeli withdrawal should be complete
     including that of the military forces,
     settlements should be dismantled and
     settlers removed. Where is this passage
     mentioned in the Camp David agreement?
     Are settlements mentioned at all in the
     Camp David accord?

iii. "The Palestinian people should exercise,
     without any external interference, the
     inalienable and fundamental right to
     self-determination, including the right
     to establish an independent state on the
     West Bank and Gaza."

     Thus, the Egyptian delegate to the
     United Nations.

     However, not one word about self-
     determination (which, of course, means
     a state), or about an independent
     (Palestinian) state appears in any one
     of the pages, paragraphs, sections,
     sub-sections etc. of the Camp David
     agreement. Dr. Ghali, speaking on
     behalf of Egypt, committed almost
     incomprehensible deviations from, and
     total contradictions, to, the Camp
     David accord which you and I signed
     and which our friend President Carter
     signed as witness, and which all of us
     are obligated to carry out in good faith

in accordance with the old golden rule: Pacta sunt servanda.[20] It is not Israel, Mr. President, which commits a breach of our peace treaty or of the other, not yet fulfilled, part of the Camp David agreement; spokesmen of Egypt, of various levels, do.

3. In this conjunction it is also my duty to turn your attention again to the fact that one of your official newspapers likened me to the "embodiment of all evil in mankind," (to use a Churchillian description), Adolph Hitler. I would not refer back to this shame, were it not for the fact that this "hostile propaganda," which Egypt undertook to abstain from conducting still goes on and on in a press which is not free of Government influence. Again I was called, by one of the Egyptian newspapers, "Shylock," an epithet hurled at the Jew by all his haters and detractors who originally, in Germany, were termed "Anti-Semites." (Of course, we Arabs and Jews are all Semites). I will refrain from listing other names, or articles, or curses. But, Mr. President, is this the way "to foster mutual understanding"?

4. On Jerusalem: With this letter I attach three documents: a) my letter to President Carter of September 17, 1978; b) the Law of the Holy Places adopted by the Knesset in June 1967; and c) the Basic Law: Jerusalem, Capital of Israel, adopted by the Knesset last week.[21]

---

20. "Agreements must be kept."
21. Item (a) is found at the end of this book in appendix 2, "Text of Camp David Accords." Items (b) and (c) are found in appendix 4, "Israeli Laws Referenced in the Correspondence."

I am aware that you wrote a letter about
Jerusalem to President Carter, who also wrote to
me a letter after having withdrawn his first draft.
About that draft we said to our American friends
that should it become official we shall not sign
the Camp David agreement which was already
completed on that Sunday, September 17, 1978.

I put to you a simple, logical question:
By what letter should we, Israel, stand? By
yours? By President Carter's? Or by the letter
of Israel's Prime Minister who, on this matter,
speaks for ninety-five per cent of the Israeli
people, without distinction of party affiliation?

I have never misled you, nor anybody else.
Time and again I repeated that Jerusalem, in
its entirety, is the capital of Israel, a city
re-united and indivisible for all generations.

Yes, indeed, there are in Jerusalem places
holy to Christians and Moslems. We respect them.
It was not so under Jordanian occupation as far
as the Jewish Holy Places were concerned. Israel
assures men and women of all religions absolutely
free access to the places sacred to them,
guaranteed by the Basic Law forever. We know
that from the point of view of religious faith
Jerusalem is holy to Christians and Moslems. To
the Jewish people Jerusalem is not only holy; it
is their history for three millennia, their heart,
their dream, the visible symbol of their national
redemption.

You assure me, Mr. President, that you are for
the unity of Jerusalem, but in your speech at the
National Press Club in Washington, a few months
ago, you demanded that "Eastern Jerusalem" be put
under Arab sovereignty. This is a contradiction
in terms. Two sovereignties over one city mean

its re-partition. Impossible. Jerusalem is and will be one, under Israel's sovereignty, its indivisible capital in which Jews and Arabs will dwell together in peace and in human dignity. Whosoever declares that the sovereign acts of our democratic Parliament are null and void makes a declaration which is null and void.

The same applies to our settlements in Judea, Samaria, the Gaza District and the Golan Heights. They are legal and legitimate and they are an integral part of our national security. None of them will ever be removed. I made a statement to this effect in Aswan, in your presence, in public, before the press and media of the world. I said the same, of course, to President Carter time and again since July, 1977.

5.   You mentioned Resolution 242. As you will recall, that Resolution refers to withdrawal of Israeli armed forces from territories – not <u>the</u> territories – and the Resolution's authors have consistently affirmed that it does not command Israel to withdraw to the pre-June 5, 1967 lines.

Mr. President, we travelled a long road towards peace. There were discussions, nocturnal sessions, crises, renewed efforts – and let us never forget those of President Carter – until our labours bore fruit. Let us continue. We would like to have representatives of the Arab inhabitants of Judea, Samaria and the Gaza District (not the PLO) around the table. But, incited and intimidated by the inflammatory and terrorist actions of the PLO they don't come ab initio.[22] We cannot force them. Can Egypt bring

---

22. The typed letter read, "they don't want to come." It was emended by hand to read "they don't come ab initio," that is, "from the beginning."

them to the table? You know the facts as well as
I do. All of us invited King Hussein; he recently
declared that he will never join negotiations
under the Camp David agreement. Can anyone of us
change his attitude? I read your speeches on this
subject.

Israel showed its good faith. We could have
said: let us rather wait with the autonomy
negotiations until Jordan and representatives of
the Palestinian Arabs join the talks. We did not
say so. You were willing to go ahead with these
negotiations; we accepted and we negotiate with
you.

However, four times Egypt unilaterally
suspended the autonomy talks. Do these repeated
suspensions contribute to the urgent need of
solving the problems under the Camp David accord?

Let us, therefore, dispense with further
unilateral suspensions. Let us renew our
negotiations. We have differences of opinion.
They do not, they should not, exclude another
agreement on full autonomy for the inhabitants
of the West Bank and Gaza (Judea, Samaria and
the Gaza District) as written in the Camp David
agreement.

Let us negotiate. Let us determine together
the date for the renewal of the talks. Let us, as
the past proves, reason together until we reach
the agreement and pave the way for peace in this
region, the cradle of human civilization.

> With my best wishes to you
> and Mrs. Sadat,
> Menachem Begin

Sadat's reply is undated but was received on August 15. The sole copy of this letter in the Begin Archives is actually a copy of the cable version distributed to government ministers and senior officials; it is printed on accordion-fold computer paper rather than typed on letterhead as most of the letters were.

Dear Prime Minister Begin,

Thank you for your letter dated August 4. I am pleased to learn that you have fully recovered and that you are able now to assume your responsibilities.

I am glad, also, that you reiterated, anew, your commitment to a comprehensive peace in the Middle East. This commitment, which we share, constitutes the very foundation of the peace process which was set in motion by my journey to Jerusalem and was reinforced by our joint effort thereafter. However, you would certainly agree with me that, for this commitment to be meaningful, it should not stop at the verbal assertion. Rather, it must be reflected in the actual behaviour of the parties concerned.

On the other hand, you spoke, in your letter of the necessity for having a dialogue among us on the essential issues under consideration. I agree. But let us first agree that a real dialogue entails a genuine exchange of views for the purpose of reaching agreement. If any party raises certain points of substance, they should be examined carefully and be given adequate attention by the other party in the spirit of mutual accommodation and understanding. Both parties should refrain from arguing for the sake of escalating the disagreement and creating unnecessary rift. The overriding factor should be seeking the truth and common interest.

Let me discuss with you another side issue before getting into the main points of substance. Several Israeli officials have been stating, privately or in public, that Israel considers all the issues negotiable and, hence, it would be quite willing to discuss them. I know that you told former British Prime Minister

Callaghan that you considered everything negotiable
except one thing: the destruction of Israel. This is
a healthy and positive attitude. But let us agree on
the meaning of the word "negotiable". To my mind: the
connotation of the term goes beyond the formal or
procedural scope of placing the subject on the agenda.
There is another substantive and practical aspect, namely
that both parties should be open-minded and defer any
judgment or action to the end of the negotiations. All
actions or measures should reflect the outcome of the
talks rather than the arbitrary will of one party. A
party who acts in good faith should do his best to
kept the issue in a "neutral position" throughout the
talks so that the negotiators may find a happy solution
freely and in the spirit of mutuality. Parties should
refrain from any action which is designed or likely to
predetermine the outcome of the negotiations. This is the
negotiability as I see it.

Having said that, I find it necessary to set the
record straight with respect to several points which you
referred to in your letter. I am doing so, not only for
the sake of the truth, but most importantly, for the sake
of peace and better understanding between our peoples.
Therefore, I will confine myself, as usual, to stating
the facts in objective terms and in the hope that this
may enable us to see events and their implications more
clearly and succinctly. In all that, I am inspired by
the unique surroundings. The thoughts which I am sharing
with you now occurred to me as I was on the peak of Mount
Moses, reciting the Koran and worshipping God in this
sacred part of the land of Egypt which witnessed the
birth of a great mission. As I was reciting the Koran on
this unparalleled spot, I became more certain of a fact
I have stated before.... That my peace initiative was a
sacred mission. The story of the Israelites began in the
land of Egypt. It is apparent that it is the will of God
Almighty that the story would find its completion in Egypt

also. This is the destiny of Egypt and its people. Such
is a sacred mission perhaps no other country is equally
qualified to fulfil.

Let us proceed, now, to examine together the
following facts.

First:

That the formula we agreed upon at Camp David with
respect to the Palestinian question does not constitute
a final solution. This is so, not only in accordance
with the explicit language used in the Framework for
Peace in the Middle East, but also because none of the
participants in that summit had the right to impose a
settlement on the Palestinian people. You would recall
that I made a statement to that effect in the first
encounter between us. What we agreed upon was merely
a transitional arrangement for a limited period of
time. Hence, all provisions and arrangements for this
transitional period are temporary in duration. It is
incorrect to claim that the insertion of the phrase "and
beyond" in the section related to security measures in
the "Framework" meant that any security arrangements
which are agree upon for the transitional period are
extended ipso facto beyond the transitional period.
This is merely a reminder of the need to devise certain
security measures in the interest of both parties, in the
course of the second phase of the negotiations.

As it is only a transitional period, certain issues
were deferred to the next set of negotiations where the
Palestinians can have their say and actively participate
in determining the outcome. These matters are related
to the final status of the West Bank and Gaza. However,
several principles and criteria were laid down in the
"Framework" so that the negotiators will not be starting
from a vacuum.

Second:

Related to this is the fact that the Camp David
Accords addressed themselves squarely to the question of

Jerusalem. It would be wrong to say that the Camp David
formula is blank so far as Jerusalem is concerned. You
will certainly recall that, throughout our conversations
in Camp David, the issue of Jerusalem figured quite
prominently. The draft "Framework for Comprehensive
Peace in the Middle East" I presented to you and to
our friend President Carter on September 6, 1978, i.e.
prior to the beginning of the Camp David talks devoted
an article to the subject and laid down a comprehensive
formula that safeguarded the interests of all those
concerned. Four U.S. drafts submitted on September 11, 12,
13, 16 contained similar, though not quite comprehensive,
provisions. When I found the proposed text inadequate
with respect to Jerusalem, I requested President Carter
to delete it. Thus, the overall solution of the problem
was deferred to the stage of the final settlement.
While the three participants in the Camp David summit
registered their respective positions, certain aspects
of the question were dealt with directly or otherwise
in the Framework even during the transitional period.
Section A of Framework institutes a transitional
regime for the West Bank and Gaza. The term "West Bank"
comprises East Jerusalem by any geographic or political
standard. This is a universal consensus of which Israel
can not detract. No nation has recognized the unilateral
annexation of Arab Jerusalem. It is on this basis that
your representatives at the autonomy talks have been
discussing with ours such issues as the voting right on
the Palestinian inhabitants of East Jerusalem within the
context of electing the SGA. On the other hand, paragraph
A(c) of the framework laid down the legal foundation for
the negotiated final settlements. Prominent on the list
was the following item:

"All the provisions and principles of UN Security
Council Resolution 242". As you well know, that
resolution contains a total prohibition against the
acquisition of territory by war. As East Jerusalem was

seized during the 1967 War, that provision applies to it,
not only in our view, but also in the view of the entire
world community. How far can these realities be ignored?
In your letter, you made a distinction between the rights
and sentiments of Muslims and Christians with regard
to Jerusalem on the one hand and the Jewish people on
the other. I think that this distinction is unwarranted
and unfounded. All believers in God, the people of the
Scripture that is, hold the city high in their thought
and heart. It is part of their cultural and spiritual
heritage. All of them have both rights and strong
spiritual attachment to that holy place which symbolizes
the oneness of the divine truth. I need not illustrate on
the historical and spiritual aspects of this unique bond.
As to the Palestinian people, Arab Jerusalem acquires the
added dimension of being part of their national rights
as well. This is a reality no one can escape from or
disregard.

You stated, also, that the formula I have proposed
for solving the problem of Jerusalem constituted what
you called "a contradiction in terms". I beg to differ.
I see no contradiction whatsoever between the existence
of two sovereignties and the administrative or municipal
unification of the city. Many Israelis and prominent
leaders of Jewish communities abroad did not fail to
see the logic of this imaginative prescription for
reconciliation and harmonious coexistence between the
followers of the world's greatest faiths. To insist on
a rigid solution based on the logic of "all or nothing
at all", as advocated by the rejectionists on both sides,
would be a grave historic mistake. It does nothing but
perpetuate the conflict and deepen friction among cousins
who should devote their efforts to a more creative and
positive endeavor.

Third:

You asked, in your letter, whether the settlements
were mentioned at all in the Camp David accord. Let

me seize this opportunity to clarify this point. You
certainly remember that, in Camp David, we spoke
extensively of the necessity to end all settlement
activities in the occupied Arab territories and withdraw
the settlers in order to rehabilitate them in their
own country instead of seizing other peoples' land. In
view of the stand you took and the considerations you
mentioned then, the commitments you made with respect to
the settlements were not entered in the main text of the
accord. Instead, they took the form of two undertakings
from you to President Carter which were conveyed to us.
The first one referred to Israeli settlements in Sinai
while the other was related to settlements in the West
Bank and Gaza. In the former undertaking, you promised
to submit a motion before the Knesset within two weeks
for a vote on the removal of Israeli settlers from Sinai.
In the second commitment, you undertook to observe a
moratorium on building new settlements for the duration
of the negotiations. It was understood by all sides that
the negotiations referred to in this commitment were
the autonomy talks. The first commitment was honored and
it contributed greatly to the beginning of the process
of implementing the peace accords. I will not dwell,
here, on the fate of the second commitment, for this is
not the purpose of my letter. Suffice it to say that the
understanding was that the issue would be subject to
review in the negotiations in which the Palestinians are
to participate. You are aware of the universal rejection
of the settlement policy pursued by your government. Its
adverse reaction is not confined to a certain group of
countries. Most of Israel's traditional supporters took
the same critical view, including Jewish communities
everywhere. It might be appropriate to mention here
what I said on this point at the national press club in
Washington on April 10, 1980: "The policy of building
Israeli settlements in Arab occupied territories is a
serious obstacle to peace. It is unfounded, ill-conceived

and illegal. It generates hatred and friction. It is
the worst formula for co-existence. In fact it is an
invitation to further violence and unrest. Much has been
said about the right of Jews to live anywhere. Certainly,
all peoples must be treated equally and without any
discrimination. However, no people has any right to live
in other peoples' territory without their consent and
free acceptance. To say otherwise would not only run
contrary to the norms of international law and legitimacy,
but it would also create a dangerous precedent none of us
can live with. The effort which is wasted on such futile
exercises should be directed towards imaginative ways and
means for promoting peace and good neighborly relations".

At this point, I think that it is useful to help you
recollect our conversation in El-Arish, a conversation
which, in my opinion, should not have given rise to any
controversy. Without getting into the details, the gist
of what I told you was that we should look at the case as
a whole and in all its aspects, rather than the Israeli-
Egyptian dimension of it. In this context, I said that
if we agree on an imaginative solution to the questions
of Jerusalem and the settlements, we would be willing
to consider providing you with water for the purpose of
rehabilitating the settlers in new quarters in the Negev,
i.e. in their own land. As I told you then, I was willing
to do that in order to find a way out of this dilemma for
all the parties involved. It is common knowledge that I
take it upon myself to find a way out for my Arab brothers
although I am under no obligation to do that. Here, I am
motivated solely by my unshakable commitment to peace
between Arabs and Jews. To this end, I have taken many
risks and I remain willing to double my effort, despite
the negative attitude of those who were supposed to bear
this responsibility with me. This is a historic mission
I fully accept. If the generous offers I make for the
sake of peace are neither appreciated nor acted upon, we
will have to start with a clean slate, but we will not be

deterred in our holy search for peace and justice for all
the peoples of the area.

I regret the fact that you made a sweeping statement
in your letter that none of the settlements in the West
Bank, the Gaza Strip and the Golan Heights will ever be
removed. This is the kind of statement that should be
avoided under all circumstances. By saving that, are you
precluding the possibility that the parties might agree
on the removal of those settlements in the future? Is
this what you call "the negotiability of all issues?"

Fourth:

I think that it is a disservice to the Camp David
accord to say that it did not contain one word about the
right of the Palestinian people to self-determination.
As you well know, the Camp David formula makes the
determination of the final status of the West Bank and
Gaza subject to the second stage negotiations to be
held within three years. However, there are certain
unmistakable indications in the "Framework" as to which
form this determination should take. Let me quote here
the following sentence from section A(c) of the Framework:

"The solution from the negotiations must also
recognize the legitimate rights of the Palestinian people
and their just requirements".

What are these rights if they do not include the
fundamental right to self-determination which is part of
the jus cogens[23] of the contemporary world?

When we call for recognizing the Palestinian people's
right to self-determination, we are by no means taking
a new position. In my address to the Israeli people on
November 17, 1977, I stated our position. In no ambiguous
terms. I said:

"If you have found the legal and moral justification
for establishing a national home on a land which was
not entirely owned by you, a fortiori, you should

---

23. "Peremptory norm."

understand the determination of the Palestinian people to reestablish their state on their land".

Fifth:

Linked to this, is your claim that Security Council Resolution 242 does not call for the withdrawal of Israeli forces to the pre-June 5, 1967 lines. Unwilling to get into an argument of this nature, I would merely mention that we should not indulge into such semantic arguments which belong to the past. The question is not one of the insertion or absence of a definite article here or there. Ideally, it should not even be one of a given text at all. The stake is too high for all of us to hinge on a word, a sentence or even on a whole text. It is a matter of will to establish a just peace of which all the parties benefit. The remaining details are nothing but technicalities. But if it is a matter of interpretation of Resolution 242, it has been established beyond doubt that the absence of the definite article is immaterial. In our peace treaty, we set a good precedent when we upheld the principle of mutual respect for each other's territorial integrity. This was a good application of Resolution 242.

It produced very positive results which were considered impossible even to dream of only a few months before. Why not follow this successful example on the other fronts? Let me also remind you of what I said in my address before the Knesset on that point:

"In all candor, and in the spirit which prompted me to come here today, I say to you that you should abandon for good all expansionist designs based on conquest. You must also stop thinking that force is the best way to deal with the Arabs....

There are Arab territories which Israel occupied and still occupies. We insist on total withdrawal from these territories, including Arab Jerusalem... Jerusalem to which I came as the city of peace which has been, and

Aug

will always remain, the living symbol of coexistence
between all followers of the three great religions".

Sixth:

In your letter, you asked the rather rhetorical
question whether Egypt can bring the Palestinians to
the table of the negotiations. In turn, let me ask you
what you did to encourage then to do so. Do you really
believe that such actions and statements on Jerusalem
and the settlements constitute any attraction for the
Palestinians?

How about the escalation of repression in the
occupied territory? The imposition of long curfews
arbitrarily, the banishment of mayors, the closing down
of universities and other institutes of learning? Do
negative statements on the future of the West Bank and
Gaza provide any incentive for the most moderate elements
among the Palestinians? As to what we did, you know
only too well the burden we accepted to bear under the
most difficult circumstances. We went as far as offering
you our life-line, the water of the Nile if we succeed
to solve the problems of Jerusalem and the settlements.
No one else would have done that for the sake of
comprehensive peace. We volunteered this offer despite
the excesses we were subjected to from our Arab brothers
and despite the misunderstanding of our intention on your
part. But this is our role to play in the area and such
is our commitment to peace.

Seventh:

You alleged in your letter that Egypt has violated
the peace treaty when it took a critical view of certain
aspects of the Israeli policy. Let me correct you on
that point which is too serious to be taken lightly.
We have stated repeatedly that we will honor all our
commitments under the peace treaty. Similarly, I have
not hesitated to recognize your carrying out of your
undertakings arising from the treaty in good faith. I
consider it a matter of top priority to reinforce our

peoples' confidence in the peace process. Therefore, I do
not think that it serves any useful purpose to raise such
a sensitive point outside the proper context.

The undertaking to abstain from hostile propaganda
does not at all mean that either party should accept the
policies or actions of the other whether he finds them
right or not.

We remain free to differ on certain issues and
criticize certain policies. This is the nature of
international life. It is the case in the dealings
among old friends. We live in an age of diversity and
multiplicity.

While I stated on previous occasions that I do not
recommend personal attacks in the press for any reason,
we can not possibly prevent our press from taking issue
with certain actions and statements. It is a law of
nature, not only of physics, that every action has a
reaction which is basically similar in kind and degree.
Thus, extremism and negativism can breed only sharp
reactions. I wish we can do without both action and
reaction.

You made a remark that the Egyptian press is not free
of Government influence. This is a gross and unfortunate
misrepresentation. You should know by now that we take
pride in the fact that we have established a democratic
system of government under which people are free to take
whatever views they deem fit. The Egyptian Government is
being criticized daily on various issues and we consider
this a shining feature of our democracy.

Finally, you complained that our officials "influence
African governments not to renew diplomatic relations
with Israel".

This allegation is based on misinformation and on the
wrong notion that African governments formulate their
policy and take their decisions on the basis of the
influence they fall under.

This is far from the truth, for our African brothers who assume the responsibility in their countries are all veteran freedom fighters who are endowed with vision and high moral standards. They make their policy according to the dictates of their conscience, their own independent evaluation of events and their perception of the pan-African interest. They value their hard-won independence very highly.

Do you really believe that actions in the West Bank and Gaza and the negative statements which have been made in the past few months were likely to win for you the support of African leaders? Has it occurred to you why all governments in different parts of the world should take this view of your policy?

Dear Prime Minister Begin,

Perhaps what I regret most is that you did not respond to several points I raised in my previous letter. Thus, the obstacles on the road to peace remain there and I can not see how we can resume the negotiations under these circumstances. As I told you, my allegiance to the cause of peace prevents me from accepting a situation where the peace negotiations degenerate into a meaningless exercise which erodes our peoples' faith and confidence in peace. It is not my intention to get involved into a verbal or rhetorical exchange which is not likely to serve the interests of any of us, not to mention the interest of peace. As we committed ourselves to continue our work until we end the dispute peacefully, I believe that the best course of action for us is to hold a summit conference in an attempt to

stem these lingering differences before they jeopardize
our mission. On the other hand, it would be unfair and
discourteous to impose this problem on our friend and
full partner President Carter at this point in view
of his other preoccupations which are obviously more
pressing.[24] You remember that I described him at Camp
David as the unknown soldier who dedicated himself to the
cause of peace. The least we can do in recognition of his
contribution is to appreciate his position and hold the
summit when these preoccupations are over. I am sure that
you share this view with me.

With best wishes,
Mohammed Anwar El Sadat

Begin's August 18 reply to Sadat was delivered on August 19, 1980.

Jerusalem, August 18, 1980

Dear President Sadat,

I thank you for your letter which reached me on August
15. I have read it with no less attention than I did your
previous communication and I will gladly respond to the
seven points you raise. But let me start with a reflection
on the passage at the end of your introduction.

You write to me: "The story of the Israelites began
in the land of Egypt. It is apparent that it is the will
of God Almighty that the story would find its completion
in Egypt also."

---

24. This letter was sent in the middle of the Iran hostage crisis. From November 4,
1979, to January 20, 1981, fifty-two Americans were held hostage by Islamist terrorists in the American embassy in Tehran. President Carter was also dealing
with major domestic problems: inflation and unemployment were soaring, cars
were lined up waiting at gas stations to buy fuel at the theretofore unheard-of
price of $2 a gallon, and the embattled president's approval ratings with the
American public were hovering at just over 30 percent.

The history of the people of Israel did not begin in
Egypt. It started in the country from which I write this
response. In those ancient days the country was called
Canaan. Abram (he was not yet Abraham) arrived in Canaan
directly from Haran, which he reached after having left
Ur-Kasdim (Mesopotamia). Thus, is it recorded in the Book
which is the inspiration of monotheism:

> "And Abram passed through the land unto the place
> of Shchem unto Eilon Moreh and the Canaanite was
> then in the land. And the Lord appeared unto Abram
> and said, unto thy seed will I give this land..."
> (Genesis, Chapter 12, Verses 6;7).

Since the days of the Prophet Samuel, Canaan was called
Eretz Israel, the Land of Israel ("Now there was no
smith found throughout all the land of Israel" - 1
Samuel, Chapter 13, Verse 19). Only in the second century
of the Christian era did the Roman Emperor Hadrianus,
having crushed the revolt of Bar Kochba with the help of
legions, from Britain and Germany, rename the land, Syria
et Palaestina. The origin of this name stems from our
ancient enemies, the Philistines, and thus did it enter
into the common usage of many nations. The mighty Emperor
also renamed, or misnamed Jerusalem, Aelia Capitolina.
Except for students of ancient history, this name is now
almost completely forgotten.

To go back to Canaan, or the Land of Israel, and to
its association with Egypt - old Abram spent a short time
in Egypt and then returned to Canaan. Only his grandson,
Jacob, named also Israel, descended (to use the Biblical
expression) with all his family to Egypt and there the
events unfolded as described in the Book. In their wake
the children of Israel returned to Canaan, just as we,
the descendents of Abraham, Isaac and Jacob - Israel,
returned through the course of history, time and again,
having never severed our ties with this land of our

ancestors. Throughout the generations Jews have never left the Land and have always dwelt in it.

None of us mortals can know the will of God Almighty, but surely as the history of the Egyptian people will find its completion in Egypt, so the history of the Jewish people will find both its expression and consummation in their own land, the Land of Israel.

1. "Both parties should refrain from arguing for the sake of escalating the disagreement and creating unnecessary rifts." These are your words. I agree with them without qualification. However, it is my duty to bring to your attention a quotation from an article which appeared in the Egyptian newspaper, Al-Gomhouriya, several days ago:

> "Begin requested clarification. We will not give a clarification, we will offer an apology. We apologize to the late Hitler. Hitler did not kill the will for peace of the nations of the world but made of it a hope and a goal. Hitler did not kill the will of the Jews to live but intensified their dedication to life. He, above all, was responsible for the establishment of the State of Israel for it was he who brought every Jew to dream about the Land of the Return as he sees it. But Menachem Begin is the one who kills the hope for peace in the hearts of men in Egypt, Israel and the Arab countries."

I shall withhold direct comment for a while.

You will recall that on May 27, 1980, I wrote to you a private, confidential letter in which I quoted from another article in a Cairo newspaper, Al-Akhbar, which wrote:

> "Hitler was an extreme racist who called for

1977

1978

1979

Aug 1980

1981

the rule of the Aryan race over the whole
world. Begin (is) an extreme racist who calls
for the rule of the Jews over all races in
the world, claiming that he belongs to the
chosen people," etc. etc.

Our Ambassador, Dr. Eliyahu Ben Elissar, brought
to you my letter. General Ali, your Foreign
Minister, was present at the meeting. Since it
was a confidential diplomatic exchange, I will not
now divulge its contents. But I can cite you as
saying that in your opinion – which you clearly
expressed – my complaint was completely justified.
In the wake of that article came the cartoon in
which Hitler bestows medals upon me, notably
the swastika, and now comes the above-mentioned
"apology" – to the late Adolph Hitler.

Mr. President, I do not complain any more. I
desist from doing so. I wish, only, to analyse
together with you what was said in the capital of
Egypt of somebody whom you called your friend.

As you know, I did not ask for any
"clarification," as the author of the above-quoted
paragraph asserts. I only drew your attention to
what was written in Al-Akhbar. But now we have
before us for all to read the "apology". It is
the most shameful profanity ever written since
a long rambling speech was published in the form
of a book called "Mein Kampf." I would wish the
editor of Al-Gomhouriya success in getting the
forgiveness of Herr Hitler.

He stated, moreover, that Hitler made peace a
"hope and a goal;" that "he did not kill the will
of peace," etc. He only killed tens of millions of
people in order to make the Aryan race the ruler
of the whole world. "Hitler did not kill the will
of the Jews to live...;" he only ordered to shoot

them, to bury them alive, to gas them, to burn
them, to drown them, to annihilate six million
men, women, children and babies. He only killed
a million-and-a-half Jewish children, torn from
the arms of their mothers. How many Einsteins,
Bergsons, Freuds, sages, philosophers, writers,
poets, might, would, have emanated out of them?
And yet the good Egyptian people is being informed
and educated on the newest theory that Hitler
"intensified the Jews' dedication to life"!

Above all, "Hitler was responsible for the
establishment of the State of Israel..." Quoting
this heresy, I cannot but say, God Almighty!
in whom we both believe – not the builders,
the pioneers, the fighters for freedom, the
prisoners, the executed heroes, the generation
of the holocaust, the revolt, the heroism, the
victory, the redemption – none of these are
responsible for the renewal of our independence;
but who is responsible? The enemy of mankind who
"scientifically" massacred millions of potential
citizens of that Jewish State.

After all this, you advise me that both
parties "should refrain from arguing for the sake
of escalating the disagreement..." But what is
even more serious and dangerous, you write in
paragraph seven: "It is a law of nature, not only
of physics, that every action has a reaction
which is basically similar in kind and degree." In
deep sorrow I must say that the venomous campaign
continues daily and even escalates, whilst
your own words could, perhaps, unintentionally
be construed by editors and journalists as
justification for all the hostility – including that
"apology" to the late Hitler – which has become the
dominant tone of the Egyptian press.

Aug

2. Hostile propaganda is clearly forbidden by our
    mutual peace treaty, and in my previous letter,
    I brought clear proofs of such conduct by your
    Minister of State for Foreign Affairs – in
    Africa, in the United Nations and elsewhere. Most
    recently there was the communique signed by him
    in Bucharest which is a complete departure from
    the Camp David agreement. It is, therefore, my sad
    duty to register for the sake of truth and for the
    record, that Egypt is not fulfilling its commitment
    under the Egyptian-Israeli peace treaty to abstain
    from hostile propaganda.

3. On settlements, you write that I gave an
    undertaking at Camp David "to observe a moratorium
    on building new settlements for the duration
    of the negotiations. It was understood by all
    sides that the negotiations referred to in this
    commitment were the autonomy talks."

    This statement does not conform to the facts
    as confirmed in the minutes of the Camp David
    talks. The document I hold before me is a letter
    addressed by me to President Carter on September
    17, 1978.
        I quote:

    "Dear Mr. President,
        I have the honor to inform you that
    during the agreed period of negotiations
    (three months) for the conclusion of the
    peace treaty no new settlements will be
    established in the area of the Government
    of Israel.
            Sincerely yours,
            Menachem Begin."

    Not only did I stress the negotiations for
    the peace treaty (meaning, of course, between

Egypt and Israel) but I intentionally noted in
parenthesis "three months," which was the time we
allotted in the Camp David Framework for Peace to
conclude our negotiations (in fact, they took six
months). This, and no other, was our commitment
we gave on settlements and that undertaking came
to an end on December 17, 1978. It never entered
my mind to give a commitment lasting for the then
indefinite duration of negotiations concerning
the autonomy for the Arab inhabitants in Judea,
Samaria and the Gaza District.

I do not claim that because of my letter to
President Carter, as quoted above, we have the
agreement of the United States Government to
construct new settlements. I merely made clear
both Israel's undertaking and when it would come
to an end. Did not your advisors inform you of the
contents of my letter on the day we signed the
Camp David accords in Washington D.C.? I, for my
part, made the matter crystal clear.

The statement I made in my last letter of
August 4 in response to your demand that all
settlements in Judea, Samaria, etc. be removed is
termed by you, "negativism". I wonder. I said in
the Aswan press conference: "We are no foreigners
to this land...we have a perfect right to live
there." And when one says that Jews and Arabs can
live together (and I remember your enthusiasm on
seeing Jews and Arabs living together in Haifa) –
what is that? Negativism? I believe that from
the moral point of view the concepts should be
reversed. We stand by our positive position.

4. On Jerusalem, I have told you everything I can,
both orally and in writing. I do not wish now
to repeat either the contents of the documents I
attached to my previous letter nor my statements

during our friendly talks. You have our position.
Jerusalem is our capital, one city, indivisible,
with guaranteed free access to the holy places
for all religions. Prince Fahd, of oil-rich Saudi
Arabia, therefore, calls on his Arab brothers to
march on Israel in a holy war – jihad. We are not
impressed. You know me by now. I hate war with
every fibre of my soul. I love peace. My colleagues
and I made great sacrifices for the sake of peace.
If there are, anywhere, ungrateful men who prefer
to forget what we did and the sacrifices we made
for the sacred cause of peace – then let them buy
oil, let them sell arms, let them be friends of
tyrants like the ruler of Iraq (to mention just
one), let them sell principles and dignity – they
will not change the irrefutable facts.

The threats of Prince Fahd are of no concern
to us. He does not know – how can he? – what this
generation of Jews who suffered the indescribable
fall and the unprecedented triumph, is capable of
sacrificing and doing in order to defend the people,
the country, Jerusalem. He may have the billions
of petro-dollars; we have the motivation in the
service of a just cause.

But let it be known to all: We do not want
military victories. We want peace – for our people
and for the other nations. And we were glad to
note that Egypt did not concur with Saudi Arabia's
war slogan.

Jerusalem, of course, is indivisible and
is a part of this peace. You write to me again
that Jerusalem should be undivided under <u>two</u>
sovereignties. This, I must admit, I do not
understand. I do not blame anybody for my
inability to comprehend. But I say to you, in full
candor, I simply do not grasp the idea. I do not

understand the project to have one city under two sovereignties, or two sovereignties over one city.

5. On Resolution 242 you mention semantics: "all the territories"; "the territories," "territories". To us, the Israelis, these are no mere semantics. The two initial formulae (containing the definite article) were proposed in those almost forgotten days of November 1967, but they were rejected. Their rejection was deliberate and meaningful. Written into Resolution 242 are the words "from territories," and by those words we are in no sense committed to carry out what is called "complete withdrawal."

This is also one of the reasons why we did not withdraw to the pre-1967 armistice lines on the southern sector. You mention Sinai. Of course, there we made the greatest sacrifices for the sake of peace. But, under the Camp David accords and the peace treaty, Israel did not withdraw behind the 1967 Gaza District armistice line. This fact, this example, should not be ignored when we deal with other sectors. There is a general consensus in Israel, by all parliamentary parties except for the Communists, not to retreat in any sector, East, North or South, to the pre-4th June, 1967, armistice lines.

6. When I asked you: Can Egypt bring representatives of the Palestinian Arabs, inhabitants of Judea, Samaria and the Gaza District, to the negotiation table, you replied with another question: "And what did you do to encourage them?" Allow me to answer.

You speak about "repression." I would be interested to know what would any country, Egypt included, have done if its citizens were assassinated, its children massacred and all this under the slogan to liquidate the "Zionist entity" which is Israel? I remember certain events in your country and the inescapable reaction of the authorities in charge. Let not the blameless be blamed for the guilt of the murderers.

Permit me to remind you again what I stressed in my last letter, that the boycott by the Palestinian Arabs of the autonomy talks began ab initio, even before we started our talks and immediately after the signing of the Camp David agreement.

7. And now, I come to the final point. As I understand it, at the end of your letter you make a double suggestion:

   a. Not to renew our autonomy talks until after November 4, 1980, on an undefined date following the elections in the United States.

   b. After that date, to hold a tripartite summit conference in which you, President Carter and I will participate.

Dear President Sadat,

If I understood you well, I feel it my duty to ask you: Why again for the fourth time does Egypt interrupt, or suspend, or disrupt our talks? Why should we not continue with our negotiations? You always contend that a solution is urgent. Were we to accept your suggestion, we would have agreed to a suspension of nearly six months or more. That is a long time indeed. Where is the sense of urgency? You, yourself, tell me that our world is one of plurality, of different opinions. Such difference of opinion exists between us as well. Of course, it takes at least two to negotiate. However, if you persist in your negative attitude, the negotiations will remain disrupted for the simple and only reason that Egypt repeatedly suspends the talks. On our side, I repeat our suggestion

to renew without any further delay the tripartite
autonomy negotiations.

And, what of the "summit" idea? I understand that
President Carter was not consulted. Permit me to say
that both he and I should have been consulted through a
diplomatic, confidential exchange. Let us at least now,
however, quietly consider the matter, the venue and the
date should all three parties accept the principle itself.
This should not, under any circumstances, preclude
the renewal and the uninterrupted continuation of the
autonomy talks. This is my concrete, positive suggestion
to you.

With best wishes,
Menachem Begin

Sadat's return letter is dated August 27, 1980.

August 27, 1980

Dear Prime Minister Begin,

Thank you for your letter dated August 18. When I
sent you my first letter, it was not my intention to
start any rhetorical or polemical exchange which would
not serve any useful purpose. Rather, I was motivated
solely by my keen desire to explore every available
avenue to ascertain whether a common ground existed for
the resumption of the autonomy talks. In my opinion, such
common ground would consist of the willingness of both
parties to create, by their actions and deeds alike, a
favorable atmosphere for reaching agreement. Having gone
that far in the current exchange of letters and views,
I think that it is neither necessary nor helpful to go
further in arguing for this or that position.

I am certain that you know quite well that we have
not violated, or attempted to violate, any commitment

we made under the peace accords. Our record bears out this fact. We said repeatedly that we would honor all our commitments and you know that we always keep our word regardless of the risks or challenges involved. Our experiment in peace-making in my opinion, needs all the understanding and sincerity we can give. I am sure that you agree with me that we should spare no effort to promote confidence and friendship between our peoples. I also believe that it is a historic inevitability that we will reach agreement sooner or later, on all outstanding issues. I do not want either of us to look back and say: was it really necessary to make all these complications? What was the whole point?

Given the present circumstances, I still believe that our common interest is better served by a summit conference at the proper time. Let us look forward to a meaningful and fruitful meeting.

With best wishes,
Mohammed Anwar El Sadat

DECEMBER 18, 1980

TALKS WITH US SPECIAL ENVOY SOL LINOWITZ

The autonomy talks once again resulted in stalemate with little progress being made on the issue of autonomy. A proposed informal summit with Carter, Begin and Sadat was cancelled after Carter lost the presidential election. On December 4, Israel's foreign minister, Yitzhak Shamir, and the Egyptian minister of state for foreign affairs, Boutros Boutros-Ghali, met in Paris. However the only result of their meeting was an announcement that talks would be suspended until President-elect Reagan's inauguration. In early December, US Special Envoy Sol Linowitz held separate talks with Prime Minister Begin in Jerusalem and President Sadat in Cairo, after which the following brief joint statement was issued on December 18, 1980.

Since the signing of the Camp David Accords we have, with the full participation of the United States, made important progress in the negotiations
aiming at the realization of the objectives of the accords.

We recognize that much more remains to be done in the weeks and
months ahead. We are confident that through perseverance and mutual
resolve we can fulfill fully the promise of Camp David. Accordingly, with
the firm conviction that the Camp David process is the only viable path
towards comprehensive peace in the Middle East today, we agree to negotiate in good faith in order to conclude the negotiations at the earliest
possible date.

We are grateful to President Carter for the part he and his advisers
played in helping us to move forward in our quest for peace in the Middle
East and are gratified by the affirmation by President-Elect Reagan that the
United States will remain committed to the Camp David process.

DECEMBER 23, 1980

BIRTHDAY WISHES

On December 23, 1980, Begin sent congratulatory birthday wishes to Sadat.

Jerusalem, December 23, 1980

Dear President Sadat,

Please accept on behalf of my wife and myself my
heartiest congratulations on the occasion of your
birthday. Many happy returns.

I am sure that we shall continue in friendship the
fruitful cooperation between our nations for the sacred
cause of peace which is our common goal.

Our best wishes go to Madam Jehan whom we
particularly congratulate on her accomplishments as a
diligent student, now a Master in Literature.

Menachem Begin

THE TWO-YEAR ANNIVERSARY OF THE TREATY

Foreign Minister Shamir visited Washington in late February and early March 1981 and met the newly inaugurated President Reagan and his top foreign and defense policy advisers, including Secretary of State Haig and Secretary of Defense Weinberger. In the following excerpt of an interview with the Israeli daily Ma'ariv *on March 15, 1981, Shamir discussed the timetable of the peace talks.*

Q: Is it now completely clear that the autonomy negotiations will not be renewed until after the Israeli elections?

A: There is no connection whatsoever between these negotiations and the Israeli elections. We have no chance of forcing any negotiating partner to continue with the negotiations. Egypt slowed down the talks when it decided to wait for the results of the US elections. Perhaps it is not surprising that now the Egyptians are waiting for the Israeli elections, and it may be that after the Israeli elections they will have another reason. We are against any postponements. The negotiations must be conducted without disruptions and without interruptions and without considerations of the Israeli elections.

Following this, Prime Minister Begin sent President Sadat a letter on March 25, 1981.

Jerusalem, March 25, 1981

Dear President Sadat,

    On the second anniversary of the Egyptian-Israel peace treaty, which you and I signed and which President Carter witnessed on behalf of the United States, please accept my heartfelt congratulations. The treaty between our two nations represents a turning point in the annals

of the Middle East and all of us aspire to continue
our efforts to bring the Camp David accord into full
realization.

With my best wishes,
Menachem Begin

Sadat replied on April 12, 1981, in a message sent on the letterhead of "The Embassy of the Arab Republic of Egypt, Tel Aviv."

12-4-1981

Dear Mr. Menachem Begin,

I received with a deep sense of recognition the
kind congratulatory message you sent me on the second
anniversary of concluding the Peace Treaty between Egypt
and Israel, which is regarded as the cornerstone for
establishing durable and fair peace in the Middle East.

We firmly believe that the peace march we started
together with President Carter should be maintained
for the prosperity and security of our two peoples. Our
accords in Camp David will remain the cornerstone for
reaching comprehensive settlement and peace in our area
and will remain an example to be followed all over the
world.

With my warmest greetings,
Mohamed Anwar El Sadat

MAY 20, 1981

THE LEBANON SITUATION

On April 28, 1981, a crisis began developing on Israel's northern border when Israeli planes downed two Syrian helicopters. They were ferrying Syrian army troops who were engaged in attacking Lebanese Christian units. US Special

Envoy Ambassador Phillip Habib arrived in the area. Against this background, Sadat wrote to Begin on May 20, 1981.

Cairo, May 20th, 1981

Dear Prime Minister Begin,

In view of the explosive situation in Lebanon, I find it my duty to write to you and exchange a few thoughts with you and your colleagues. You would certainly agree with me that our overriding concern should be the maintenance of peace and stability in the region. This is essential for the success of the efforts we are exerting within the framework of a comprehensive and lasting peace. On the other hand, this is the strategy which serves the interests of each and every nation in the area and, in fact, all nations in the four corners of the World.

You would recall that I have spoken to you time and again about the situation in Lebanon and the danger inherent in any escalation of tension in this troubled part of the Arab World.

Specifically, I mentioned to you that it is our duty to work for a greater degree of stability there. Any outside interference is certain to exacerbate the situation and render it more precarious. It leads inevitably to a vicious circle of foreign intervention of which none of us can benefit. Any step towards the escalation of tension is apt to give rise to excessive reaction by other parties.

Any Israeli action in Lebanon today would rally the Arab World against Israel at a time when we are endeavoring to generate support for our peace policy in many countries in the Middle East and the Third World at large. The crises over the Syrian missiles in my view should be solved by quiet diplomacy and not by precipitating military action. This is the course that could reinforce the people[']s belief in the possibilities of solving the entire dispute through peaceful means. All states in the region are well advised to adopt a hands-off policy in order to enable the Lebanese people to solve their differences and come to terms with the necessity for coexistence. Such policy will also deprive outside powers of the chance to exploit the situation to their advantage and intervence [sic]. Any temporary gain Israel may realize through a military operation is more than outweighed by the long term damage it will definitely cause to the prospects for peace and the trend towards coexistence. In short, I can not emphasize to you enough the importance of self-restraint and patience.

I believe that the efforts of President Reagan's special envoy should be given every chance of success. It might take some time to agree on a formula that would avert any further escalation of tension. However, one should not be discouraged by that. The interests involved necessitate a policy of moderation and reason on the part of all those concerned. I am sending you this message as a friend who is most concerned about peace between Israel and the Arab nation.

Best wishes to you and Mrs. Begin from Jihan and myself.

Sincerely,
Mohammed Anwar El Sadat

JUNE 4, 1981

SHARM EL-SHEIKH PRESS CONFERENCE

On June 4, 1981, Prime Minister Begin and President Sadat met at Sharm el-Sheikh to discuss agreements and solutions. High on the agenda was the ongoing tense situation in Lebanon, and possible hostilities with Syria, who had maintained a military presence in Lebanon since 1976. Ever mindful of the effect of regional hostilities on the peace process, both Sadat and Begin took pains to reaffirm their commitment to the Camp David Framework agreements. At the conclusion of the meeting a press conference was held.

OPENING STATEMENT BY PRIME MINISTER MENACHEM BEGIN

Mr. President, Members of the Governments of Egypt and Israel, Ambassador of Israel to Egypt, Ladies and Gentlemen of the press:

This is a welcome and a taking leave combined. I welcome the President of the Arab Republic of Egypt, my friend, President Sadat, that he accepted my invitation, and now we say goodbye to each other, after we finish answering your questions, until we meet again, as we hope soon, in Alexandria. We had a talk which lasted for an hour and a half. We made important agreements, we reached serious solutions. We are not going today to disclose the contents of those solutions and agreements. And for that I have to apologize. You will have to remain patient: the problems and the solutions will develop, and become known in the process of their realization. However, I can say, that during those ninety minutes, we achieved much, the reason being, that we are friends, that we made peace, that we keep our mutual pledge never to raise arms against each other, that this is the quietest corner in the world, the Israeli and Egyptian border, and that we always speak with complete candor. Therefore, I can say with all humility, that this day, the fourth of June, 1981 will be noted as one of the good days in the lives of my friend President Sadat and in my life; and in the history of our nations. Thank you, Ladies and Gentlemen...

EXCERPTS FROM THE PRESS CONFERENCE

Q: Mr. President, what's your attitude towards the Lebanese crisis, and did you find some common point of view on this issue with our prime minister?

Sadat: Well, as I have already stated before, the Lebanese problem is a tragedy, really a tragedy, and the way it started also is a tragedy, in '75.[25] We have discussed this problem, Premier Begin and

---

25. In 1971, Jordan expelled the PLO from its country, and the majority of the expelled terrorists went to Lebanon, where they set up camp along the southern

me, for sure, and I have expressed my ideas to him, like he said quite frankly; whenever we sit together, we are always frank, and candid.

I think the whole tragedy started in '75 by [Syria's] President Assad.[26] Now we are living the tragedy in the area, and mainly the Lebanese and the Palestinians that started it really, President Assad, is inflicting upon both. For the Lebanese, my view is that the Syrian forces should withdraw from Lebanon. It was the cause for everything six years before in '75 when President Assad thought at that time that he will be like it was printed in France, "Le Lion de la Grande Syrie."[27] Well, the area is suffering now of instability because of this. If we remove the cause, the whole thing will be straightened. And until then, I asked my friend, Premier Begin, to give the Americans the ample time, without deadlines, because I remember before we knew each other, and we were sometimes in confrontation before we reached Camp David and knew each

---

border and used Lebanon as a base for military attacks on Israel. Their presence led to what would turn out to be a fifteen-year-long devastating civil war in Lebanon, which erupted in 1975 when Palestinian acts of terrorism against Christian Lebanese groups were met with retaliations in an escalating series of attacks that eventually engulfed the entire nation. The following year, in 1976, Syrian president Hafez al-Assad sent troops to occupy Lebanon and help put down the insurgence. The conflict continued to rage, however, off and on until 1990, eventually killing an estimated 100,000 people.

26. Although Assad did not openly send troops to Lebanon until 1976, Sadat here intimates that Syria was involved from the beginning of the conflict. It was understood that Assad was always involved behind the scenes in Lebanese politics, since Lebanon is viewed as part of "Greater Syria." Due to both the Baathist ideology and the nationalist ideology of the Syrian Social Nationalist Party, Syrian elites view their country as one based on geoculturalism rather than political boundaries, identifying with the concept of a Syrian Fertile Crescent or Greater Syria. This territory is perceived as extending from the Taurus range in the northwest and the Zagros Mountains in the northeast to the Suez Canal and the Red Sea (including the Sinai Peninsula and the Gulf of Aqaba) in the south, and from the eastern Mediterranean Sea (including the island of Cyprus) in the west, to the arch of the Arabian Desert and the Persian Gulf in the east.

27. "The lion of Greater Syria," Greater Syria being understood as an empire as conceived by a nationalist ideology of territorial reclamation comprising the modern-day states of Syria, Lebanon, Jordan, and Israel, parts of Iraq, a province of Turkey, and the Sinai.

1977

1978

1979

1980

June 1981

other, he was always against deadlines. Let us give the Americans the opportunity and the ample time to find a solution, and it will not be difficult. I also asked my friend, Premier Begin, to end the raids on the Palestinians. Apart from this, I think we agree upon the fact that the status quo should return and the legitimate president of Lebanon should for one time tell the whole world if he needs the Syrian forces as deterrent, like it is called, or the so-called deterrent forces, if he needs it or not. I pray for God that he finds the courage to say the word for the whole world.

Begin: With the permission of my friend, the President, I am in full agreement with the President that the decisive cause of the trouble is the invasion of the Syrian occupation army into Lebanon. It is no Arab deterrent army whatsoever. It is a Syrian army, which now uses its guns, tanks, missiles and its divisions, equipped with deadly Soviet weapons, against the civilian population, mainly in Beirut and Zahle. As in the past they used it against Muslims and now they use them against Christians, and carry out daily the massacre of civilians: men, women and children.

The second reason of the trouble in Lebanon is the so-called PLO, also armed with deadly Soviet weapons, like the Katyushas, forty launchers on one truck, and when those forty launchers issue forth missiles, and those forty missiles with one strike hit a house, almost everybody is either killed or maimed and the house crumbles. Now I accept the request of my friend President Sadat to give more time to Mr. Philip Habib, to try to solve the crisis in Lebanon – caused by the Syrians – by peaceful means. We don't want war, we don't want any war with Syria. But of course, as the President rightly said, the status quo ante must be restored. This is also the opinion of Mr. Habib and this opinion was also expressed by the Secretary of State, Mr. Haig, who yesterday said that it is logical. Of course, we give Mr. Habib additional time, but this can't go on for an undefined period of time. But he will have ample time as the President asked me. As far as our preventive operations against the bases of the PLO is concerned, I would like to make clear that we don't have any ambition to hit even those bases. But what we do is an act of legitimate self-defense in the highest moral sense.

There are now 30,000 armed PLO men in Lebanon. As I said, with the most sophisticated arms, and missiles, and tanks and heavy guns. And they plan day and night to carry out incursions into our country, to take hostages, to kill men, women and children. It became clear that the only way to defend our people, our citizens, our men, women and children, is to carry out those preventive operations. And therefore every man of good will, when he hears this explanation, accepts; they hear we face an absolute necessity to defend our own people, our own citizens…

Q: …Did you agree anything in regard to the fate of the Israeli citizens who are now living in Ophira [Sharm el-Sheikh]?

Begin: I am going to meet them after this press conference…. The President listened to them after we finished our talk. He was kind enough to have with them a very sincere and open talk for half an hour…. After the President leaves…I will meet with the settlers….

Q: Mr. President, will the peace process between Israel and Egypt be harmed in any way if war breaks out between Syria and Israel, and did you discuss this question today?

Sadat: Well, for sure, we have discussed this question, because this is a main topic. And let me tell you this: the decision of war and peace in the area on the Arab side is in the hands of Egypt and on the Israeli side is in the hands of Israel. We have pledged together that the October War will be the last war. We have agreed upon this today also, and let me tell you this: since Camp David, it is now about three years, dramatic changes have taken place in the area that we live in. But, there is only one fact that prevails. This fact is the Camp David, and the treaty between Egypt and Israel, and the peace process.

Q: Gentlemen: you obviously have different opinions with regard to military actions by the Palestinians. But what about political actions? What is the situation with regard to the autonomy talks? And since all the Palestinians at the moment continue to say that they are not interested in negotiating autonomy in the present

1977

1978

1979

1980

June 1981

framework, that it's being suggested, what do you think can be done to get the Palestinians involved?

Sadat: Well, we have started the peace process, and we have not asked the permission of anyone. And we shall continue the peace process. Regarding the autonomy talks, we didn't discuss it today. But, if you ask me my own idea, I think, after the Israeli elections, we shall be preparing ourselves on both sides, with our friends the Americans, to start again, and as usual by nature and by fact, I'm optimistic. I'm hopeful that before the end of this year, by God's will, we shall be reaching full autonomy and giving much more, I mean, push to the peace process. And whenever you hear the Palestinians or the Alawis in Syria, saying that they will not join or so, quote me saying that I am waiting for them in El Arish. To come take their chance in their hands, and meet with the Israelis in El Arish.

Begin: …As the President said, the question of autonomy negotiations was not raised today. I did not raise it. I will explain why: because President Sadat said, several months ago – and several weeks ago he repeated the statement – that the negotiations concerning the autonomy for the Palestinian Arabs residing in Judea, Samaria and the Gaza district will not start before the elections take place in Israel. In other words: they will start only after the elections; that is a statement I have to respect. We cannot impose ourselves on the President and the Egyptian government, or anybody else. And therefore it would be useless to raise this question. But now I would like to tell you, another question arises: who is going to conduct the negotiations after the elections? So there are two possibilities: Either I am reelected, if the people wish it so, then the chairman of the Autonomy Committee representing Israel will be Dr. Burg. If Mr. Peres is elected, Dr. Burg doesn't stand a chance to be the chairman of the commission. So maybe he himself will preside over the commission…I don't know. We must all now be patient…. I do believe with all my heart, that whoever negotiates on behalf of Israel will reach an agreement with our Egyptian friends concerning the autonomy, the full autonomy for the Arab

Palestinian inhabitants of Judea, Samaria and the Gaza District, in accordance with the Camp David Agreement...

[President Sadat was now asked in Arabic about the mechanics of a proposed Arab sovereignty over East Jerusalem. He replied, also in Arabic, that the city could remain unified but that there should be Arab sovereignty over the Arab part of the city. One unified city council could be made up of half Arabs and half Jews, and the city council would appoint alternatingly Arab and Jewish mayors. President Sadat noted that Prime Minister Begin was not in agreement with this proposal.]

Begin: I would like to add that the question of Jerusalem did not come up today in the conversation between the President and myself. As far as the merits of the issue are concerned, I cannot speak on behalf of the President, and I do not wish to criticize his opinion. He's entitled to his opinion. I can only explain to you what is my standpoint on this issue, and there are four points.

One: Jerusalem is one city, undivided, and indivisible. Secondly, Jerusalem is the capital of Israel, since the days of King David, for eternity. Thirdly, there cannot be any division of any kind, of Jerusalem, and there cannot be two sovereignties in Jerusalem; the only sovereignty is that of Israel. And fourthly, guaranteed by law forever, free access to the holy shrines to all members of all religions, whether Muslim, Christian or Jew.

[At this point a question was asked about how the summit meeting might impact on the Israeli elections. President Sadat declined comment, but Prime Minister Begin chastised the questioner: "It didn't even occur to us...we have so serious problems to discuss and you mix in the elections."]

Q: You both have expressed that you are nearly agreed on the formation of the multinational forces to come into the Sinai border area next April. Yet you have not announced agreement. What are the differences that divide you and why have you not done that today?

Begin: That question didn't come up; only we stated when the multinational force should be formed. We have colleagues and advisors who conduct the negotiations very efficiently, and we both believe that very soon there will be a complete agreement between us and the Americans.

Sadat: There are no real difficulties in it at all.

Q: There was a report…what was involved was the possibility of a trade-off: a speedier withdrawal, perhaps, by Israel, in exchange for an acceptance of [*unintelligible*], leaving some of the facilities intact for Egypt. Did you discuss that?

Begin: Please be patient, you will see in a very short time that we solved all these problems connected with the multinational force.…

JUNE 9, 1981

THE BOMBING OF THE IRAQI NUCLEAR REACTOR

On June 7, 1981, Israel Air Force planes conducted a preventive strike, bombing and destroying the Iraqi nuclear facility Tammuz 1-Ossirak, south of Baghdad. Two days later, Begin wrote to Sadat.

Jerusalem, June 9, 1981

Dear President Sadat,

The first letter about the most recent occurrence I wrote to President Reagan and the second I write to you.

Saddam Hussein – "more vicious than Gaddafi" – planned to develop, mainly with the help of France, several atomic bombs of the Hiroshima type. He would then have tried to either bring Israel to her knees or to destroy her menfolk and infrastructure. Three such bombs would have inflicted on us 600,000 casualties. In Egyptian terms it would have meant more than eight million people. Could or would Egypt have stood by? Israel, likewise, could not. We had to act before the reactor became "hot", which was to have happened, in accordance with our most reliable information, either in July or the latest in September, this year. (Yesterday, a news item was broadcast which I heard for the first time that the reactor would have become operational and "hot" after a fortnight!)

It is now clear to every man of goodwill that this was the last hour for us to prevent a mortal danger to our people. Had the reactor become "hot" we could have done nothing against it. In such circumstances the "opening" of the nuclear plant would have caused a horrible wave of lethal radio-activity over Baghdad with hundreds of thousands of casualties amongst innocent people, residents of the Iraqi capital. I, for one, would never have taken such a decision nor do I believe that any of my colleagues would ever have supported such a proposal. Nothing would have been left for us than to sit passively by for a period of between two or four years until Saddam Hussein would have readied his three or four or five nuclear bombs.

Mr. President, this description is simple but factual. We did our duty to defend our people and prevent disaster from taking place in our country. And so we shall in the future when the necessity arises. So help me God.

With your permission, I attach our official communique. Please read it; it is brief, it explains much.

Alisa is still in hospital but is feeling much better. I was deeply perturbed, the doctors having suspected a stroke of the brain. Now, the improvement is great and the terrible anxiety is relieved. With God's help, she will soon come home.

Alisa joins me in sending our warmest wishes to you and Madam Jihan.

Yours sincerely,
Menachem Begin

JULY 2 – 3, 1981

AN EXCHANGE OF FRIENDLY GREETINGS

On the occasion of the onset of the month of Ramadan, Begin sent greetings to Sadat on July 2, 1981.

Jerusalem, July 2, 1981

Dear President Sadat,

I am happy to extend to you, to your dear family and to all your Moslem citizens my warmest greetings and best wishes on the occasion of the commencement of the holy month of Ramadan.

Providence has enabled us to join our two ancient nations in peace and we thank the Almighty for its blessings. May our common path continue to prosper as we endeavor, together, to extend the peace throughout our region.

God grant you health and strength.

Yours sincerely and in
friendship,
Menachem Begin

Sadat reciprocated by cable, delivered via the Egyptian embassy in Tel Aviv, on July 3, 1981.

Mr. Menahem Begin
Prime Minister of Israel

Dear Mr. Prime Minister,

I have received with thanks your cable of congratulations on the occasion of the month of Ramadan.

I have the pleasure to express my greatest thanks to you for your noble feelings towards me and the people of Egypt which have paved the way for a just and lasting peace to prevail in our area.

We pray to God almighty that peace process will be consolidated thus guaranteeing stability and security all over the Middle East.

> My best wishes to you for
> health and happiness.
> Mohamed Anwar El-Sadat

OCTOBER 5, 1981

THE LAST LETTER

On October 5, 1981, Begin wrote what turned out to be his last communication with Sadat, who would be assassinated the next day.

> Jerusalem, October 5, 1981

His Excellency
Mohammed Anwar El-Sadat
The President of the Arab Republic of Egypt
Cairo

Dear Mr. President,

On behalf of the people and Government of Israel and in my own name I send you my best wishes on the occasion of Id al-Adha.

We hope that the next months of fruitful negotiations will bring to our nations the desired result of cementing the peace and deepening further our friendship and cooperation.

My wife joins me in sending to you and Mrs. Sadat our warmest wishes.

> Yours sincerely,
> Menachem Begin

Oct

OCTOBER 6, 1981

FINAL RESPECTS

In the summer of 1981, Egypt had experienced an explosion of civilian violence between Muslim extremists and Coptic Christians that led to a gruesome massacre of some eighty Copts. Egypt was also beset by economic problems and by internal dissension, some of which originated in the relationship President Sadat had established with the State of Israel. In the months afterwards, tensions simmered throughout Egypt, and in September President Sadat began a sweeping, highly unpopular crackdown that led to the arrests of fifteen hundred people, including Muslim fundamentalists, Copts, and political opponents of Sadat. On October 6, 1981, President Sadat was attending an annual military parade (ironically, it commemorated Egypt's "victory" of crossing the Suez Canal in the 1973 Yom Kippur War attack on Israel) when a team of assassins from the Egyptian Islamic Jihad, dressed in Egyptian military uniforms, lobbed grenades and opened fire on the reviewing stand. When the firing stopped, twenty-eight people (including four American diplomats) were injured, and twelve, including the president, lay dying. Prime Minister Menachem Begin released the following statement to the press lamenting the death of President Sadat.

President Sadat fell victim to a criminal assassination. The people of Israel share in the mourning of the people of Egypt. We send our deepest condolences to Mrs. Sadat and the children.

President Sadat was murdered by the enemies of peace. His decision to come to Jerusalem and the reception accorded to him by the people, the Knesset and the Government of Israel will be remembered as one of the great events of our time.

President Sadat did not pay attention to abuse and hostility, and went ahead with endeavors to abolish the state of war with Israel and to make peace with our nation. It was a difficult road. The President of the United States, Mr. Carter, the President of the Arab Republic of Egypt, President Sadat, and myself as Prime Minister of Israel and our colleagues resolved to do our utmost to reach the noble goal of establishing peace in our region. Unforgettable are the days of Camp David, and so is the hour in which the President of Egypt and the Prime Minister of Israel signed a treaty of peace between our two countries, and the President of the United States attached his signature as a witness to that historic act. Millions of peace-loving people throughout the world rejoiced.

During our many meetings, personal friendship was established between us. I therefore lost today not only a partner to the peace process, but also a friend. The hearts of my wife and myself go out to Mrs. Sadat and to all the bereaved family. May God console them in their grief. We hope that the peace process, despite the cruel act of his enemies, will continue, as we know President Sadat would wish with all his heart.

•　　•　　•

1977

1978

1979

1980

1981

Oct

Prime Minister Menachem Begin meeting with Rabbi Joseph Baer Soloveitchik of Boston
at the Waldorf Astoria Hotel in New York. Photographer: Yaacov Saar – July 17, 1977

Prime Minister Menachem Begin being welcomed with bread and salt on arrival at northern Sinai development
town Yamit celebrating its second anniversary. Photographer: Moshe Milner – September 29, 1977

Prime Minister Menachem Begin addressing residents during the official inauguration of the Avraham Ofer quarter at Yamit. Photographer: Moshe Milner – September 29, 1977

Egyptian president Anwar Sadat standing on top of the El Al ramp after landing at Ben-Gurion Airport. Photographer: Moshe Milner – November 19, 1977

Egyptian president Anwar Sadat accompanied by Prime Minister Menachem Begin (second right) at Yad Vashem Holocaust Martyrs' and Heroes' Remembrance Authority, Jerusalem. Photographer: Avi Simhoni – November 20, 1977

Prime Minister Menachem Begin and President Anwar Sadat in conversation on the couch in President Sadat's drawing room in Ismailia, Egypt. Photographer: Yaacov Saar – December 25, 1977

President Sadat and Prime Minister Begin walking down the steps after their first conference at Sadat's residence in Ismailia. Photographer: Yaacov Saar – December 25, 1977

Left to right: Senator Jacob Javits, New York commissioner of cultural affairs Bess Myerson, New York mayor Ed Koch and Israel's ambassador to the UN Chaim Herzog applauding Prime Minister Menachem Begin while marching at the head of the Salute to Israel Parade on Fifth Avenue in New York. Photographer: Yaacov Saar – May 5, 1978

"After you, sir." Prime Minister Menachem Begin and President Anwar Sadat about to enter President Carter's Aspen Lodge at Camp David. Photographer: Moshe Milner – September 6, 1978

Prime Minister Menachem Begin accidentally bumping into President Sadat during a leisurely morning stroll at Camp David with Egyptian deputy foreign minister Boutros-Ghali looking on.
Photographer: Moshe Milner – September 6, 1978

Left, Egyptian president Anwar Sadat; center, US president Jimmy Carter; right, Israeli prime minister Menachem Begin at Gettysburg, near Camp David. Photographer: Moshe Milner – September 9, 1978

President Carter taking part in traditional Shabbat eve meal arranged for Prime Minister Begin at Hickory Lodge at Camp David. Photographer: Moshe Milner – September 9, 1978

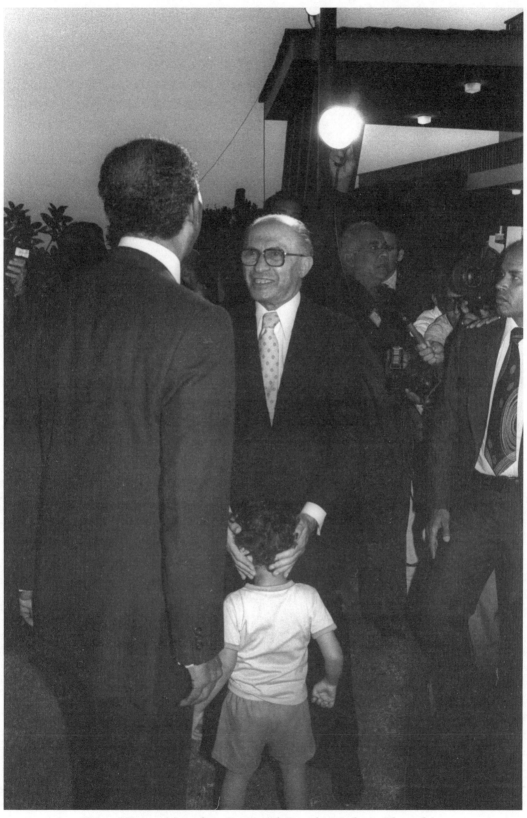

Prime Minister Menachem Begin with President Sadat in Alexandria.
Photographer: Moshe Milner – July 10, 1979

Prime Minister Menachem Begin with President Sadat in Alexandria.
Photographer: Moshe Milner – July 10, 1979

Prime Minister Menachem Begin with Jews in the synagogue in Alexandria.
Photographer: Moshe Milner – July 10, 1979

A representative of the Jewish community in Alexandria welcomes Prime Minister Menachem Begin on his arrival. Photographer: Moshe Milner – July 10, 1979

Prime Minister Menachem Begin meets the people of Alexandria in the street.
Photographer: Moshe Milner – July 10, 1979

Prime Minister Menachem Begin speaks at a dinner held in his honor by President Sadat.
Photographer: Moshe Milner – April 2, 1979

Prime Minister Menachem Begin and President Sadat in a meeting at Aswan.
Photographer: Moshe Milner – January 7, 1980

Prime Minister Menachem Begin caressing Sadat's grandson at Aswan meeting.
Photographer: Moshe Milner – January 7, 1980

Prime Minister Menachem Begin and President Sadat on their way to the helicopter tour
in front of Lake Nasser, a massive reservoir that resulted from construction of the Aswan High Dam.
Photographer: Moshe Milner – October 1, 1980

Prime Minister Menachem Begin and President Sadat at the end of their meeting in Aswan.
In the background: the old Aswan Dam. Photographer: Moshe Milner – October 1, 1980

Prime Minister Menachem Begin with President Sadat in Alexandria.
Photographer: Chanania Herman – August 25, 1981

Prime Minister Menachem Begin at the Tomb of the Unknown Soldier in Alexandria.
Photographer: Chanania Herman – August 25, 1981

Prime Minister Menachem Begin at the Tomb of the Unknown Soldier in Alexandria.
Photographer: Chanania Herman – August 25, 1981

Prime Minister Menachem Begin with President Sadat's family in Alexandria.
Photographer: Chanania Herman – August 25, 1981

Egyptian vice president Hosni Mubarak (left) receives Prime Minister Menachem Begin
after his arrival in Cairo to attend the funeral of the assassinated Egyptian president, Anwar Sadat.
Photographer: Chanania Herman – October 9, 1981

Prime Minister Menachem Begin (left), after his arrival in Cairo to attend the funeral of Anwar Sadat, with the late president's widow Jehan and son Gamal. Photographer: Chanania Herman – October 9, 1981

(Left to right) Prime Minister Menachem Begin and Ministers Yosef Burg, Ariel Sharon, and Yitzhak Shamir, walking from their lodgings in traditional observance of the Shabbat day, to the funeral of assassinated Egyptian president Anwar Sadat. Photographer: Chanania Herman – October 10, 1981

General view of Yamit against the background of palm trees and the Mediterranean Sea.
Photographer: Yaacov Saar – December 12, 1981

General view of Yamit in the last stages of complete demolition.
Photographer: Beni Tel Or – April 22, 1982

PERSONALITIES

Assad, Hafez al- (1930–2000) was the president of Syria from 1971 until his death.

Atherton, Alfred Leroy "Roy" Jr. (1921–2002) was a United States Foreign Service officer and diplomat. He served as United States ambassador to Egypt 1979–1983.

Begin, Menachem (1913–1992), a former commander of the pre-state Irgun resistance movement, was the sixth prime minister of the State of Israel, 1977–1983.

bin Talal, Hussein (1935–1999) was the King of Jordan from 1952 until his death.

Boutros-Ghali, Boutros (1922–) served as Egypt's minister of state for foreign affairs from 1977 until early 1991 and was the sixth secretary-general of the United Nations (UN) from 1992 to 1997.

Carter, James Earl "Jimmy" Jr. (1924–) served as the thirty-ninth president of the United States from 1977 to 1981.

Dayan, Moshe (1915–1981), a former IDF chief of staff (1953–1958), was foreign minister of Israel, 1977–1979.

Gamassy, Mohamed Abdel Ghany, lieutenant general, was chief of staff of Egypt's armed forces.

Khalil, Mustafa (1920–2008) served as the prime minister of Egypt from 1978 to 1980, and also as the Egyptian foreign minister from 1979 until 1980.

Sadat, Muhammad Anwar, or **Anwar al- or el-** (1918–1981) was the third President of Egypt, serving from 1970 until his assassination on October 6, 1981.

Vance, Cyrus Roberts (1917–2002) was the United States secretary of state under President Jimmy Carter from 1977 to 1980.

Weizman, Ezer (1924–2005) was minister of defense of Israel 1977–1980, and later served as the seventh president of Israel, 1993–2000.

APPENDICES

Appendix 1

Speeches in the Knesset Plenum

In order to permit the reader to gain a better comprehension of the atmosphere in which the peace negotiations were conducted within the Israeli political system, the following excerpts from speeches Menachem Begin made in the Knesset chamber were selected.

SITTING 61 OF THE NINTH KNESSET DECEMBER 28, 1977

The Speaker, Yitzhak Shamir: I hereby open the Knesset sitting.... I welcome the prime minister back from the peace mission to Ismailia. I give the floor to the prime minister.

The Prime Minister, Menachem Begin: Mr. Speaker, Knesset Members, once peace is established we propose introducing administrative autonomy for the Arab inhabitants of Judea, Samaria, and the Gaza district, on the basis of the following principles:

The administration of the Military Government in Judea, Samaria, and the Gaza district will be cancelled, to be replaced by administrative autonomy of and for the Arab inhabitants....

The inhabitants of Judea, Samaria, and the Gaza district, irrespective of citizenship, and including those without citizenship, will be given the option of receiving Israeli or Jordanian citizenship.... The inhabitants of those areas who opt for Israeli citizenship will be entitled to vote for and be elected to the Knesset, in accordance with the Elections Law; those who have or opt for Jordanian citizenship will be entitled to vote for and be elected to the parliament of the Hashemite Kingdom of Jordan, in accordance with that country's elections law....

Questions arising from the vote of inhabitants of Judea, Samaria, and the Gaza district to the Jordanian parliament will be clarified by negotiations between Israel and Jordan....

The inhabitants of Israel will be entitled to purchase land and settle in Judea, Samaria, and the Gaza district. The Arab inhabitants of Judea, Samaria, and the Gaza district who have opted for Israeli citizenship will be entitled to purchase land and settle in Israel....

The inhabitants of Israel, Judea, Samaria, and the Gaza district will be assured freedom of movement and economic activity in Israel, Judea, Samaria, and the Gaza district. The Administrative Council will appoint one of its members to represent it before the government of Israel in order to discuss current concerns, and one of its members to represent it before the government of Jordan for the same purpose....

Clause 11 of our plan reads: "Security and public order in Judea, Samaria and the Gaza District will be in the hands of the Israeli authorities." Without that clause there is no significance to the program for administrative autonomy....

Tawfiq Toubi (Democratic Front for Peace and Equality): It is the continuation of the occupation. How can there be peace if the occupation continues...?

Begin: If it were proposed that we withdraw our army from Judea, Samaria, and Gaza, on no account would we allow the murderous organization known as the PLO, the basest organization of murderers in history, apart from the Nazi organizations, to assume control in those areas.... It boasts of the murders it has perpetrated and threatens to solve the problems of the Middle East with one bullet in the heart of President Sadat of Egypt, as its predecessors did in the al-Aqsa Mosque with King Abdullah.... Small wonder that the Egyptian government has said that if that bullet is fired it will reply with a million bullets. We want to say that on no account will that organization be allowed to take control of Judea, Samaria, and Gaza. If we were to withdraw, that is precisely what would happen.

Consequently, let it be clear to anyone who wishes to reach an agreement with us that the IDF will remain in Judea, Samaria, and Gaza and that there will also be other security arrangements, so that all the Jewish and Arab inhabitants of the Land of Israel can live in peace and security....

Clause 24 reads: "Israel insists on its right and claim to sovereignty over Judea, Samaria and the Gaza District. Knowing that there are other claims, it proposes for the sake of the agreement and the peace that the problem of sovereignty in these areas remain open."

I said these things to both President Carter of the US and President Sadat of Egypt. We have the right and the claim to sovereignty over those parts of the Land of Israel. It is our country, and belongs to the Jewish people by right. We want an agreement and peace; we know that there are at least two other claims to sovereignty over those areas. If there is a mutual desire to reach an agreement and bring peace, what is the way to do it? If these conflicting claims remain and there is no answer to the clash between them, there will be no agreement between the sides. Consequently, in order to enable an agreement to be made and peace to be attained, there is only one way: to decide to agree that the question of sovereignty remain open and to deal with people, with nations, namely: the Arabs of the Land of Israel should receive administrative autonomy, and the Jews of the Land of Israel true security. That is the fairness of the content of the proposal, and that is how it was received abroad too....

I went with this peace plan to President Carter of the US. I met with him tête-à-tête and on that occasion as well as during the talks between the US and the Israeli delegations he expressed his positive assessment of the plan....

While I was in the US I asked the secretary of state to inform President Sadat that I wished to consult him, whether in Cairo, a neutral spot, or, if he so wished, in Ismailia. I mentioned Ismailia because when President Sadat visited Jerusalem we spoke of it as a possible meeting place. The president of Egypt informed me via the secretary of state that he had chosen Ismailia as the site of our meeting. I agreed. And so, a few days after the conclusion of my mission to the US and Britain, the meeting in Ismailia took place.

Mr. Speaker, it was a successful meeting. Its success came at its beginning. President Sadat and I held a personal conversation, and the main point – the continuation of the negotiations between the two countries for the attainment of a "peace treaty," rather than the phrase "peace agreement" – was achieved during the first five minutes of the conversation. These negotiations will be held at a high level, the committees being: political, to be situated in Jerusalem, and military, to be situated in Cairo. The chairmen of the committees will be the foreign ministers and ministers of defense of Egypt and Israel. The chairmanship of the committees will alternate: our foreign minister will open the committee meetings in Jerusalem; the Egyptian foreign minister will open the meetings of the military committee in Cairo. One week later the chairmen will rotate. The political committee will deal with the civilian settlements in the Sinai Peninsula, and with what might be termed the Jewish-Arab moral issue of the Arabs of the Land of Israel. The military committee will deal with all the military problems connected with the peace treaty regarding the Sinai Peninsula.

And so, Mr. Speaker, for the first time after almost thirty years, in another two weeks, direct, face-to-face negotiations will begin between accredited, ministerial representatives of Israel, and accredited representatives of Egypt, its foreign minister and minister of defense. No third man shall take the chair at those committees, as was customary in all the meetings between us and the Arab countries, the ministers themselves conducting the meetings and alternating the chairmanship.

The negotiations will be thorough and detailed, focusing on both political and security aspects, so that agreement and a peace treaty may be attained. Because this is happening for the first time since the establishment of the state, for the first time after five wars, for the first time after statements from various sides that the State of Israel must be destroyed, we must welcome this shift and hope and pray that during the weeks or months while the committees are working they will reach agreement, and if there is agreement, that it will serve as a basis for the peace treaty which in this case will be signed by the authorized representatives of Israel and Egypt.

It can be said that at the Ismailia meeting both sides agreed to make a joint statement, but it was not issued because the two delegations did not reach agreement regarding the problem which we, rightly, call the problem of the Arabs of the Land of Israel, and which the Egyptians – as is their right – term the Palestinian problem. We tried, we made a great effort to reach a joint formulation. But it transpired that we could not.… We postponed Sunday's meeting to Monday on the assumption that if both sides made an effort a solution would be found, as was indeed the case.

Agreement of a kind was reached on a joint formula, on the basis of the precedents of international conferences, after we proposed – and this was accepted – that each side should determine its position and use its phraseology. Consequently, the statement regarding the problem of the Arabs of the Land of Israel, as was read out by the president of Egypt at our joint press conference, was in two parts, namely: "The position of Egypt is that a Palestinian state should be established in the West Bank and the Gaza Strip." And the second part: "The Israeli position is that the Palestinian Arabs residing in Judea, Samaria and the Gaza District should enjoy self rule."

Because of the difference on this issue the statement on which there was complete agreement was not published. We did not see fit to press for the publication of a joint communiqué if the Egyptian side said that under those conditions it could not sign it. But I should point out that the actual content was agreed on by both delegations.

Aharon Yadlin (Alignment): What content?

Begin: If it was not published, why should it be published in the Knesset?

…Mr. Speaker, with the completion of the meeting at Ismailia we have done our part. We have given what we can. Henceforth, the ball is in the other court. For peace, for a peace treaty, we have taken upon ourselves a heavy burden of responsibility and risks.…

At this very moment and ever since my return from the US, a difficult and painful discussion has been conducted between my best friends and myself. From this podium I will say, as I told them, that if it has been ordained that I should conduct this argument, I will do it with love. They are my friends. We have gone a long way together, in good times and bad, and I love and respect them, as I will continue to do. But there is no alternative. You have to accept responsibility with the same degree of civil courage without which there are no political decisions.

It is obvious to me that we are taking the right course to enable a peace treaty to be negotiated and signed. After examining all the other courses...I have no doubt that the only way to enable negotiations to be held and a peace treaty to be signed is the one proposed by the government. Consequently, if it is necessary to argue on this issue with dear and close friends, we will do so....

If the routine thinking of officials in the Egyptian Foreign Ministry leads them to assume that they will be able to exert international pressures on us to accept their positions, to which we do not agree and which we will not accept, they are mistaken. We are accustomed to having pressure exerted on us and refusing to give in.... But I am sure that no international pressure will be put on Israel.... The people who praised our peace plan as being fair, constructive, and a breakthrough are very serious men. They are aware of its full content, apart from certain adjustments which do not alter the essence of the plan and which have been brought to the notice of our American friends. This is the plan I brought before President Carter and President Sadat, and they cannot change their minds at the behest of the routine thinkers of the Egyptian Foreign Ministry....

We have today massive moral support throughout the US, both in the administration, in both houses of Congress, and, last but not least, among US public opinion.... That is why the routine thinkers of the Egyptian Foreign Ministry are deluding themselves if they think that we will accept their outdated formulae which are totally divorced from reality if international pressure is brought to bear on us. It will not be brought to bear, and we will continue on our course of bringing peace to the nation in Israel and the Middle East, because that has been my desire not since May or June of 1977 but since November and December of 1947 when, after an interval of peaceful relations between the Arabs and Jews of Palestine, the first shot was fired at a Jew by an Arab, and when I appealed to the Arabs of Palestine from the underground not to shed Jewish blood and to build the country together to the benefit of both peoples. But the bloodshed continued, there were five wars and we want to put an end to them by establishing peace and signing peace treaties.

Toubi: How can the country be built up, how can there be cooperation, when one side wants to suppress the other?

Begin: Is your sitting here an expression of suppression?

Toubi: Don't obscure the issue of a nation which wants independence and its own state.

Begin: Our object, and, I am sure, that of the whole House, with the possible exception of one party group, is to bring peace to this country after having liberated it....

SITTING 71 OF THE NINTH KNESSET JANUARY 23, 1978

The Prime Minister, Menachem Begin: ...[W]hen President Sadat decided to visit the Land of Israel and appeal to the Knesset, and thereby to the entire nation, and in effect to many countries throughout the world, he knew full well what we were and were not prepared to accept.

We met in Jerusalem. In our long talk during the night President Sadat assured me that with regard to the Sinai the Egyptian army would not cross the line of the Gidi and Mitla passes.... To this day there has been no denial of that presidential statement. On the contrary, when we met at Ismailia I repeated that assurance and submitted it to the President in writing. There was complete silence from the other side.... On the basis of that statement we built our peace plan for the Sinai Peninsula.

The distance between the line of the Gidi and Mitla passes and the international border, between the Land of Israel and the Sinai, is between 180 and 200 kilometers. But when General Gamasi gave the demarcation and demilitarization line to the Minister of Defense, Ezer Weizman, it transpired that the Egyptian line was only 40 kilometers from the international border, a difference of between 140 and 160 kilometers.

I must point out that for us that difference is crucial. No verbal acrobatics can change the fact that the Sinai Desert was the basis for aggression against Israel five times in 30 years.... That is why we made up our minds that in any peace treaty between Israel and Egypt the Sinai should be demilitarized. I said as much to President Sadat, and he gave me the assurance I have just cited....

I remember the argument at Yalta about the future of Poland. On one side were the Russians, on the other the US and the British. The Russians convinced the American president by saying that Poland had been an open corridor for Germany's aggression against Russia twice in this generation and several times in the past, and that that corridor had to be closed.... The reference was to an inhabited country, not a desert, and that view was accepted.

No country should be turned into a base for aggression. Five times we fought in the Sinai Desert because Egypt attacked this tiny nation. Particularly in 1948, one day after the proclamation of our independence, when we had virtually no weapons, when our sons had hardly anything with which to defend this small nation, when we were in danger of physical annihilation by the armies that were approaching its heart in the south, the north, and the east; the Egyptian army was only 20 kilometers from Tel Aviv in 1948. We encountered it at Zarnuga; it was situated outside Ramat Rachel, on the southern outskirts of Jerusalem the capital, together with other armies. And we were standing at the edge of the abyss, on the verge of destruction.

All that happened because the Sinai Desert had become what the French call *place d'armes*. On no account will we permit a peace treaty to leave open the possibility of making the Sinai Desert a base for aggression again. I therefore appeal to President Sadat from this podium to instruct the Egyptian army chiefs to submit to us a plan for the demilitarization of the Sinai in accordance with his assurance....

Since the meeting at Ismailia, articles have appeared in the Egyptian press referring to me as "Shylock," in a rabidly anti-Semitic sense.... Peace negotiations are being conducted between us. President Sadat came to the Knesset, stood on this very podium and said that he had come here to knock down the walls of prejudice between us. And in the course of those negotiations one of his aides refers to me in anti-Semitic terms, thereby rebuilding the wall once again....

Elsewhere in the Egyptian press our peace plan has been described as "an invitation to Egypt to commit suicide." The Knesset has been made privy to all the details of the plan. Is it an invitation to Egypt to commit suicide? The object of statements like the one I have just quoted and others, such as the one defining Jews as "a nation of haggling moneylenders" – a phrase we have heard already in our time – is to make the Egyptian nation hate us.… And all this at a time when peace negotiations are being conducted between our two countries.… Voices have even been heard threatening renewed war against Israel.…

On January 14 an interview with President Sadat appeared in the weekly called *October*. I have read it more than once and can only say that it astonished me greatly. I asked myself if this was the same Anwar Sadat who came to us, spoke to us, talked with me until three in the morning, and concluded with the heartwarming words: "You are my friend." What has happened in between? In the interview he accuses us of harboring dishonest and malicious intentions behind the facade of our peace plan.… And all this is embellished with anti-Semitic expressions, in the midst of peace negotiations, after Israel has displayed goodwill.…

Two days ago President Sadat addressed the Egyptian People's Assembly, and said the following, amongst other things: "We have heard official Israeli statements saying that the peace negotiations will take five years." As the House well knows, no one in Israel has said any such thing. We suggested that they should take a few months. Of course time is needed. Important details have to be worked out. Someone chooses to see that as Jewish haggling and arrogance. What is there to haggle over? After all, they must do my bidding because I, the president of Egypt, went to Jerusalem.…

[As President Sadat said in the Egyptian People's Assembly,] "Moreover, they wanted to make that into a national issue within Israel, making use of the psychological makeup of that nation, which immigrated to the Palestinian lands and imposed its existence on it year after year by establishing settlements on it and making it a base for imposing its continued existence." That, it appears, is the history of Zionism: we imposed ourselves on the Palestinian lands.

With all due respect, I would like to say once more to President Sadat that that is not the way things were. We returned to the Land of Israel. We did not take anyone's land away from him. We returned to our land by right. We had to build it, that is true. We had to make the desert bloom, as the Bible says. We returned to it and built it and fought for it by right. That is the true history of Zionism, the liberation movement of the Jewish people.…

President Sadat also said that I apologized for what I said at what is known as the incident at the dinner at the Hilton. There is nothing to be ashamed of in apologizing. It is my conviction that if one makes a mistake, one should apologize. But the point is that I did not apologize, because I had nothing to apologize for. The Egyptian foreign minister came to the Knesset. I welcomed him warmly, of course, as is customary in Israel. I chided him for all those anti-Semitic remarks. I – he apologized to me, particularly for the reference to Shylock. He told me that when he was tried in Egypt in 1956, he was defended by a famous Jewish lawyer, to whom he is grateful to this day. We concluded on a friendly note, saying that each side must refrain from making inflammatory statements that spoil the atmosphere.

The truth is that for ten days we restrained ourselves. As the House will recall, we did not react to the term "Shylock" nor to various other things that were said. We did not argue with Sadat about his interview in *October*.... The Egyptian foreign minister agreed that we would both refrain from making inflammatory statements in the future. It did not occur to me to assure him that I would not make a political speech at the dinner.... It has happened to me on my visits abroad – to the US, Romania, and London, for example – that heads of state said things with which I did not agree. When appropriate, I replied, giving our point of view, as was my right....

What did I say at that dinner? It should be remembered that upon arriving in Lod and after having been welcomed warmly by our foreign minister, the Egyptian foreign minister stated that Israel must withdraw to the borders of June 4, 1967, and give back the Old City of Jerusalem.... It was my national duty to respond to that statement at the appropriate occasion, making it clear that Jerusalem will not be divided again, that we will not withdraw to the borders of June 4, 1967, and that we will not permit the pernicious use of the phrase "the right to national self-defense." I did not apologize. There was nothing to apologize for. No agreement was broken. On the contrary, it was kept. But that is what President Sadat told the Egyptian People's Assembly.... He also claimed that it was arrogance on my part to say that we have never asked Egypt for recognition of our right to exist.

At the conclusion of his address to the Knesset, President Sadat said that he had not come to ask us to withdraw from the Arab land that was occupied in 1967, that it was obvious that Israel would have to withdraw from all of it and that there could be no argument on that point. My reply is that, with all due respect, it is not taken for granted, it is not acceptable to us, and we will give no such undertaking to anyone. We must not give it. We will not mislead anyone, and we have made our position on that score perfectly clear....

The Six-Day War was a defensive war, and as such affords two rights: first, in the absence of a peace treaty, the armed forces remain where they were when the ceasefire came into force or on the basis of signed agreements, and I would like all concerned to understand that no Israeli soldier will move away without there being a peace treaty.... Secondly, it is well known that territorial changes come in the wake of a defensive war. They are legitimate under international law and practice, as we saw occur in Europe after every war. It is true that such changes are subject to a peace treaty, and derive from right rather than might, but the right exists and we will insist on what is rightly ours....

In conclusion, I would like to clarify the government's position regarding the events of the last few days. Without any justification, taking us completely by surprise, President Sadat instructed the political committee to return to Cairo. As the US secretary of state announced, in the negotiations we had progressed to a new joint statement of principles, not the one we had agreed on at Ismailia.... We were then asked to send our delegation, headed by the minister of defense, to Ismailia, to continue the deliberations of the military committee. The government decided to delay the departure of our delegation.

Statements like the ones I have quoted to the House which are being made in Cairo do not create the appropriate atmosphere for Israel's minister of defense, chief of the general staff and senior officers to go there and negotiate.... Our decision also states explicitly that we will resume the talks if the atmosphere improves and the statements that are offensive to the Jewish people and the Jewish state cease.... For it is also our bound duty to defend the honor of the Jewish people.... We respect the Egyptian nation, and did not write or say anything insulting or offensive about it, but we will not brook any disrespect to the Jewish people....

We have left the door wide open for the renewal of the negotiations, within the frameworks of both the military and the political committees, as well as the bilateral relations between Egypt and Israel. If we see that in the next few days there are no further insults, there will be no reason for our military delegation not to go to Cairo and participate in the deliberations of the military committee.

We expressed our views regarding the settlements at Ismailia.... Naturally, we are aware of President Sadat's opposition to the existence of settlements between Rafah and El Arish, and it is his right to oppose them.... At Ismailia I submitted our two-part peace proposal to him, which contained a clause to the effect that the settlements should benefit from our defense, since the experience of our generation has taught us that no Jewish settlement can be left undefended. I added that, just as we respect his principles, we ask him to respect ours....

At Ismailia President Sadat explained to us why he could not accept our viewpoint. That is why negotiations were held. But did they stop at Ismailia because of that Israeli demand? On the contrary, the meeting ended with friendship and understanding and a joint decision to continue negotiations within the framework of the two committees.... There was no ultimatum, no demand; quite the contrary, everything was on an extremely amicable level and concluded with a joint press conference....

Before submitting our peace plan at Ismailia, we showed it to the president, vice president and senior officials of the US, former US president Ford, well-known senators, and the prime minister and foreign minister of Britain. All of them, without exception, were full of praise for it, using such phrases as "there is a great deal of flexibility," "a long step forward," and "a notable contribution," to mention but a few.... That, Mr. Speaker, was the general opinion expressed about Israel's peace plan, and that is what it will remain.

SITTING 145 OF THE NINTH KNESSET SEPTEMBER 25, 1978

The Prime Minister, Menachem Begin: Mr. Speaker, distinguished Knesset –

Geula Cohen (Likud): I call on the prime minister to resign before the Knesset approves the Camp David Accords.

The Speaker, Yitzhak Shamir: Please be quiet. Will the prime minister kindly continue.

Cohen: The commander of the IZL [*Irgun Tzvai Leumi, also known as Etzel, a resistance organization that opposed the British Mandate government*].

Begin: Mr. Speaker, Knesset Members, I bring before the Knesset, and thereby before the entire nation, the tidings of the establishment of peace between Israel and the largest Arab country and, in the course of time, inevitably, with all our neighbors. The documents that were agreed upon at the Camp David conference, and which were signed by me on behalf of the government of Israel –

Cohen: Not on behalf of the nation in Israel.

Begin: – are in front of you. Therefore I will not take up the Knesset's time by reading them. However, I am unable to disclose the contents of two other documents, the Egyptian one that was submitted to President Carter and myself at our first meeting at Camp David on the first day of our talks, and the American one –

Cohen: Why can't you disclose it? Tell the nation.

Begin: – that was submitted to us during the course of the talks –

Cohen: Mr. Prime Minister, tell the nation what's in it. Stop deceiving the nation. [*From the floor:* That's going too far. Have some respect.] I have respect for Israel, not for you....

Begin: Will the Speaker kindly protect me from MK Cohen.

Cohen: I am trying to protect the Land of Israel from the prime minister.... We sent people to die for the Land of Israel....

Begin: ...One day it will be possible to publish the two documents; today it is not, for reasons which I will call psychological-political....

Cohen: You cannot bring a statement of that kind before the nation....

Shamir: MK Cohen, I call you to order.

Cohen: I'm in order. It's the others who aren't.

Shamir: MK Cohen, kindly be quiet.

Cohen: The prime minister has already been removed from this Knesset because –

Shamir: MK Cohen, I call you to order for the second time....

Cohen: The performance isn't here, it was at Camp David. The speaker –

Shamir: I call you to order for the third time.

Cohen: I heard you. I'm telling you that I will not let the prime minister tell the nation things that are deceptive and misleading – I was elected by tens of thousands of Jews to continue – It was not because of Begin that I was elected but because of the love of Israel which Begin once shared....

Shamir: MK Cohen, I am calling you to order for the last time....

Cohen: Settlers have already been removed from the Land of Israel. You can remove me by force from the Knesset too....

Shamir: Under clause 69 of the Knesset rules of procedure the Knesset will vote without a debate on the proposal to remove MK Cohen from the chamber. [*The proposal to remove MK Cohen from the chamber is adopted.*]

Shamir: Will MK Cohen kindly leave the chamber.

Cohen: I'm going. I respect the Knesset. I don't respect the prime minister.... I think that he is bringing us neither peace, security, nor honor. He is bringing the repartition of the Land of Israel. [*MK Cohen leaves the chamber.*]

Begin: ...I realize that at present we are going through a period of what might be called "birth pangs." This is a free nation, with differing views within it. This is a democratic parliament, with different parties, and differences of opinion within parties. But this is one of the major events of our generation. After thirty years, after five wars, bloodshed, bereavement, and orphanhood, we have reached the moment when, by making great sacrifices, we can sign a peace treaty with an Arab nation numbering more than

40 million people. After that there is hope, a basis for believing, that the day is not far off when we will sign a peace treaty with our other neighbors. It is a turning point which can without a doubt be called historic. We pray that our course succeeds and that the peace we all long for comes. We have made every effort and sacrificed as much as we could so that that day may come.

We lay the documents before you. Each one of you must think the matter through, consult his conscience, and vote as he thinks fit. I call on all the Knesset Members, irrespective of party group, to do this. I only ask all the Knesset Members, the representatives of a noble nation which has suffered a great deal, fought a great deal, sacrificed a great deal, to appreciate the moral significance of this turning point. For 30 years we hoped that the moment would come when we would sit down face-to-face to sign a peace treaty, with the complete normalization of relations, the cessation of wars, the assurance of life not only to our generation but to our children and our children's children. This is a great moment....

Mr. Speaker, Knesset Members, at this late hour I do not wish to give a speech, but prefer to talk to friends with whom I have worked for more than 30 years, regardless of party differences, and to this I will add some personal thoughts, for which I beg your indulgence. Why is this night different from all other nights?[1] Because on other nights we fought and signed armistice agreements, yet the state of war remained in force. Because on other days we signed ceasefire agreements, and the state of war remained in force. Because at other times we signed interim agreements; nonetheless the state of war still obtained. But this night we are discussing the signing of a peace treaty, the first sentence of which will read: "The state of war between Egypt and Israel is terminated." That is the first sentence of all peace treaties.

I would like to tell the entire House that we are fortunate in having lived to see this night. For the first time since the establishment of the state one of our neighbors will announce publicly that the state of war between us is terminated....

---

1. A reference to the wording of the Passover Haggadah.

I would like to say that in my 50 years of service to the nation and Zionism my belief in the justice of Zionism has not become weaker by a single iota....

But to get to the main point, Camp David.... For twelve days and nights we explained incessantly to the American president and all his aides how vital the settlements were in security and moral terms, and how right former governments had been to establish them. President Carter was convinced and tried to persuade President Sadat, and I would like to thank President Carter for that.... He tried twice and encountered complete rejection.... I consulted our team, and we found ourselves unable to agree to remove the settlements, both because we believed that they should remain and because ours is a parliamentary, not a presidential, regime, and our task is to implement the policy that the Knesset has decided to undertake.... But in that case the Camp David talks would have failed, no agreement would have been signed, the Egyptians would have returned to Cairo, we would have come back to Jerusalem, and the Americans would have gone to Washington.

But as prime minister I knew in my heart of hearts that if Israel was responsible for the breakdown of the talks it would find itself up against America, Europe, US Jewry and world Jewry.... I know what it is to withstand pressure. I have no need to brag.... During the past nine months hardly a single newspaper in Israel or the world has had one good word to say about me.... That pressure had no effect, however.... But I knew that if Camp David collapsed, Israel would stand alone and would eventually have to submit, of that I am convinced....

And so, it was my responsibility. I proposed a third approach to my colleagues, neither saying yes nor no, but agreeing to bring the subject before the Knesset for its decision....

The choice before the House is, then, whether to embark on peace negotiations, with the attendant dismantling of the settlements, or not. There is no third possibility.... As someone with a sense of responsibility, it is my duty to tell the House that this is the only practical way of attaining a peace treaty for the first time in 30 years. The peace treaty is virtually ready. What has been agreed concerning the bilateral relations between Egypt and

Israel is almost the entire peace treaty.... If you decide that the settlements should remain, all our efforts at Camp David will have been for nothing and the peace treaty will be lost....

Settlements are very dear to me.... I make no distinction between party affiliation when it comes to settlements. Everyone knows that I love each individual settler.... But as prime minister it is my duty to think of the consequences of this decision, when I know that a peace treaty is in our grasp. In making my calculations I am thinking of the sons of those settlers who will have to be uprooted. Those sons will not have to fall in battle, because we will have peace.... For it is the duty of a prime minister to see to it that there is no more bloodshed, no more orphans and widows and bereaved parents, and that has been my approach throughout the decades of service to the nation, not since 1967 but since 1947....

For four and a half years we fought against the British, and not one Arab injured any Jew, but after the UN resolution the clashes began, with the first casualties.... Since then no one in Israel has wanted peace more than myself. This is a confession.... For 31 years this man has dreamed of peace with the Arabs, has respected the Arabs and extended his hand to them, calling on them to build this country together and cease the bloodshed. Now the opportunity is within our reach, the document is all but ready, it just needs some minor revisions, and then, who knows, perhaps then the biblical verse "and the land had rest 40 years" will be fulfilled. A prime minister has a duty to concern himself with such things, does he not?

And so, I had no choice. Those who abstain may have a choice. I had to decide, together with my colleagues.... The peace treaty was on one side of the scales and the settlements on the other. According to every moral code to which I subscribe, the scales tipped on the side of the peace treaty. There is no other way. With the pain, the insults, the shouts – no other way. To my dying day I will believe that this is the right choice. For the entire nation, for the people living in the Rafah area, it is the right choice. We made a proviso that the period must be fixed by an agreement between the two sides. After the peace treaty has been signed, over a period of between three and nine months, we must withdraw with our forces to the Ras Muhammad–El Arish line, where we will remain for another two years. We have time to think about everything and do everything. But one thing must be clear: it is a clear cut decision that we are making today. We will not delude anyone. If the Knesset so decides, the decision will be implemented....

The Egyptians have asked us, via our friends the Americans, to appoint a delegation without delay to be in direct contact with them, so that negotiations on a peace treaty may begin forthwith.... I suggest that the House does not wait or impose delays, but works quickly and makes a clear-cut decision, as the government has requested.... Once the decision has been made and the negotiations for a peace treaty begin, we will examine every eventuality by means of the Knesset's Foreign Affairs and Defense Committee. I would be grateful if you were to heed my advice.... I beseech each and every one, for God's sake, vote as you wish but let a clear-cut decision be made by the majority in the Knesset so that tomorrow we can begin the work of preparing the negotiations and, God willing, sign a peace treaty....

It is three a.m. It is enough.... In the wake of that confession I want to say: the nation is in the throes of birth pangs. It is true to say that everything that is great is born through suffering. The greatest miracle in the universe – the birth of a baby – is accompanied by pain. What we are talking about here is the greatest turning point in the Middle East, the possibility of signing a peace treaty between Israel and Egypt. I am not surprised by the pains. I am not complaining about the demonstrations, though I would prefer it if they were not held at night as my neighbors suffer, their children suffer.... But I forgive everything, because there is pain.

Peace is born, first and foremost, of our blood. For this peace we have sacrificed 12,000 of our best boys, in five wars, one war after another, one battlefield after another. We want to put an end to that. This is the opportunity, this is the chance. I do not know what difficulties still lie ahead of us, but it is evident that this is the opportunity.... We want to preserve the lives of our children, who are the apples of our eyes, and the lives of our grandchildren. We don't want there to be war every five years. Can anyone be blamed for the fact that we have to make sacrifices? Can we be accused of making concessions on those grounds?

I do not think so, because this is something we all want, something in which we all believe. One-third of our nation has been lost in this generation – 12,000 of our best, most heroic and sacred boys; bereaved families; tears, pain, and sorrow –we want to put an end to that. This is the moment. Now is the hour. That is why this is such a great moment and why I appeal to all the Members of the Knesset, irrespective of party group, to unite around the chance of peace, adopt the proposal and begin discussions. Perhaps, God willing, within the next year we will be able to say that peace has come to Israel....

THE VOTE
Those in favor: 84
Those against: 19
Abstentions: 17

[The coalition proposal that the Knesset approve the Camp David agreements, authorizing the government to resolve all the attendant problems, dismantle the settlements in the Sinai, and resettle their inhabitants, if this is necessitated by the peace negotiations between Egypt and Israel, which should be reflected by a written document, is adopted.]

Appendix 2

Text of Camp David Accords
September 17, 1978

THE FRAMEWORK FOR PEACE
IN THE MIDDLE EAST

Muhammad Anwar al-Sadat, President of the Arab Republic of Egypt, and Menachem Begin, Prime Minister of Israel, met with Jimmy Carter, President of the United States of America, at Camp David from September 5 to September 17, 1978, and have agreed on the following framework for peace in the Middle East. They invite other parties to the Arab-Israel conflict to adhere to it.

PREAMBLE

The search for peace in the Middle East must be guided by the following:

- The agreed basis for a peaceful settlement of the conflict between Israel and its neighbors is United Nations Security Council Resolution 242, in all its parts.

- After four wars during 30 years, despite intensive human efforts, the Middle East, which is the cradle of civilization and the birthplace of three great religions, does not enjoy the blessings of peace. The people of the Middle East yearn for peace so that the vast human and natural resources of the region can be turned to the pursuits of peace and so that this area can become a model for coexistence and cooperation among nations.

- The historic initiative of President Sadat in visiting Jerusalem and the reception accorded to him by the parliament, government and people of Israel, and the reciprocal visit of Prime Minister Begin to Ismailia, the peace proposals made by both leaders, as well as the warm reception of these missions by the peoples of both countries, have created an unprecedented opportunity for peace which must not be lost if this generation and future generations are to be spared the tragedies of war.

- The provisions of the Charter of the United Nations and the other accepted norms of international law and legitimacy now provide accepted standards for the conduct of relations among all states.

- To achieve a relationship of peace, in the spirit of Article 2 of the United Nations Charter, future negotiations between Israel and any neighbor prepared to negotiate peace and security with it are necessary for the purpose of carrying out all the provisions and principles of Resolutions 242 and 338.

- Peace requires respect for the sovereignty, territorial integrity and political independence of every state in the area and their right to live in peace within secure and recognized boundaries free from threats or acts of force. Progress toward that goal can accelerate movement toward a new era of reconciliation in the Middle East marked by cooperation in promoting economic development, in maintaining stability and in assuring security.

- Security is enhanced by a relationship of peace and by cooperation between nations which enjoy normal relations. In addition, under the terms of peace treaties, the parties can, on the basis of reciprocity, agree to special security arrangements such as demilitarized zones, limited armaments areas, early warning stations, the presence of international forces, liaison, agreed measures for monitoring and other arrangements that they agree are useful.

FRAMEWORK

Taking these factors into account, the parties are determined to reach a just, comprehensive, and durable settlement of the Middle East conflict through the conclusion of peace treaties based on Security Council resolutions 242 and 338 in all their parts. Their purpose is to achieve peace and good neighborly relations. They recognize that for peace to endure, it must involve all those who have been most deeply affected by the conflict. They therefore agree that this framework, as appropriate, is intended by them to constitute a basis for peace not only between Egypt and Israel, but also between Israel and each of its other neighbors which is prepared to negotiate peace with Israel on this basis. With that objective in mind, they have agreed to proceed as follows:

A. West Bank and Gaza

1. Egypt, Israel, Jordan and the representatives of the Palestinian people should participate in negotiations on the resolution of the Palestinian problem in all its aspects. To achieve that objective, negotiations relating to the West Bank and Gaza should proceed in three stages:

   a. Egypt and Israel agree that, in order to ensure a peaceful and orderly transfer of authority, and taking into account the security concerns of all the parties, there should be transitional arrangements for the West Bank and Gaza for a period not exceeding five years. In order to provide full autonomy to the inhabitants, under these arrangements the Israeli military government and its civilian administration will be withdrawn as soon as a self-governing authority has been freely elected by the inhabitants of these areas to replace the existing military government. To negotiate the details of a transitional arrangement, Jordan will be invited to join the negotiations on the basis of this framework. These new arrangements should give due consideration both to the principle of self-government by the inhabitants of these territories and to the legitimate security concerns of the parties involved.

   b. Egypt, Israel, and Jordan will agree on the modalities for establishing elected self-governing authority in the West Bank and Gaza. The delegations of Egypt and Jordan may include Palestinians from the West Bank and Gaza or other Palestinians as mutually agreed. The parties will negotiate an agreement which will define the powers and responsibilities of the self-governing authority to be exercised in the West Bank and Gaza. A withdrawal of Israeli armed forces will take place and there will be a redeployment of the remaining Israeli forces into specified security locations. The agreement will also include arrangements for assuring internal and external security and public order. A strong local police force will be established, which may include Jordanian citizens. In addition, Israeli and Jordanian forces will participate in joint patrols and in the manning of control posts to assure the security of the borders.

c. When the self-governing authority (administrative council) in the West Bank and Gaza is established and inaugurated, the transitional period of five years will begin. As soon as possible, but not later than the third year after the beginning of the transitional period, negotiations will take place to determine the final status of the West Bank and Gaza and its relationship with its neighbors and to conclude a peace treaty between Israel and Jordan by the end of the transitional period. These negotiations will be conducted among Egypt, Israel, Jordan and the elected representatives of the inhabitants of the West Bank and Gaza. Two separate but related committees will be convened, one committee, consisting of representatives of the four parties which will negotiate and agree on the final status of the West Bank and Gaza, and its relationship with its neighbors, and the second committee, consisting of representatives of Israel and representatives of Jordan to be joined by the elected representatives of the inhabitants of the West Bank and Gaza, to negotiate the peace treaty between Israel and Jordan, taking into account the agreement reached in the final status of the West Bank and Gaza. The negotiations shall be based on all the provisions and principles of UN Security Council Resolution 242. The negotiations will resolve, among other matters, the location of the boundaries and the nature of the security arrangements. The solution from the negotiations must also recognize the legitimate right of the Palestinian peoples and their just requirements. In this way, the Palestinians will participate in the determination of their own future through:

i.   The negotiations among Egypt, Israel, Jordan and the representatives of the inhabitants of the West Bank and Gaza to agree on the final status of the West Bank and Gaza and other outstanding issues by the end of the transitional period.

ii. Submitting their agreements to a vote by the elected representatives of the inhabitants of the West Bank and Gaza.

iii. Providing for the elected representatives of the inhabitants of the West Bank and Gaza to decide how they shall govern themselves consistent with the provisions of their agreement.

iv. Participating as stated above in the work of the committee negotiating the peace treaty between Israel and Jordan.

2. All necessary measures will be taken and provisions made to assure the security of Israel and its neighbors during the transitional period and beyond. To assist in providing such security, a strong local police force will be constituted by the self-governing authority. It will be composed of inhabitants of the West Bank and Gaza. The police will maintain liaison on internal security matters with the designated Israeli, Jordanian, and Egyptian officers.

3. During the transitional period, representatives of Egypt, Israel, Jordan, and the self-governing authority will constitute a continuing committee to decide by agreement on the modalities of admission of persons displaced from the West Bank and Gaza in 1967, together with necessary measures to prevent disruption and disorder. Other matters of common concern may also be dealt with by this committee.

4. Egypt and Israel will work with each other and with other interested parties to establish agreed procedures for a prompt, just and permanent implementation of the resolution of the refugee problem.

B. Egypt-Israel

1. Egypt-Israel undertake not to resort to the threat or the use of force to settle disputes. Any disputes shall be settled by peaceful means in accordance with the provisions of Article 33 of the U.N. Charter.

2. In order to achieve peace between them, the parties agree to negotiate in good faith with a goal of concluding within three months from the signing of the Framework a peace treaty between them while inviting the other parties to the conflict to proceed simultaneously to negotiate and conclude similar peace treaties with a view to achieving a comprehensive peace in the area. The Framework for the Conclusion of a Peace Treaty between Egypt and Israel will govern the peace negotiations between them. The parties will agree on the modalities and the timetable for the implementation of their obligations under the treaty.

C. Associated Principles

1. Egypt and Israel state that the principles and provisions described below should apply to peace treaties between Israel and each of its neighbors – Egypt, Jordan, Syria and Lebanon.

2. Signatories shall establish among themselves relationships normal to states at peace with one another. To this end, they should undertake to abide by all the provisions of the U.N. Charter. Steps to be taken in this respect include:

   a. full recognition;

   b. abolishing economic boycotts;

   c. guaranteeing that under their jurisdiction the citizens of the other parties shall enjoy the protection of the due process of law.

3. Signatories should explore possibilities for economic development in the context of final peace treaties, with the objective of contributing to the atmosphere of peace, cooperation and friendship which is their common goal.

4. Claims commissions may be established for the mutual settlement of all financial claims.

5. The United States shall be invited to participated in the talks on matters related to the modalities of the implementation of the agreements and working out the timetable for the carrying out of the obligations of the parties.

6. The United Nations Security Council shall be requested to endorse the peace treaties and ensure that their provisions shall not be violated. The permanent members of the Security Council shall be requested to underwrite the peace treaties and ensure respect or the provisions. They shall be requested to conform their policies an actions with the undertaking contained in this Framework.

> For the Government of the Arab Republic of Egypt:
> [Muhammad Anwar el-Sadat]

> For the Government of Israel:
> [Menachem Begin]

> Witnessed by:
> Jimmy Carter,
> President of the United States of America

FRAMEWORK FOR THE CONCLUSION OF A PEACE TREATY BETWEEN EGYPT AND ISRAEL

In order to achieve peace between them, Israel and Egypt agree to negotiate in good faith with a goal of concluding within three months of the signing of this framework a peace treaty between them:

It is agreed that:

- The site of the negotiations will be under a United Nations flag at a location or locations to be mutually agreed.

- All of the principles of U.N. Resolution 242 will apply in this resolution of the dispute between Israel and Egypt.

- Unless otherwise mutually agreed, terms of the peace treaty will be implemented between two and three years after the peace treaty is signed.

  The following matters are agreed between the parties:

1. the full exercise of Egyptian sovereignty up to the internationally recognized border between Egypt and mandated Palestine;

2. the withdrawal of Israeli armed forces from the Sinai;

3. the use of airfields left by the Israelis near al-Arish, Rafah, Ras en-Naqb, and Sharm el-Sheikh for civilian purposes only, including possible commercial use only by all nations;

4. the right of free passage by ships of Israel through the Gulf of Suez and the Suez Canal on the basis of the Constantinople Convention of 1888 applying to all nations; the Strait of Tiran and Gulf of Aqaba are international waterways to be open to all nations for unimpeded and nonsuspendable freedom of navigation and overflight;

5. the construction of a highway between the Sinai and Jordan near Eilat with guaranteed free and peaceful passage by Egypt and Jordan; and

6. the stationing of military forces listed below.

STATIONING OF FORCES

- No more than one division (mechanized or infantry) of Egyptian armed forces will be stationed within an area lying approximately 50 km. (30 miles) east of the Gulf of Suez and the Suez Canal.

- Only United Nations forces and civil police equipped with light weapons to perform normal police functions will be stationed within an area lying west of the international border and the Gulf of Aqaba, varying in width from 20 km. (12 miles) to 40 km. (24 miles).

- In the area within 3 km. (1.8 miles) east of the international border there will be Israeli limited military forces not to exceed four infantry battalions and United Nations observers.

- Border patrol units not to exceed three battalions will supplement the civil police in maintaining order in the area not included above.

- The exact demarcation of the above areas will be as decided during the peace negotiations.

- Early warning stations may exist to insure compliance with the terms of the agreement.

- United Nations forces will be stationed:
    1. in part of the area in the Sinai lying within about 20 km. of the Mediterranean Sea and adjacent to the international border, and
    2. in the Sharm el-Sheikh area to insure freedom of passage through the Strait of Tiran; and these forces will not be removed unless such removal is approved by the Security Council of the United Nations with a unanimous vote of the five permanent members.

- After a peace treaty is signed, and after the interim withdrawal is complete, normal relations will be established between Egypt and Israel, including full recognition, including diplomatic, economic and cultural relations; termination of economic boycotts and barriers to the free movement of goods and people; and mutual protection of citizens by the due process of law.

INTERIM WITHDRAWAL

Between three months and nine months after the signing of the peace treaty, all Israeli forces will withdraw east of a line extending from a point east of El Arish to Ras Muhammad, the exact location of this line to be determined by mutual agreement.

> For the Government of the Arab Republic of Egypt:
> [Muhammad Anwar el-Sadat]

> For the Government of Israel:
> [Menachem Begin]

> Witnessed by:
> Jimmy Carter,
> President of the United States of America

ACCOMPANYING LETTERS

ON JERUSALEM

Begin to Carter
The President
Camp David
Thurmont, Maryland

September 17, 1978

Dear Mr. President,

I have the honor to inform you, Mr. President, that on 28 June 1967 – Israel's Parliament (The Knesset) promulgated and adopted a law to the effect: "the Government is empowered by a decree to apply the law, the jurisdiction and administration of the State to any part of Eretz Israel (Land of Israel – Palestine), as stated in that decree."

On the basis of this law the Government of Israel decreed in July 1967 that Jerusalem is one city indivisible, the capital of the State of Israel.

> Sincerely,
> (signed)
> Menachem Begin

Sadat to Carter
His Excellency Jimmy Carter
President of the United States

September 17, 1978

Dear Mr. President,

I am writing you to reaffirm the position of the Arab
Republic of Egypt with respect to Jerusalem:

1. Arab Jerusalem is an integral part of the West
Bank. Legal and historical Arab rights in the City must
be respected and restored.

2. Arab Jerusalem should be under Arab sovereignty.

3. The Palestinian inhabitants of Arab Jerusalem are
entitled to exercise their legitimate national rights,
being part of the Palestinian People in the West Bank.

4. Relevant Security Council resolutions, particularly
Resolutions 242 and 267, must be applied with regard to
Jerusalem. All the measures taken by Israel to alter
the status of the City are null and void and should be
rescinded.

5. All peoples must have free access to the City and
enjoy the free exercise of worship and the right to visit
and transit to the holy places without distinction or
discrimination.

6. The holy places of each faith may be placed under
the administration and control of their representatives.

7. Essential functions in the City should be undivided
and a joint municipal council composed of an equal number
of Arab and Israeli members can supervise the carrying
out of these functions. In this way, the City shall be
undivided.

Sincerely,
(signed)
Mohamed Anwar El Sadat

Carter to Sadat

His Excellency
Anwar Al-Sadat
President of the Arab Republic of Egypt
Cairo

September 22, 1978

Dear Mr. President:

I have received your letter of September 17, 1978, setting forth the Egyptian position on Jerusalem. I am transmitting a copy of that letter to Prime Minister Begin for his information.

The position of the United States on Jerusalem remains as stated by Ambassador Goldberg in the United Nations General Assembly on July 14, 1967, and subsequently by Ambassador Yost in the United Nations Security Council on July 1, 1969.[1]

Sincerely,
(signed)
Jimmy Carter

ON SINAI SETTLEMENTS

Begin to Carter

The President
Camp David
Thurmont, Maryland

September 17, 1978

Dear Mr. President:

I have the honor to inform you that during two weeks after my return home I will submit a motion before Israel's Parliament (the Knesset) to decide on the following question:

If during the negotiations to conclude a peace treaty between Israel and Egypt all outstanding issues are agreed upon, "are you in favor of the removal of the

---

1. These statements are reproduced below.

Israeli settlers from the northern and southern Sinai areas or are you in favor of keeping the aforementioned settlers in those areas?"

The vote, Mr. President, on this issue will be completely free from the usual Parliamentary Party discipline to the effect that although the coalition is being now supported by 70 members out of 120, every member of the Knesset, as I believe, both on the Government and the Opposition benches will be enabled to vote in accordance with his own conscience.

Sincerely,
(signed)
Menachem Begin

Sadat to Carter

His Excellency Jimmy Carter
President of the United States

September 17, 1978

Dear Mr. President,

In connection with the "Framework for a Settlement in Sinai" to be signed tonight, I would like to reaffirm the position of the Arab Republic of Egypt with respect to the settlements:

1. All Israeli settlers must be withdrawn from Sinai according to a timetable within the period specified for the implementation of the peace treaty.

2. Agreement by the Israeli Government and its constitutional institutions to this basic principle is therefore a prerequisite to starting peace negotiations for concluding a peace treaty.

3. If Israel fails to meet this commitment, the "Framework" shall be void and invalid.

Sincerely,
(signed)
Mohamed Anwar El Sadat

Carter to Begin

His Excellency
Menachem Begin
Prime Minister of Israel

September 22, 1978

Dear Mr. President:

I have received your letter of September 17, 1978, describing how you intend to place the question of the future of Israeli settlements in Sinai before the Knesset for its decision.

Enclosed is a copy of President Sadat's letter to me on this subject.

Sincerely,
(signed)
Jimmy Carter

Enclosure: Letter from President Sadat

Carter to Sadat

His Excellency
Anwar Al-Sadat
President of the Arab Republic of Egypt
Cairo

September 22, 1978

Dear Mr. President:

I transmit herewith a copy of a letter to me from Prime Minister Begin setting forth how he proposes to present the issue of the Sinai settlements to the Knesset for the latter's decision.

In this connection, I understand from your letter that Knesset approval to withdraw all Israeli settlers from Sinai according to a timetable within the period specified for the implementation of the peace treaty is

a prerequisite to any negotiations on a peace treaty
between Egypt and Israel.

> Sincerely,
> (signed)
> Jimmy Carter

Enclosure: Letter from Prime Minister Begin

IMPLEMENTATION OF COMPREHENSIVE SETTLEMENT

Sadat to Carter

His Excellency
Jimmy Carter
President of the United States
The White House
Washington, D.C.

September 17, 1978

Dear Mr. President,

In connection with the "Framework for Peace in the Middle East," I am writing you this letter to inform you of the position of the Arab Republic of Egypt, with respect to the implementation of the comprehensive settlement.

To ensure the implementation of the provisions related to the West Bank and Gaza and in order to safeguard the legitimate rights of the Palestinian people, Egypt will be prepared to assume the Arab role emanating from these provisions, following consultations with Jordan and the representatives of the Palestinian people.

> Sincerely,
> (signed)
> Mohamed Anwar El Sadat

Carter to Begin
His Excellency
Menachem Begin
Prime Minister of Israel

September 22, 1978

Dear Mr. Prime Minister:

I hereby acknowledge that you have informed me as follows:

A. In each paragraph of the Agreed Framework Document the expressions "Palestinians" or "Palestinian People" are being and will be construed and understood by you as "Palestinian Arabs."

B. In each paragraph in which the expression "West Bank" appears, it is being, and will be, understood by the Government of Israel as Judea and Samaria.

Sincerely,
(signed)
Jimmy Carter

STATEMENT REGARDING US POSITION ON JERUSALEM

Statement by Ambassador Arthur J. Goldberg, US representative to the United Nations, in plenary session, in explanation of the vote on the resolution on Jerusalem, July 14, 1967.

Mr. President, the goal of the United States in the Middle East, one we believe shared by the great preponderance of the world community, is a durable peace and enduring settlement. We conceive of this goal as requiring throughout the area far more than a return to the temporary and fragile truce which erupted into tragic conflict on June 5.

We are convinced, both by logic and the unforgettable experience of a tragic history, that there can be progress toward the durable peace in the entire area only if certain essential steps are taken. One immediate, obvious and imperative step is the disengagement of all forces and the withdrawal of Israeli forces to their own territory. A second and equally immediate, obvious and imperative step is the termination of any claims to a state of war or belligerence on the part of Arab states in the area.

These two steps are essential to progress toward a durable peace. They are equally essential if there is to be substance and concrete meaning to the basic charter right of every state in the area, a right to which the United States remains firmly committed: the right to have its territorial integrity and political independence respected by all and free from the threat or use of force by all.

The United States stands ready to give its full support to practical measures to help bring about these steps – withdrawal of forces and the termination of belligerent acts or claims as soon as possible.

But if our goal is a durable peace, it is imperative that there be greater vision both from this organization and from the parties themselves. It is imperative that all look beyond the immediate causes and effects of the recent conflict. Attention must also be focused, and urgently:

- on reaching a just and permanent settlement of the refugee problem, which has been accentuated by recent events;

- on means to ensure respect for the right of every member of the United Nations in the area to live in peace and security as an independent national state;

- on arrangements so that respect for the territorial integrity and political independence of all states in the area is assured;

- on measures to ensure respect for the rights of all nations to freedom of navigation and of innocent passage through international waterways;

- on reaching agreement, both among those in the area and those outside, that economic development and the improvement of living standards should be given precedence over a wasteful arms race in the area.

In each and every one of the separate but related imperatives of peace, we recognize fully that agreement cannot be imposed upon the parties from outside. At the same time, we also believe that the machinery, experience and resources of the United Nations can be of immeasurable help in implementing agreements acceptable to the parties.

The offer of such assistance by this organization is dictated not only by the roots of United Nations responsibility and involvement in the Middle East, which have grown deep and strong over two decades, it is also dictated by our common determination, even duty, under the charter to save succeeding generations in the Middle East from the scourge of another war.

It is against the background of this overall policy that my Government has developed its attitudes toward the question of Jerusalem – and I wish to make that attitude very explicit. The views of my government on Jerusalem have been expressed by the President of the United States and other high level officials.

On June 28, the White House released the following statement:

The President said on June 19 that in our view "there must be adequate recognition of the special interest of three great religions in the holy places of Jerusalem." On this principle he assumes that before any unilateral action is taken on the status of Jerusalem there will be appropriate consultation with religious leaders and others who are deeply concerned. Jerusalem is holy to Christians, to Jews, and to Moslems. It is one of the great continuing tragedies of history that a city which is so much the center of man's highest values has also been, over and over, a center of conflict. Repeatedly the passionate beliefs of one element have led to exclusion or unfairness for others. It has been so, unfortunately, in the last 20 years. Men of all religions will agree that we must now do better. The world must find an answer that is fair and recognized to be fair....

The second statement, released on the same day by the Department of State, read:

The hasty administrative action taken today cannot be regarded as determining the future of the places or the status of Jerusalem in relation to them.

The United States has never recognized such unilateral actions by any of the states in the area as governing the international status of Jerusalem....

During my own statement to the General Assembly on July 3, I said that the "safeguarding of the holy places and freedom of access to them for all, should be internationally guaranteed; and the status of Jerusalem in relation to them should be decided not unilaterally but in consultation with all concerned." These statements represent the considered and continuing policy of the United States Government.

With regard to the specific measures taken by the Government of Israel on June 28, I wish to make it clear that the United States does not accept or recognize these measures as altering the status of Jerusalem. My Government does not recognize that the administrative measures taken by the Government of Israel on June 28 can be regarded as the last word on the matter, and we regret that they were taken. We insist that the measures taken cannot be considered other than interim and provisional, and not prejudging the final and permanent status of Jerusalem. Unfortunately and regrettably, the statements of the Government of Israel on this matter have thus far, in our view, not adequately dealt with this situation.

Many delegations are aware that we were prepared to vote for a separate resolution on Jerusalem which would declare that the Assembly would not accept any unilateral action as determining the status of Jerusalem and calling on the Government of Israel to desist from any action purporting to define permanently the status of Jerusalem. However, the sponsors made clear then, as was their right, that they preferred to proceed with their own text in document A/2253, and now with their resolution in A/L. 528/ Rev. 2. The latter draft does include changes which we consider represent a marked improvement over the original version, particularly in that it no longer tends to prejudge action in the Security Council. Nevertheless, since the resolution just adopted expressly builds on Resolution 2253, on which we abstained for reasons which we stated publicly, consistent with that vote we also abstained today.

Even as revised, the resolution does not fully correspond to our views, particularly since it appears to accept by its call for recision of measures that the administrative measures which were taken constitute annexation of Jerusalem by Israel, and because we do not believe the problem of Jerusalem can realistically be solved apart from the other related aspects of Jerusalem and of the Middle Eastern situation. Therefore, the United States abstained.

We have, of course, recently expressed ourselves in a more formal sense by voting for a resolution dealing with the question of Jerusalem. This was the Latin American Resolution contained in document A/L. 523/Rev. 1, which dealt with Jerusalem as one of the elements involved in a peaceful settlement in the Middle East.

It is in the treatment of one aspect of the problem of Jerusalem as an isolated issue, separate from the other elements of Jerusalem and of a peaceful settlement in the Middle East, that we were unable to support Resolution 2253. Certainly, Jerusalem, as has been pointed out universally, I think, by every speaker, is an important issue and, in our opinion, one which must necessarily be considered in the context of a settlement of all problems arising out of the recent conflict. In Jerusalem there are transcendent spiritual interests. But there are also other important issues. And we believe that the most fruitful approach to a discussion of the future of Jerusalem lies in dealing with the entire problem as one aspect of the broader arrangements that must be made to restore a just and durable peace in the area. And we believe, consistent with the resolution we were ready to sponsor, that this Assembly should have dealt with the problem by declaring itself against any unilateral change in the status of Jerusalem.

Mr. President, since we are approaching the end of this session on this important subject, in which remarks were made not relating specifically to Jerusalem but ranging very broadly on other subjects, I cannot let this occasion pass without reference to some of the allegations made regarding my Government's role in the recent conflict in the Middle East. The charges that the United States instigated, encouraged, or in any way participated in this tragic struggle are too unfounded to dignify by individual comment. I dealt with many of these falsehoods explicitly in the Security Council and will not take the time of the Assembly to go over the same ground here. I reaffirm what I said to the Security Council with respect to each and every one of these charges.

I will merely say that one positive note in this session has been the abandonment of the most vicious falsehood of all – which could have been productive of the most disastrous consequences – that the United States planes and military personnel participated in the war on the side of Israel. Before the war broke out we sought to prevent it by all means at our command. And once it began, we did everything in our power to bring it to an early end. The record of our diplomacy is very clear in this matter, despite comments which have been read from newspapers which scarcely characterize that diplomacy. And the record of the Security Council is plain and clear for everyone to read as to the actions we took, supported, and initiated in the Security Council to bring the conflict to an end.

There is one charge about our position to which I believe no nation in this hall faithful to the charter would feel any necessity to plead. That is the charge that we supported the right of every sovereign state member of the United Nations to an independent national existence, its right to live in a spirit of peaceful coexistence and good neighborliness with all in the area. That is a charge which the charter of the United Nations places on us all and which we should all readily accept and acknowledge.

Our view has remained steadfast – before, during, and now after the conflict. We extend the hand of friendship to all states in the Middle East and express the fervent hope that as time heals the scars of war, we can soon again join our common efforts in helping build a better, more enduring order in every state and throughout the area, with peace, justice, security, and liberty for all.

Mr. President, so much vituperation has taken place in this Assembly, so unseemly in a world forum, that I could not help recalling today a statement made by my distinguished predecessor, who died two years ago today in the cause of peace, Adlai Stevenson. Adlai Stevenson, talking about our beloved Eleanor Roosevelt, said, "She would rather light a candle than curse the darkness." And I share that spirit. I do not see that anything is gained in the cause of peace in the Middle East by the vituperation which has taken place, vituperation not only against my country but against other, small countries, vituperation which has no place in this forum.

The time has come – indeed, the time is long overdue – for vituperation and bitterness to be tempered by sober realization of the difficulties ahead and the willingness to face them squarely and to do something about them.

What is needed is the wisdom and statesmanship of all those directly concerned and the members of the United Nations so that conditions of hate, too much ventilated in this hall, can be eventually replaced by conditions of good neighborliness.

What is needed, above all, in the area is a spirit of reconciliation which will someday hopefully make possible a peace of reconciliation. I fervently hope that all in the area and all in this hall will approach the days ahead in this spirit.

STATEMENT REGARDING US POSITION ON SITUATION IN JERUSALEM

Statement by Ambassador Charles W. Yost, US Representative to the United Nations, in the Security Council, on the situation in Jerusalem, July 1, 1969:

Once again the Council has been summoned to deal with certain actions taken by the Government of Israel in Jerusalem. We have listened carefully to the statements of the representatives of Jordan and several other Arab states, as well as to the reply of the representative of Israel.

The discussion thus far has made amply clear that the status of Jerusalem is not an isolated problem, but, rather, an integral part of a whole complex of issues in the current Middle Eastern conflict which must be resolved. This is not a novel conclusion. The Council clearly recognized that fact in Resolution 242, which treats the entire Middle Eastern situation as a package. This resolution remains the basis of our approach to a just and lasting peace in the area. You are all well aware of the strenuous efforts my own government is making to help Ambassador Jarring promote a peaceful settlement. Progress in these efforts has, admittedly, been slow. This is perhaps not surprising when one reflects on how deep the roots of the conflict go. But the important thing is that some progress is being made. The fact that it has not been crowned with dramatic success should not give grounds for despair. Nor should it be exploited as justification for action which will make greater progress even more difficult. This applies to actions in Jerusalem as elsewhere in the area. Indeed, Jerusalem occupies a very special place in all our minds and all our hearts as one of the holiest cities in the entire world. For Jerusalem is a sacred shrine to three of the world's largest and oldest religious faiths: Islam, Christianity and Judaism. By virtue of that fact the United States has always considered that Jerusalem enjoys a unique international standing and that no action should be taken there, without full regard to Jerusalem's special history and special place in the world community. Unfortunately there have been acts of many kinds which have broken the peace in Jerusalem and which are of deep concern to my government and to the international community. Mr. President, we understand the deep emotional concerns which move all parties to the Arab-Israeli dispute on the subject of Jerusalem. We do not believe, however, that any of these concerns are served by what is now taking place in East Jerusalem, whether it be actions by those now exercising authority there or by individuals considering themselves aggrieved and therefore justified in resorting to violence. The expropriation or confiscation of land, the construction of housing on such land, the demolition or confiscation of buildings, including those having historic or religious significance, and the application of Israeli law to occupied portions of the city are detrimental to our common interests in the city. The United States considers that the part of Jerusalem that came under the control of Israel in the June war, like other areas occupied by Israel, is occupied territory and hence subject to the provisions of international law governing the rights and obligations of an occupying Power. Among the provisions of international law which bind Israel, as they would bind any occupier, are the provisions that the occupier has no right to make changes in laws or in administration other than those which are temporarily necessitated by his security interests, and that an occupier may not confiscate or destroy private property. The pattern of behavior authorized under the Geneva convention and international law is clear: the occupier must maintain the occupied area as intact and unaltered as possible, without interfering with the customary life of the area, and any changes must be necessitated by immediate needs of the occupation. I regret to say that the actions of Israel in the occupied portion of Jerusalem present a different picture, one which gives rise to understandable concerns that the eventual disposition of East Jerusalem may be prejudiced, and that the private rights and activities of the population are already being affected and altered.

My Government regrets and deplores this pattern of activity, and it has so informed the Government of Israel on numerous occasions since June 1967. We have consistently refused to recognize these measures as having anything but a provisional character and do not accept them as affecting the ultimate status of Jerusalem.

I have explained in some detail the opposition of the United States to certain measures taken by the Government of Israel in Jerusalem, since this is the precise object of the complaint brought before us by the government of Jordan. But, as I suggested earlier, we cannot logically and intelligently consider the problem of Jerusalem without putting it in its proper perspective – the Middle East situation as a whole. In this connection, I would recall that one of the first major policy decisions taken by President Nixon after assuming office this year was that the United States Government should take new initiatives in helping to try to bring peace to the Middle East. For the past several months we have been devoting our best efforts to this task. We shall continue to do so, but for these efforts to succeed we will require the goodwill and cooperation of the parties themselves. A just and lasting peace in the Middle East is long and tragically overdue. It will not be found through terror bombings, which inevitably harm innocent civilians, any more than it will through unilateral attempts to alter the status of Jerusalem. It will be found only through the instruments and processes of negotiation, accommodation and agreement. It will come only through the exercise by the parties of the utmost restraint – not just along the cease-fire lines or in public statement, but also on the ground, in Jerusalem itself.

In treating the problem of Jerusalem, since we deal with it in the context of the total situation in the Middle East, my delegation will subject any proposal for Council action, first of all, to the test of whether that proposal is likely to help or hinder the peaceful settlement process. I hope all members will do likewise. For example, one constructive move the Council might make would be to request the parties to lay aside their recriminations, to desist from any action, in Jerusalem or elsewhere, that might be construed as prejudicing or prejudging a final, comprehensive settlement, a just and lasting peace. Thus, our consideration of the situation in Jerusalem could provide a fitting occasion on which to insist once more that the parties to a dispute which keeps the world's holiest city in turmoil act responsibly to resolve the whole dispute; and until it is resolved, that they take no action anywhere which could further jeopardize its resolution.

Appendix 3

Text of the Peace Treaty between Israel and Egypt

March 26, 1979

Ratified by Egypt April 10, 1979, and by Israel April 20, 1979.

The Government of the Arab Republic of Egypt and the Government of the State of Israel;

PREAMBLE

Convinced of the urgent necessity of the establishment of a just, comprehensive and lasting peace in the Middle East in accordance with Security Council Resolutions 242 and 338;

Reaffirming their adherence to the "Framework for Peace in the Middle East Agreed at Camp David," dated September 17, 1978;

Noting that the aforementioned Framework as appropriate is intended to constitute a basis for peace not only between Egypt and Israel but also between Israel and each of its other Arab neighbors which is prepared to negotiate peace with it on this basis;

Desiring to bring to an end the state of war between them and to establish a peace in which every state in the area can live in security;

Convinced that the conclusion of a Treaty of Peace between Egypt and Israel is an important step in the search for comprehensive peace in the area and for the attainment of settlement of the Arab–Israeli conflict in all its aspects;

Inviting the other Arab parties to this dispute to join the peace process with Israel guided by and based on the principles of the aforementioned Framework;

Desiring as well to develop friendly relations and cooperation between themselves in accordance with the United Nations Charter and the principles of international law governing international relations in times of peace;

Agree to the following provisions in the free exercise of their sovereignty, in order to implement the "Framework for the Conclusion of a Peace Treaty Between Egypt and Israel":

ARTICLE I

1. The state of war between the Parties will be terminated and peace will be established between them upon the exchange of instruments of ratification of this Treaty.
2. Israel will withdraw all its armed forces and civilians from the Sinai behind the international boundary between Egypt and mandated Palestine, as provided in the annexed protocol (Annex I), and Egypt will resume the exercise of its full sovereignty over the Sinai.
3. Upon completion of the interim withdrawal provided for in Annex I, the Parties will establish normal and friendly relations, in accordance with Article III (3).

ARTICLE II

The permanent boundary between Egypt and Israel is the recognized international boundary between Egypt and the former mandated territory of Palestine, as shown on the map at Annex II, without prejudice to the issue of the status of the Gaza Strip. The Parties recognize this boundary as inviolable. Each will respect the territorial integrity of the other, including their territorial waters and airspace.

ARTICLE III

1. The Parties will apply between them the provisions of the Charter of the United Nations and the principles of international law governing relations among states in times of peace. In particular:
   a. They recognize and will respect each other's sovereignty, territorial integrity and political independence;
   b. They recognize and will respect each other's right to live in peace within their secure and recognized boundaries;
   c. They will refrain from the threat or use of force, directly or indirectly, against each other and will settle all disputes between them by peaceful means.

2. Each Party undertakes to ensure that acts or threats of belligerency, hostility, or violence do not originate from and are not committed from within its territory, or by any forces subject to its control or by any other forces stationed on its territory, against the population, citizens or property of the other Party. Each Party also undertakes to refrain from organizing, instigating, inciting, assisting or participating in acts or threats of belligerency, hostility, subversion or violence against the other Party, anywhere, and undertakes to ensure that perpetrators of such acts are brought to justice.

3. The Parties agree that the normal relationship established between them will include full recognition, diplomatic, economic and cultural relations, termination of economic boycotts and discriminatory barriers to the free movement of people and goods, and will guarantee the mutual enjoyment by citizens of the due process of law. The process by which they undertake to achieve such a relationship parallel to the implementation of other provisions of this Treaty is set out in the annexed protocol (Annex III).

ARTICLE IV

1. In order to provide maximum security for both Parties on the basis of reciprocity, agreed security arrangements will be established including limited force zones in Egyptian and Israeli territory, and United Nations forces and observers, described in detail as to nature and timing in Annex I, and other security arrangements the Parties may agree upon.

2. The Parties agree to the stationing of United Nations personnel in areas described in Annex I. The Parties agree not to request withdrawal of the United Nations personnel and that these personnel will not be removed unless such removal is approved by the Security Council of the United Nations, with the affirmative vote of the five Permanent Members, unless the Parties otherwise agree.

3. A Joint Commission will be established to facilitate the implementation of the Treaty, as provided for in Annex I.

4. The security arrangements provided for in paragraphs 1 and 2 of this Article may at the request of either party be reviewed and amended by mutual agreement of the Parties.

ARTICLE V

1. Ships of Israel, and cargoes destined for or coming from Israel, shall enjoy the right of free passage through the Suez Canal and its approaches through the Gulf of Suez and the Mediterranean Sea on the basis of the Constantinople Convention of 1888, applying to all nations, Israeli nationals, vessels and cargoes, as well as persons, vessels and cargoes destined for or coming from Israel, shall be accorded non-discriminatory treatment in all matters connected with usage of the canal.

2. The Parties consider the Strait of Tiran and the Gulf of Aqaba to be international waterways open to all nations for unimpeded and non-suspendable freedom of navigation and overflight. The parties will respect each other's right to navigation and overflight for access to either country through the Strait of Tiran and the Gulf of Aqaba.

ARTICLE VI

1. This Treaty does not affect and shall not be interpreted as affecting in any way the rights and obligations of the Parties under the Charter of the United Nations.

2. The Parties undertake to fulfill in good faith their obligations under this Treaty, without regard to action or inaction of any other party and independently of any instrument external to this Treaty.

3. They further undertake to take all the necessary measures for the application in their relations of the provisions of the multilateral conventions to which they are parties, including the submission of appropriate notification to the Secretary General of the United Nations and other depositaries of such conventions.

4. The Parties undertake not to enter into any obligation in conflict with this Treaty.

5. Subject to Article 103 of the United Nations Charter in the event of a conflict between the obligation of the Parties under the present Treaty and any of their other obligations, the obligations under this Treaty will be binding and implemented.

ARTICLE VII

1. Disputes arising out of the application or interpretation of this Treaty shall be resolved by negotiations.

2. Any such disputes which cannot be settled by negotiations shall be resolved by conciliation or submitted to arbitration.

ARTICLE VIII

The Parties agree to establish a claims commission for the mutual settlement of all financial claims.

ARTICLE IX

1. This Treaty shall enter into force upon exchange of instruments of ratification.

2. This Treaty supersedes the Agreement between Egypt and Israel of September, 1975.

3. All protocols, annexes, and maps attached to this Treaty shall be regarded as an integral part hereof.

4. The Treaty shall be communicated to the Secretary General of the United Nations for registration in accordance with the provisions of Article 102 of the Charter of the United Nations.

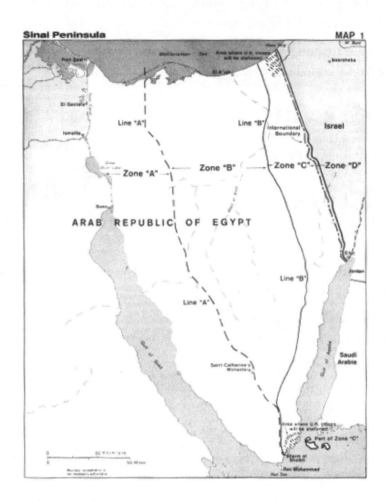

Map 1: The Zones. "Documents Pertaining to the Conclusion of Peace," information booklet published by the embassy of Israel, Washington, DC, April 1979.

ANNEX I
PROTOCOL CONCERNING ISRAELI WITHDRAWAL AND SECURITY AGREEMENTS

ARTICLE I
CONCEPT OF WITHDRAWAL

1. Israel will complete withdrawal of all its armed forces and civilians from the Sinai not later than three years from the date of exchange of instruments of ratification of this Treaty.

2. To ensure the mutual security of the Parties, the implementation of phased withdrawal will be accompanied by the military measures and establishment of zones set out in this Annex and in Map 1, hereinafter referred to as "the Zones."

3. The withdrawal from the Sinai will be accomplished in two phases:
   a. The interim withdrawal behind the line from east of El Arish to Ras Mohammed as delineated on Map 2 within nine months from the date of exchange of instruments of ratification of this Treaty.

   b. The final withdrawal from the Sinai behind the international boundary not later than three years from the date of exchange of instruments of ratification of this Treaty.

4. A Joint Commission will be formed immediately after the exchange of instruments of ratification of this Treaty in order to supervise and coordinate movements and schedules during the withdrawal, and to adjust plans and timetables as necessary within the limits established by paragraph 3, above. Details relating to the Joint Commission are set out in Article IV of the attached Appendix. The Joint Commission will be dissolved upon completion of final Israeli withdrawal from the Sinai.

ARTICLE II
DETERMINATION OF FINAL LINES AND ZONES

1. In order to provide maximum security for both Parties after the final withdrawal, the lines and the Zones delineated on Map 1 are to be established and organized as follows:

a. Zone A

    i. Zone A is bounded on the east by line A (red line) and on the west by the Suez Canal and the east coast of the Gulf of Suez, as shown on Map 1.

    ii. An Egyptian armed force of one mechanized infantry division and its military installations, and field fortifications, will be in this Zone.

    iii. The main elements of that Division will consist of:

        (a) Three mechanized infantry brigades.

        (b) One armed brigade.

        (c) Seven field artillery battalions including up to 126 artillery pieces.

        (d) Seven anti-aircraft artillery battalions including individual surface-to-air missiles and up to 126 anti-aircraft guns of 37 mm and above.

        (e) Up to 230 tanks.

        (f) Up to 480 armored personnel vehicles of all types.

        (g) Up to a total of twenty-two thousand personnel.

b. Zone B

    i. Zone B is bounded by line B (green line) on the east and by line A (red line) on the west, as shown on Map 1.

    ii. Egyptian border units of four battalions equipped with light weapons and wheeled vehicles will provide security and supplement the civil police in maintaining order in Zone B. The main elements in the four Border Battalions will consist of up to a total of four thousand personnel.

    iii. Land based, short range, low power, coastal warning points of the border patrol units may be established on the coast of this Zone.

    iv. There will be in Zone B field fortifications and military installations for the four border battalions.

c. Zone C

    i. Zone C is bounded by line B (green line) on the west and the International Boundary and the Gulf of Aqaba on the east, as shown on Map 1.

    ii. Only United Nations forces and Egyptian civil police will be stationed in Zone C.

    iii. The Egyptian civil police armed with light weapons will perform normal police functions within this Zone.

    iv. The United Nations Force will be deployed within Zone C and perform its functions as defined in Article VI of this annex.

    v. The United Nations Force will be stationed mainly in camps located within the following stationing areas shown on Map 1, and will establish its precise locations after consultations with Egypt:

       (a) In that part of the area in the Sinai lying within about 20 km of the Mediterranean Sea and adjacent to the International Boundary.

       (b) In the Sharm el-Sheikh area.

d. Zone D

    i. Zone D is bounded by line D (blue line) on the east and the international boundary on the west, as shown on Map 1.

    ii. In this Zone there will be an Israeli limited force of four infantry battalions, their military installations, and field fortifications, and United Nations observers.

    iii. The Israeli forces in Zone D will not include tanks, artillery and anti-aircraft missiles except individual surface-to-air missiles.

    iv. The main elements of the four Israeli infantry battalions will consist of up to 180 armored personnel vehicles of all types and up to a total of four thousand personnel.

2. Access across the international boundary shall only be permitted through entry check points designated by each Party and under its control. Such access shall be in accordance with laws and regulations of each country.

3. Only those field fortifications, military installations, forces, and weapons specifically permitted by this Annex shall be in the Zones.

ARTICLE III
AERIAL MILITARY REGIME

1. Flights of combat aircraft and reconnaissance flights of Egypt and Israel shall take place only over Zones A and D, respectively.

2. Only unarmed, non-combat aircraft of Egypt and Israel will be stationed in Zones A and D, respectively.

3. Only Egyptian unarmed transport aircraft will take off and land in Zone B and up to eight such aircraft may be maintained in Zone B. The Egyptian border unit.,., may be equipped with unarmed helicopters to perform their functions in Zone B.

4. The Egyptian civil police may be equipped with unarmed police helicopters to perform normal police functions in Zone C.

5. Only civilian airfields maybe built in the Zones.

6. Without prejudice to the provisions of this Treaty, only those military aerial activities specifically permitted by this Annex shall be allowed in the Zones and the airspace above their territorial waters.

ARTICLE IV
NAVAL REGIME

1. Egypt and Israel may base and operate naval vessels along the coasts of Zones A and D, respectively.

2. Egyptian coast guard boats, lightly armed, may be stationed and operate in the territorial waters of Zone B to assist the border units in performing their functions in this Zone.

3. Egyptian civil police equipped with light boats, lightly armed, shall perform normal police functions within the territorial waters of Zone C.

4. Nothing in this Annex shall be considered as derogating from the right of innocent passage of the naval vessels of either party.

5. Only civilian maritime ports and installations may be built in the Zones.

6. Without prejudice to the provisions of this Treaty, only those naval activities specifically permitted by this Annex shall be allowed in the Zones and in their territorial waters.

ARTICLE V
EARLY WARNING SYSTEMS

Egypt and Israel may establish and operate early warning systems only in Zones A and D respectively.

ARTICLE VI
UNITED NATIONS OPERATIONS

1. The Parties will request the United Nations to provide forces and observers to supervise the implementation of this Annex and employ their best efforts to prevent any violation of its terms.

2. With respect to these United Nations forces and observers, as appropriate, the Parties agree to request the following arrangements:
   a. Operation of check points, reconnaissance patrols, and observation posts along the international boundary and line B, and within Zone C.
   b. Periodic verification of the implementation of the provisions of this Annex will be carried out not less than twice a month unless otherwise agreed by the Parties.
   c. Additional verifications within 48 hours after the receipt of a request from either Party.
   d. Ensuring the freedom of navigation through the Strait of Tiran in accordance with Article V of the Treaty of Peace.

3. The arrangements described in this article for each zone will be implemented in ones A, B, and C by the United Nations Force and in Zone D by the United Nations Observers.

4. United Nations verification teams shall be accompanied by liaison officers of the respective Party.

5. The United Nations Force and observers will report their findings to both Parties.

6. The United Nations Force and Observers operating in the Zones will enjoy freedom of movement and other facilities necessary for the performance of their tasks.

7. The United Nations Force and Observers are not empowered to authorize the crossing of the international boundary.

8. The Parties shall agree on the nations from which the United Nations Force and Observers will be drawn. They "ill be drawn from nations other than those which are permanent members of the United Nations Security Council.

9. The Parties agree that the United Nations should make those command arrangements that will best assure the effective implementation of its responsibilities.

ARTICLE VII
LIAISON SYSTEM

1. Upon dissolution of the Joint Commission, a liaison system between the Parties will be established. This liaison system is intended to provide an effective method to assess progress in the implementation of obligations under the present Annex and to resolve any problem that may arise in the course of implementation, and refer other unresolved matters to the higher military authorities of the two countries respectively for consideration. It is also intended to prevent situations resulting from errors or misinterpretation on the part of either Party.

2. An Egyptian liaison office will be established in the city of El Arish and an Israeli liaison office will be established in the city of Beer-Sheba. Each office will be headed by an officer of the respective country, and assisted by a number of officers.

3. A direct telephone link between the two offices will be set up and also direct telephone lines with the United Nations command will be maintained by both offices.

ARTICLE VIII
RESPECT FOR WAR MEMORIALS

Each Party undertakes to preserve in good condition the War Memorials erected in the memory of soldiers of the other Party, namely those erected by Egypt in Israel, and shall permit access to such monuments.

ARTICLE IX
INTERIM ARRANGEMENTS

The withdrawal of Israeli armed forces and civilians behind the interim withdrawal line, and the conduct of the forces of the Parties and the United Nations prior to the final withdrawal, will be governed by the attached Appendix and Map 2.

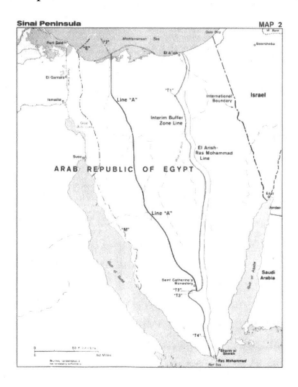

Map 2: Withdrawal of Israeli Armed Forces. "Documents Pertaining to the Conclusion of Peace," information booklet published by the embassy of Israel, Washington, DC, April 1979.

APPENDIX TO ANNEX I
ORGANIZATION OF MOVEMENTS
IN THE SINAI

ARTICLE I
PRINCIPLES OF WITHDRAWAL

1. The withdrawal of Israeli armed forces and civilians from the Sinai will be accomplished in two phases as described in Article I of Annex I. The description and timing of the withdrawal are included in this Appendix. The Joint Commission will develop and present to the Chief Coordinator of the United Nations forces in the Middle East the details of these phases not later than one month before the initiation of each phase of withdrawal.

2. Both parties agree on the following principles for the sequences of military movements.

    a. Notwithstanding the provisions of Article IX, paragraph 2, of this Treaty, until Israeli armed forces complete withdrawal from the current J and M Lines established by the Egyptian-Israeli Agreement of September 1975, hereinafter referred to as the 1975 Agreement, up to the interim withdrawal line, all military arrangements existing under that Agreement will remain in effect, except those military arrangements otherwise provided for in this Appendix.

    b. As Israeli armed forces withdraw, United Nations forces will immediately enter the evacuated areas to establish interim and temporary buffer zones as shown on Maps 2 and 3, respectively, for the purpose of maintaining a separation of forces. United Nations forces' deployment will precede the movement of any other personnel into these areas.

    c. Within a period of seven days after Israeli armed forces have evacuated any area located in Zone A, units of Egyptian armed forces shall deploy in accordance with the provisions of Article II of this Appendix.

    d. Within a period of seven days after Israeli armed forces have evacuated any area located in Zones A or B, Egyptian border units shall deploy in accordance with the provisions of Article II of this Appendix, and will function in accordance with the provisions of Article II of Annex I.

e. Egyptian civil police will enter evacuated areas immediately after the United Nations forces to perform normal police functions.

f. Egyptian naval units shall deploy in the Gulf of Suez in accordance with the provisions of Article II of this Appendix.

g. Except those movements mentioned above, deployments of Egyptian armed forces and the activities covered in Annex I will be offered in the evacuated areas when Israeli armed forces have completed their withdrawal behind the interim withdrawal line.

ARTICLE II
SUBPHASES OF THE WITHDRAWAL
TO THE INTERIM WITHDRAWAL LINE

1. The withdrawal to the interim withdrawal line will be accomplished in subphases as described in this Article and as shown on Map 3. Each subphase will be completed within the indicated number of months from the date of the exchange of instruments of ratification of this Treaty:

   a. First subphase: within two months, Israeli armed forces will withdraw from the area of El Arish, including the town of El Arish and its airfield, shown as Area I on Map 3.

   b. Second subphase: within three months, Israeli armed forces will withdraw from the area between line M of the 1975 Agreement and line A, shown as Area II on Map 3.

   c. Third subphase: within five months, Israeli armed forces will withdraw from the area east and south of Area II, shown as Area III on Map 3.

   d. Fourth subphase: within seven months, Israeli armed forces will withdraw from the area of El Tor-Ras El Kenisa, shown as Area IV on Map 3.

   e. Fifth subphase: Within nine months, Israeli armed forces will withdraw from the remaining areas west of the interim withdrawal line, including the areas of Santa Katrina and the areas east of the Giddi and Mitla passes, shown as Area V on Map 3, thereby completing

Israeli withdrawal behind the interim withdrawal line.

2. Egyptian forces will deploy in the areas evacuated by Israeli armed forces
   as follows:
   a. Up to one-third of the Egyptian armed forces in the Sinai in accordance
      with the 1975 Agreement will deploy in the portions of Zone A lying
      within Area I, until the completion of interim withdrawal. Thereafter,
      Egyptian armed forces as described Article II of Annex I will be
      deployed in Zone A up to the limits of the interim zone.

   b. The Egyptian naval activity in accordance with Article IV of Annex I
      will commence along the coasts of areas I, III and IV, upon completion
      of the second, third, and fourth subphases, respectively.

   c. Of the Egyptian border units described in Article II of Annex I, upon
      completion of the first subphase one battalion will be deployed in Area
      I. A second battalion will deployed in Area II upon completion of the
      second subphase. A third battalion will deployed in Area Ill upon
      completion of the third subphase. The second and third battalions
      mentioned above may also be deployed in any of the subsequently
      evacuated areas of the southern Sinai.

3. United Nations forces in Buffer Zone I of the 1976 Agreement will rede-
   ploy enable the deployment of Egyptian forces described above upon
   the completion of the subphase, but will otherwise continue to function
   in accordance with the provisions of that Agreement in the remainder
   of that zone until the completion of interim withdrawal, as indicated in
   Article I of this Appendix.

4. Israeli convoys may use the roads south and east of the main road junc-
   tion east of El Arish to evacuate Israeli forces up to the completion of
   interim withdrawal. These convoys will proceed in daylight upon four
   hours notice to the Egyptian liaison group and United Nations forces,
   will be escorted by United Nations forces, and will be in accordance with
   schedules coordinated by the Joint Commission. An Egyptian liaison
   officer will accompany convoys to assure uninterrupted movement. The
   Joint Commission may approve other arrangements for convoys.

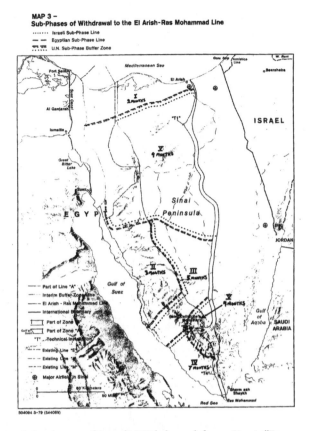

Map 3: Sub-phases of Israeli Withdrawal from Sinai. "Documents Pertaining to the Conclusion of Peace," information booklet published by the embassy of Israel, Washington, DC, April 1979.

ARTICLE III
UNITED NATIONS FORCES

1. The Parties shall request that United Nations forces be deployed as necessary to perform the functions described in the Appendix up to the time of completion of final Israeli withdrawal. For that purpose, the Parties agree to the redeployment of the United Nations Emergency Force.

2. United Nations forces will supervise the implementation of this Appendix and will employ their best efforts to prevent any violation of its terms.

3. When United Nations forces deploy in accordance with the provisions of Article and II of this Appendix, they will perform the functions of verification in limited force zones in accordance with Article VI of Annex

I, and will establish check points, reconnaissance patrols, and observation posts in the temporary buffer zones described in Article II above. Other functions of the United Nations forces which concern the interim buffer zone are described in Article V of this Appendix.

ARTICLE IV
JOINT COMMISSION AND LIAISON

1. The Joint Commission referred to in Article IV of this Treaty will function from the date of exchange of instruments of ratification of this Treaty up to the date of completion of final Israeli withdrawal from the Sinai.

2. The Joint Commission will be composed of representatives of each Party headed by senior officers. This Commission shall invite a representative of the United Nations when discussing subjects concerning the United Nations, or when either Party requests United Nations presence. Decisions of the Joint Commission will be reached by agreement of Egypt and Israel.

3. The Joint Commission will supervise the implementation of the arrangements described in Annex I and this Appendix. To this end, and by agreement of both Parties, it will:

   a. coordinate military movements described in this Appendix and supervise their implementation;

   b. address and seek to resolve any problem arising out of the implementation of Annex I and this Appendix, and discuss any violations reported by the United Nations Force and Observers and refer to the Governments of Egypt and Israel any unresolved problems;

   c. assist the United Nations Force and Observers in the execution of their mandates, and deal with the timetables of the periodic verification when referred to it by the Parties as provided for in Annex I and this Appendix;

   d. organize the demarcation of the international boundary and all lines and zones described in Annex I and this Appendix;

   e. supervise the handing over of the main installations in the Sinai from Israel to Egypt;

f. agree on necessary arrangements for finding and returning missing bodies of Egyptian and Israeli soldiers;

g. organize the setting up and operation of entry check points along the El Arish-Ras Mohammed line in accordance with the provisions of Article 4 of Annex III;

h. conduct its operations through the use of joint liaison teams consisting of one Israeli representative and one Egyptian representative, provided from a standing Liaison Group, which will conduct activities as directed by the Joint Commission;

i. provide liaison and coordination to the United Nations command implementing provisions of the Treaty, and, through the joint liaison teams, maintain local coordination and cooperation with the United Nations Force stationed in specific areas or United Nations Observers monitoring specific areas for any assistance as needed;

j. discuss any other matters which the Parties by agreement may place before it.

4. Meetings of the Joint Commission shall be held at least once a month. In the event that either Party of the Command of the United Nations Force requests a specific meeting, it will be convened within 24 hours.

5. The Joint Committee will meet in the buffer zone until the completion of the interim withdrawal and in El Arish and Beer-Sheba alternately afterwards. The first meeting will be held not later than two weeks after the entry into force of this Treaty.

ARTICLE V
DEFINITION OF THE INTERIM BUFFER ZONE AND ITS ACTIVITIES

1. An interim buffer zone, by which the United Nations Force will effect a separation of Egyptian and Israeli elements, will be established west of and adjacent to the interim withdrawal line as shown on Map 2 after implementation of Israeli withdrawal and deployment behind the interim withdrawal line. Egyptian civil police equipped with light weapons will perform normal police functions within this zone.

2. The United Nations Force will operate check points, reconnaissance patrols, and observation posts within the interim buffer zone in order to ensure compliance with the terms of this Article.

3. In accordance with arrangements agreed upon by both Parties and to be coordinated by the Joint Commission, Israeli personnel will operate military technical installations at four specific locations shown on Map 2 and designated as T1 (map central coordinate 57163940), T2 (map central coordinate 59351541), T3 (map central coordinate 5933-1527), and T4 (map central coordinate 61130979) under the following principles:

   a. The technical installations shall be manned by technical and administrative personnel equipped with small arms required for their protection (revolvers, rifles, sub-machine guns, light machine guns, hand grenades, and ammunition), as follows:

      i. T1 – up to 150 personnel

      ii. T2 and T3 – up to 350 personnel

      iii. T4 – up to 200 personnel

   b. Israeli personnel will not carry weapons outside the sites, except officers who may carry personal weapons.

   c. Only a third party agreed to by Egypt and Israel will enter and conduct inspections within the perimeters of technical installations in the buffer zone. The third party will conduct inspections in a random manner at least once a month. The inspections will verify the nature of the operation of the installations and the weapons and personnel therein. The third party will immediately report to the Parties any divergence from an installation's visual and electronic surveillance or communications role.

   d. Supply of the installations, visits for technical and administrative purposes, and replacement of personnel and equipment situated in the sites, may occur uninterruptedly from the United Nations check points to the perimeter of the technical installations, after checking and being escorted by only the United Nations forces.

   e. Israel will be permitted to introduce into its technical installations items required for the proper functioning of the installations and personnel.

f. As determined by the Joint Commission, Israel will be permitted to:

  i. Maintain in its installations fire-fighting and general maintenance equipment as well as wheeled administrative vehicles and mobile engineering equipment necessary for the maintenance of the sites. All vehicles shall be unarmed.

  ii. Within the sites and in the buffer zone, maintain roads, water lines, and communications cables which serve the site. At each of the three installation locations (T1, T2 and T3, and T4), this maintenance may be performed with up to two unarmed wheeled vehicles and by up to twelve unarmed personnel with only necessary equipment, including heavy engineering equipment if needed. This maintenance may be performed three times a week, except for special problems, and only after giving the United Nations four hours notice. The teams will be escorted by the United Nations.

g. Movement to and from the technical installations will take place only during daylight hours. Access to, and exit from, the technical installations shall be as follows:

  i. T1: Through a United Nations check point, and via the road between Abu Aweigila and the intersection of the Abu Aweigila road and the Gebel Libni road (at Km. 161), as shown on Map 2.

  ii. T2 and T3: through a United Nations checkpoint and via the road constructed across the buffer zone to Gebel Katrina, as shown on Map 2.

  iii. T2, T3, and T4: via helicopters flying within a corridor at the times, and according to a flight profile, agreed to by the Joint Commission. The helicopters will be checked by the United Nations Force at landing sites outside the perimeter of the installations.

h. Israel will inform the United Nations Force at least one hour in advance of each intended movement to and from the installations.

i. Israel shall be entitled to evacuate sick and wounded and summon medical experts and medical teams at any time after giving immediate notice to the United Nations Force.

4. The details of the above principles and all other matters in this Article requiring coordination by the Parties will be handled by the Joint Commission.

5. These technical installations will be withdrawn when Israeli forces withdraw from the interim withdrawal line, or at a time agreed by the parties.

ARTICLE VI
DISPOSITION OF INSTALLATIONS AND MILITARY BARRIERS

Disposition of installations and military barriers will be determined by the Parties in accordance with the following guidelines:

1. Up to three weeks before Israeli withdrawal from any area, the Joint Commission will arrange for Israeli and Egyptian liaison and technical teams to conduct a joint inspection of all appropriate installations to agree upon condition of structures and articles which will be transferred to Egyptian control and to arrange for such transfer. Israel will declare, at that time, its plans for disposition of installations and articles within the installations.

2. Israel undertakes to transfer to Egypt all agreed infrastructures, utilities, and installations intact, inter alia, airfields, roads, pumping stations, and ports. Israel will present to Egypt the information necessary for the maintenance and operation of the facilities. Egyptian technical teams will be permitted to observe and familiarize themselves with the operation of these facilities for a period of up to two weeks prior to transfer.

3. When Israel relinquishes Israeli military water points near El Arish and El Tor, Egyptian technical teams will assume control of those installations and ancillary equipment in accordance with an orderly transfer process arranged beforehand by the Joint Commission. Egypt undertakes to continue to make available at all water supply points the normal quantity of currently available water up to the time Israel withdraws behind the international boundary, unless otherwise agreed in the Joint Commission.

4. Israel will make its best effort to remove or destroy all military barriers, including obstacles and minefields, in the areas and adjacent waters from which it withdraws, according to the following concept:

   a. Military barriers will be cleared first from areas near populations, roads and major installations and utilities.

   b. For those obstacles and minefields which cannot be removed or destroyed prior to Israeli withdrawal, Israel will provide detailed maps to Egypt and the United Nations through the Joint Commission not later than 15 days before entry of United Nations forces into the affected areas.

   c. Egyptian engineers will enter those areas after United Nations forces enter to conduct barrier clearance operations in accordance with Egyptian plans to be submitted prior to implementation.

ARTICLE VII
SURVEILLANCE ACTIVITIES

1. Aerial surveillance activities during the withdrawal will be carried out as follows:

   a. Both Parties request the United States to continue airborne surveillance flights in accordance with previous agreements until the completion of final Israeli withdrawal.

   b. Flight profiles will cover the Limited Forces Zones to monitor the limitations on forces and armaments, and to determine that Israeli armed forces have withdrawn from the areas described in Article II of Annex I, Article II of this Appendix, and Maps 2 and 3, and that these forces thereafter remain behind their lines. Special inspection flights may be flown at the request of either Party or of the United Nations.

   c. Only the main elements in the military organizations of each Party, as described in Annex I and in this Appendix, will be reported.

2. Both Parties request the United States operated Sinai Field Mission to continue its operations in accordance with previous agreements until completion of the Israeli withdrawal from the area east of the Giddi and Mitla Passes. Thereafter, the Mission be terminated.

ARTICLE VIII
EXERCISE OF EGYPTIAN SOVEREIGNTY

Egypt will resume the exercise of its full sovereignty over evacuated parts of the Sinai upon Israeli withdrawal as provided for in Article I of this Treaty.

ANNEX II
MAP OF ISRAEL-EGYPT
INTERNATIONAL BOUNDARY

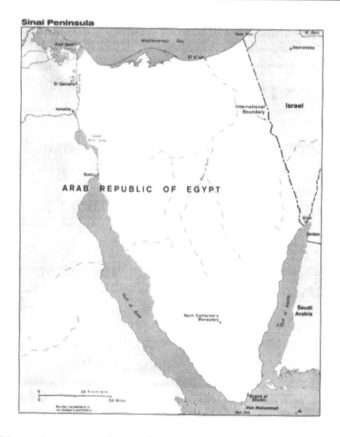

Map 4: International Boundary. "Documents Pertaining to the Conclusion of Peace," information booklet published by the embassy of Israel, Washington, DC, April 1979.

ANNEX III
PROTOCOL CONCERNING
RELATIONS OF THE PARTIES

ARTICLE 1
DIPLOMATIC AND CONSULAR RELATIONS
The Parties agree to establish diplomatic and consular relations and to exchange ambassadors upon completion of the interim withdrawal.

ARTICLE 2
ECONOMIC AND TRADE RELATIONS
1. The Parties agree to remove all discriminatory barriers to normal economic relations and to terminate economic boycotts of each other upon completion of the interim withdrawal.

2. As soon as possible, and not later than six months after the completion of the interim withdrawal, the Parties will enter negotiations with a view to concluding an agreement on trade and commerce for the purpose of promoting beneficial economic relations.

ARTICLE 3
CULTURAL RELATIONS
1. The Parties agree to establish normal cultural relations following completion of the interim withdrawal.

2. They agree on the desirability of cultural exchanges in all fields, and shall, as soon as possible and not later than six months after completion of the interim withdrawal, enter into negotiations with a view to concluding a cultural agreement for this purpose.

ARTICLE 4
FREEDOM OF MOVEMENT
1. Upon completion of the interim withdrawal, each Party will permit the free movement of the nationals and vehicles of the other into and within

its territory according to the general rules applicable to nationals and vehicles of other states. Neither Party will impose discriminatory restrictions on the free movement of persons and vehicles from its territory to the territory of the other.

2. Mutual unimpeded access to places of religious and historical significance will be provided on a non-discriminatory basis.

ARTICLE 5
COOPERATION FOR DEVELOPMENT AND GOOD NEIGHBORLY RELATIONS

1. The Parties recognize a mutuality of interest in good neighbourly relations and agree to consider means to promote such relations.

2. The Parties will cooperate in promoting peace, stability and development in their region. Each agrees to consider proposals the other may wish to make to this end.

3. The Parties shall seek to foster mutual understanding and tolerance and will, accordingly, abstain from hostile propaganda against each other.

ARTICLE 6
TRANSPORTATION AND TELECOMMUNICATIONS

1. The Parties recognize as applicable to each other the rights, privileges and obligations provided for by the aviation agreements to which they are both party, particularly by the Convention on International Civil Aviation, 1944 ("The Chicago Convention") and the International Air Services Transit Agreement, 1944.

2. Upon completion of the interim withdrawal any declaration of national emergency by a party under Article 89 of the Chicago Convention will not be applied to the other party on a discriminatory basis.

3. Egypt agrees that the use of airfields left by Israel near El Arish, Rafah, Ras El-Nagb and Sharm el-Sheikh shall be for civilian purposes only, including possible commercial use by all nations.

4. As soon as possible and not later than six months after the completion of the interim withdrawal, the Parties shall enter into negotiations for the purpose of concluding a civil aviation agreement.

5. The Parties will reopen and maintain roads and railways between their countries and will consider further road and rail links. The Parties further agree that a highway will be constructed and maintained between Egypt, Israel and Jordan near Eilat with guaranteed free and peaceful passage of persons, vehicles and goods between Egypt and Jordan, without prejudice to their sovereignty over that part of the highway which falls within their respective territory.

6. Upon completion of the interim withdrawal, normal postal, telephone, telex, data facsimile, wireless and cable communications and television relay services by cable, radio and satellite shall be established between the two Parties in accordance with all relevant international conventions and regulations.

7. Upon completion of the interim withdrawal, each Party shall grant normal access to its ports for vessels and cargoes of the other, as well as vessels and cargoes destined for or coming from the other. Such access will be granted on the same conditions generally applicable to vessels and cargoes of other nations. Article 5 of the Treaty of Peace will be implemented upon the exchange of instruments of ratification of the aforementioned treaty.

ARTICLE 7
ENJOYMENT OF HUMAN RIGHTS
The Parties affirm their commitment to respect and observe human rights and fundamental freedoms for all, and they will promote these rights and freedoms in accordance with the United Nations Charter.

ARTICLE 8
TERRITORIAL SEAS
Without prejudice to the provisions of Article 5 of the Treaty of Peace each Party recognizes the right of the vessels of the other Party to innocent passage through its territorial sea in accordance with the rules of international law.

AGREED MINUTES

ARTICLE I

Egypt's resumption of the exercise of full sovereignty over the Sinai provided for in paragraph 2 of Article I shall occur with regard to each area upon Israel's withdrawal from the area.

ARTICLE IV

It is agreed between the parties that the review provided for in Article IV (4) will be undertaken when requested by either party, commencing within three months of such a request, but that any amendment can be made only by mutual agreement of both parties.

ARTICLE V

The second sentence of paragraph 2 of Article V shall not be construed as limiting the first sentence of that paragraph. The foregoing is not to be construed as contravening the second sentence of paragraph 2 of Article V, which reads as follows: "The Parties will respect each other's right to navigation and overflight for access to either country through the Strait of Tiran and the Gulf of Aqaba."

ARTICLE VI (2)

The provisions of Article VI shall not be construed in contradiction to the provisions of the framework for peace in the Middle East agreed at Camp David. The foregoing is not to be construed as contravening the provisions of Article VI (2) of the Treaty, which reads as follows: "The Parties undertake to fulfill in good faith their obligations under this Treaty, without regard to action of any other Party and independently of any instrument external to this Treaty."

ARTICLE VI (5)

It is agreed by the Parties that there is no assertion that this Treaty prevails over other Treaties or agreements or that other Treaties or agreements prevail over this Treaty. The foregoing is not to be construed as contravening the provisions of Article VI (5) of the Treaty, which reads as follows:

"Subject to Article 103 of the United Nations Charter, in the event of a conflict between the obligations of the Parties under the present Treaty and any of their other obligations, the obligation under this Treaty will be binding and implemented."

ANNEX I

Article VI, Paragraph 8, of Annex I provides as follows:

> The Parties shall agree on the nations from which the United Nations forces and observers will be drawn. They will be drawn from nations other than those which are permanent members of the United Nations Security Council.

The Parties have agreed as follows:

> With respect to the provisions of paragraph 8, Article VI, of Annex 1, if no agreement is reached between the Parties, they will accept or support a U.S. proposal concerning the composition of the United Nations force and observers.

ANNEX III

The Treaty of Peace and Annex III thereto provide for establishing normal economic relations between the Parties. In accordance herewith, it is agreed that such relations will include normal commercial sales of oil by Egypt to Israel, and that Israel shall be fully entitled to make bids for Egyptian-origin oil not needed for Egyptian domestic oil consumption, and Egypt and its oil concessionaires will entertain bids made by Israel, on the same basis and terms as apply to other bidders for such oil.

> For the Government of the Arab Republic of Egypt:
> [Muhammad Anwar el-Sadat]

> For the Government of Israel:
> [Menachem Begin]

> Witnessed by:
> Jimmy Carter,
> President of the United States of America

Memorandum of Agreement between the Governments of the United States of America and the State of Israel

March 26, 1979

Recognizing the significance of the conclusion of the Treaty of Peace between Israel and Egypt and considering the importance of full implementation of the Treaty of Peace to Israel's security interests and the contribution of the conclusion of the Treaty of Peace to the security and development of Israel as well as its significance to peace and stability in the region and to the maintenance of international peace and security; and

Recognizing that the withdrawal from Sinai imposes additional heavy security, military and economic burdens on Israel;

The Governments of the United States and the State of Israel, subject to their constitutional processes and applicable law, confirm as follows:

1. In the light of the role of the United States in achieving the Treaty of Peace and the parties' desire that the United States continue its supportive efforts, the United States will take appropriate measures to promote full observance of the Treaty of Peace.

2. Should it be demonstrated to the satisfaction of the United States that there has been a violation or threat of violation of the Treaty of Peace, enhance friendly and peaceful relations between the parties and promote peace in the region, and will take such remedial measures as it deems appropriate, which may include diplomatic, economic and military measures as described below.

3. The United States will provide support it deems appropriate for proper actions taken by Israel in response to such demonstrated violations of the Treaty of Peace. In particular, if a violation of the Treaty of Peace is deemed to threaten the security of Israel, including, inter alia, a blockade of Israel's use of international waterways, a violation of the provisions of the Treaty of Peace concerning limitation of forces or an armed attack against Israel, the United States will be prepared to consider, on an urgent basis, such measures as the strengthening of the United States presence in the area,

the providing of emergency supplies to Israel, and the exercise of maritime rights in order to put an end to the violation.

4. The United States will support the parties' rights to navigation and overflight for access to either country through and over the Strait of Tiran and the Gulf of Aqaba pursuant to the Treaty of Peace.

5. The United States will oppose and, if necessary, vote against any action or resolution in the United Nations which in its judgments adversely affects the Treaty of Peace.

6. Subject to Congressional authorization and appropriation, the United States will endeavor to take into account and will endeavor to be responsive to military and economic assistance requirements of Israel.

7. The United States will continue to impose restrictions on weapons supplied by it to any country which prohibit their unauthorized transfer to any third party. The United States will not supply or authorize transfer of such weapons for use in an armed attack against Israel, and will take steps to prevent such unauthorized transfer.

8. Existing agreements and assurances between the United States and Israel are not terminated or altered by the conclusion of the Treaty of Peace, except for those contained in Articles 5, 6, 7, 8, 11, 12, 15 and 16 of Memorandum of Agreement between the Government of Israel and the Government of the United States (United States–Israeli Assurances) of September 1, 1975.

9. This Memorandum of Agreement sets forth the full understandings of the United States and Israel with regard to the subject matters covered between them hereby, and shall be implemented in accordance with its terms.

Appendix 4

Israeli Laws Referenced in the Correspondence

PROTECTION OF HOLY PLACES LAW
ADOPTED BY THE KNESSET ON JUNE 27, 1967

1. The Holy Places shall be protected from desecration and any other violation and from anything likely to violate the freedom of access of the members of the different religions to the places sacred to them or their feelings with regard to those places.

2. a. Whosoever desecrates or otherwise violates a Holy Place shall be liable to imprisonment for a term of seven years.

    b. Whosoever does anything likely to violate the freedom of access of the members of the different religions to the places sacred to them or their feelings with regard to those places shall be liable to imprisonment for a term of five years.

3. This Law shall add to, and not derogate from, any other law.

4. The Minister of Religious Affairs is charged with the implementation of this Law, and he may, after consultation with, or upon the proposal of, representatives of the religions concerned and with the consent of the Minister of Justice make regulations as to any matter relating to such implementation.

5 This Law shall come into force on the date of its adoption by the Knesset.

Levi Eshkol,
Prime Minister

Zerach Warhaftig,
Minister of Religious Affairs

Shneur Zalman Shazar,
President

BASIC LAW:
JERUSALEM, CAPITAL OF ISRAEL
ADOPTED BY THE KNESSET ON JULY 30, 1980

1. Jerusalem, complete and united, is the capital of Israel.

2. Jerusalem is the seat of the President of the State, the Knesset, the Government and the Supreme Court.

3. The Holy Places shall be protected from desecration and any other violation and from anything likely to violate the freedom of access of the members of the different religions to the places sacred to them or their feelings towards those places.

4. a. The Government shall provide for the development and prosperity of Jerusalem and the well-being of its inhabitants by allocating special funds, including a special annual grant to the Municipality of Jerusalem (Capital City Grant) with the approval of the Finance Committee of the Knesset.

   b. Jerusalem shall be given special priority in the activities of the authorities of the State so as to further its development in economic and other matters.

   c. The Government shall set up a special body or special bodies for the implementation of this section.

Menachem Begin,
Prime Minister

Yitzchak Navon, President of the State

SOURCES

Archives, Menachem Begin Heritage Center, Jerusalem

Website, Ministry for Foreign Affairs, Israel (www.mfa.gov.il)

Website, El-Sadat, Egypt (www.anwarsadat.org/index.asp)

Website, Nobel Peace Prize, Norway (www.nobelprize.org/)

Website, Knesset, Israel (www.knesset.gov.il/main/eng/home.asp)

FOR FURTHER READING

Avner, Yehuda. *The Prime Ministers: An Intimate Narrative of Israeli Leadership*. Jerusalem: Toby Press, 2010.

Blitzer, Wolf. *Between Washington and Jerusalem: A Reporter's Notebook*. New York: Oxford University Press, 1985.

Boutros-Ghali, Boutros. *Egypt's Road to Jerusalem: A Diplomat's Story of the Struggle for Peace in the Middle East*. New York: Random House, 1997.

Carter, Jimmy. *Keeping Faith: Memoirs of a President*. Toronto: Bantam Books, 1982.

Chaim Herzog Center for Middle East Studies and Diplomacy. *The Camp David Accords and Related Documents*. Beersheba: Ben-Gurion University of the Negev, 1998.

Charney, Leon H. *Special Counsel*. New York: Philosophical Library, 1984.

Finkelstone, Joseph. *Anwar Sadat: Visionary Who Dared*. London and Portland, OR: Frank Cass, 1996.

Heikal, Mohamed H. *Secret Channels: The Inside Story of Arab-Israeli Peace Negotiations*. London: HarperCollins, 1996.

Israeli, Raphael. "'I, Egypt': Aspects of President Anwar Al-Sadat's Political Thought." *Jerusalem Papers on Peace Problems*, no. 34. Jerusalem: Magnes Press, 1981.

Jureidini, Paul A., and R.D. McLaurin. *Beyond Camp David: Emerging Alignments and Leaders in the Middle East*. Syracuse, NY: Syracuse University Press, 1981.

Kamel, Mohamed Ibrahim. *The Camp David Accords: A Testimony*. London: KPI, 1986.

Katz, Shmuel. *The Hollow Peace*. Jerusalem: Jerusalem Post, 1981.

Quandt, William B. *Camp David: Peacemaking and Politics*. Washington, DC: The Brookings Institution, 1986.

——, and Richard Quandt. *Peace Process: American Diplomacy and the Arab-Israeli Conflict since 1967*. 3rd ed. Berkeley: University of California Press, 2005.

el-Sadat, Anwar. *In Search of Identity: An Autobiography*. New York: Harper and Row, 1978.

Sadat, Jehan. *A Woman of Egypt: Jehan Sadat's Story of Her Love for Anwar Sadat and for Her Country*. New York: Pocket Books, 1989.

Stein, Kenneth W. *Heroic Diplomacy: Sadat, Kissinger, Carter, Begin and the Quest for Arab-Israeli Peace*. New York and London: Routledge, 1999.

Steinberg, Gerald. "Where Credit Is Due: Reclaiming Begin's Contribution to Making Peace." In *Twenty-five Years of Israel-Egypt Peace: The Role of Leaders*. Jerusalem: The Menachem Begin Heritage Center, 2004.

Weizman, Ezer. *The Battle for Peace*. New York: Bantam Books, 1981.

HEBREW TITLES

For the researcher and Hebrew reader,
we recommend the following additional titles.

Ben-Elissar, Eliyahu. *Lo od milchama* [No more war].
Tel Aviv: Maariv, 1995.

Dayan, Moshe. *Halanetzach tochal cherev* [Will the sword devour forever?].
Tel Aviv: Yedioth Ahronoth, 1981.

Haber, Eitan, and Zev Schiff. *Shnat hayonah* [The year of the dove].
Tel Aviv: Zmora, Bitan, Modan, 1980.

Kalfon, Moshe. *Memilchama leshalom* [From war to peace].
Tel Aviv: Hakibbutz Hameuchad, 2002.

Katz, Yochanan. *Hayonah hazehirah: Bikuro shel Sadat b'Yisrael v'reishit tahalich hashalom* [The careful dove: Sadat's visit to Israel and the beginning of the peace process]. Tel Aviv: Yaron Golan, 2008.

Rubinstein, Elyakim. *Darchei shalom* [Paths of peace].
Tel Aviv: Ministry of Defense, 1992.

Segev, Shmuel. *Sadat: Haderech l'shalom* [Sadat: The path to peace].
    Tel Aviv: Masada, 1978.

Weizman, Ezer. *Hakrav al hashalom: Tatzpit ishit* [Battle for peace:
    A personal observation]. Tel Aviv: Yedioth Ahronoth, 1981.